Chris Owen is a British hist⌐
appointed MBE for his work i⌐
fessional life, he has written e
history, the life of L. Ron H
became interested in the story ⌐⌐ ⌐⌐⌐⌐⌐⌐⌐ ⌐ ⌐⌐⌐ ⌐⌐⌐⌐⌐
reading about it in Russell Miller's biography *Bare-Faced Messiah*. Owen has also advised other authors on aspects of Hubbard's life and career.

CW01497996

RON

THE WAR HERO

The True Story of
L. Ron Hubbard's
Calamitous Military Career

CHRIS OWEN

SILVERTAIL BOOKS • *London*

Contents

INTRODUCTION

Pasts Imperfect

Between 1941 and 1945, over sixteen million American men and women served in the United States Armed Forces. Some went on after the war to achieve fame in politics, sports and the arts. One veteran, though, made his mark in another and quite unexpected way: a few years after demobilizing, Lieutenant Lafayette Ronald Hubbard, United States Naval Reserve, became the founder and leader of the controversial Church of Scientology.

Hubbard's wartime service with the United States Navy was a pivotal time in his life. Before the war he had dreamed of achieving greatness, even boasting that he would "smash his name into history."[1] He was now a participant in the biggest conflict in history. What better opportunity was there for glory?

To Scientologists, L. Ron Hubbard is a much-decorated war hero and "master mariner" who served his country with distinction. He commanded warships, fought bravely against the Japanese and Germans and suffered serious combat injuries. He had a miraculous recovery through the use of his own revolutionary mental techniques, which he developed into Dianetics and Scientology. At the war's end, he received numerous decorations in recognition of his valor and accomplishments.

To the US Navy, the Veterans Administration, and those who served with him, the picture is very different. His naval record shows that he briefly had command of two small vessels and was removed from both of them when he made serious errors of leadership. Several of his superiors were strongly critical of him and considered him incapable of serving independently without close

I

supervision. He spent most of his war service ashore, far from any combat zones. He never saw combat. He was not wounded but instead spent extended periods being treated for commonplace physical afflictions. He was awarded only a handful of standard decorations for his war service.

Echoes of Hubbard's time in the US Navy can be seen throughout Scientology. He awarded himself the rank of Commodore and assembled a small fleet of ships in the 1960s, from which he oversaw the activity of the Church of Scientology for several years. He established an inner "religious order" of dedicated Scientologists who even today use quasi-naval ranks and uniforms. And he created an intelligence service within the Church of Scientology to mimic Naval Intelligence, serving as a formidable worldwide apparatus for crushing internal and external threats to Scientology and his own interests.

Hubbard's war service also provides the justification for the Church of Scientology's existence. Tommy Davis, formerly the Church's principal spokesman, has said that if it was true that Hubbard had not been injured, "the injuries that he handled by the use of Dianetics procedures were never handled, because they were injuries that never existed; therefore, Dianetics is based on a lie; therefore, Scientology is based on a lie. The fact of the matter is that Mr. Hubbard was a war hero."[2]

What, then, is the true story of "Ron the War Hero"? This book takes a look at the conflicting accounts in order to sift out the grains of truth. It includes copies of key documents from Hubbard's service history and contrasts them with what Hubbard and the Church of Scientology have claimed.

History, writes the Irish historian T.W. Moody, is "a continuing, probing, critical search for truth about the past ... History of a matter of facing the facts of the ... past, however painful some of them may be; mythology is a way of refusing to face the historical facts. The study of history not only enlarges truth about our past, but opens the mind to the reception of ever new accessions of truth. On the other hand the obsession with myths, and especially the more destructive myths, perpetuates the closed mind."[3]

The Church of Scientology is rightly critical of erroneous or conjectural statements made by its critics and spends much time pointing out their errors. It is only fair that its own statements should be subjected to the same critical treatment in order to find the truth about Hubbard's military career. The story that emerges is not so heroic but is still remarkable in its own way.

CHAPTER I

Scientology's Account

I am the last person to advertise war. I served the US Government and then the US Navy for several years, was honorably discharged as an officer and really don't care to say much more about it. – L. Ron Hubbard [1]

According to L. Ron Hubbard and the Church of Scientology, he excelled as a machine gunner with the National Guard[2] and served with distinction in the US Marine Corps[3] before being commissioned into the US Navy, either before the war[4] or alternatively, on its outbreak.[5] Just before he joined the Navy, he was responsible for the establishment of the US Army Air Force.[6]

He carried out a two thousand mile voyage to Alaska in 1940 on behalf of the US Navy[7] and subsequently rewrote the Navy's Hydrographic Office Publications.[8] His work on navigation was so far-reaching that the Navy was anxious to enlist him[9] and he was summoned to Washington, D.C. for a debriefing by Rear Admiral Chester Nimitz, later famous for his role in the Pacific.[10]

After the US entered the war, he was ordered to the Philippines, which he had known as a youngster[11] and was the first of three theaters of the war in which he saw combat[12] and fought with distinction.[13] Alternatively, he was posted to the USS *Edsall*, on which he was the Gunnery Officer, and landed on the north coast of Java in the Dutch East Indies on the same day as Japan attacked Pearl Harbor (December 7, 1941). He was cut off near Surabaya by invading Japanese forces in February 1942. After a gruelling trek through the jungle to the south coast, he scrambled into a rubber raft and sailed across the Timor Sea to within a hundred miles of the Australian coast before being picked up by a friendly destroyer.[14] He used the skills he learned in the Boy Scouts to keep himself alive.[15]

An alternative version is that he first served in Australia where he coordinated naval intelligence activities and was Senior Officer Present Ashore.[16] Another alternative is that he was in Australia working to coordinate relief for General Douglas MacArthur's forces.[17] He worked as a counter-intelligence officer to organize relief for the beleaguered American forces on Bataan.[18]

While escaping from the Japanese on Java, he suffered severe injuries after being machine-gunned in the back.[19] Alternatively, he fractured an ankle while evading the Japanese,[20] or was wounded in the thigh while serving in the Battle of the Java Sea.[21] He was flown home in the Secretary of the Navy's private plane as the first US casualty returned from the Far East,[22] having seen "hard action in the South Pacific".[23]

Another account states that during 1941–42 he served in Brisbane as a mail officer manning the only anti-aircraft battery in Australia.[24] His posting ended when he was relieved by "fifteen officers of rank".[25]

Alternatively, he commanded a gunboat in the Pacific, sailed to a Japanese-occupied island, tied up at the dock, went ashore and wandered around by himself for three days.[26]

Arriving back in the US in 1942, he recuperated from his injuries while serving in the Cable Censor's Office in New York before being posted to the North Atlantic theatre.[27] Alternatively, the shortage of skilled officers was so bad that after a week in hospital he was ordered at once to the command of a North Atlantic corvette[28] which had formerly been in British service as the *Mist*. He saw service for the remainder of that year with British and American anti-submarine vessels in the North Atlantic.[29] He rose to command the Fourth British Corvette Squadron[30] and drew on his extensive experience as a world traveller to train naval crews[31] in amphibious landing techniques.[32]

Another version has it that he commanded the subchaser USS *YP-422* (aka USS *Mist*) and turned its crew – all hardened criminals transferred from Portsmouth Naval Prison – into the finest crew in the fleet.[33] *YP-422* was said to be an anti-submarine escort vessel with Atlantic convoys.[34]

In 1943, he was transferred to the North Pacific where he was made Commodore of Corvette Squadrons.[35] Alternatively, he commanded a sixty-man subchaser, USS *PC-815*.[36] He fought and sunk either one or two Japanese submarines off the Oregon coast in May 1943.[37]

The following years, 1944–45, he worked as an instructor at the Small Craft Training Center in San Pedro, California[38] and trained 15,000 naval personnel.[39] He subsequently served with amphibious forces[40] as Navigation Officer aboard the USS *Algol*,[41] a ship which he described as having "about 700 men aboard it... in the middle of the Pacific Ocean".[42] During his post aboard the *Algol* he wrote a revolutionary textbook that greatly simplified the art of navigation.[43] He also "pressed on with research into the plight of the human spirit ... despite all else" while serving on *Algol*.[44] Some of his adventures on *Algol* were later made into a popular Hollywood film, *Mister Roberts*, by his screenwriter friends.[45]

He later attended Princeton University as a postgraduate[46] or, alternatively, attended the US Navy's School of Government at Princeton as a student,[47] where he advised students and staff on the subjects of "Oriental Justice and law enforcement."[48] Another account says that Hubbard saw action aboard a destroyer in the Aleutians in late 1944.[49] An alternative account says that his final active service post in the US Navy was in the Office of the Provost Marshal in Korea in 1945.[50]

Hubbard ended the war (in either 1944 or 1945) "highly decorated and grievously wounded".[51] He was crippled and blinded after an unexploded shell, which had landed on the deck of his ship and which he was throwing overboard, exploded in his face.[52]

Alternatively, he had suffered flash-burn injuries to his eyes while serving as Gunnery Officer aboard the USS *Edsall* earlier in the war, resulting in him being declared "legally blind".[53] Yet another alternative is that he had been left lame by shrapnel fragments in hip and back,[54] or possibly in the chest.[55] He was "twice pronounced dead", which was "a matter of medical record."[56] He was taken to Oak Knoll Naval Hospital in California where he was treated for injured optic nerves and physical injuries to his hip and back.[57]

By applying his own revolutionary mental therapies, which later became the basis of Scientology, he recovered so fully that he was reclassified for full combat duty, to the amazement of the Naval authorities.[58] He spent a full year in Oak Knoll Hospital and was fully recovered by 1947,[59] as a result of which he lost his retirement pension.[60] This fact shook the medical and psychiatric officers of the Navy's Retiring Board, as their "fixed ideas and practices had received a hard blow".[61]

Hubbard was "given a perfect score on mental and physical fitness reports" in 1950,[62] and was officially assessed as having "no neurotic or psychotic tendencies of any kind whatsoever".[63] He also healed eleven patients suffering from serious war-related conditions.[64]

Hubbard's wartime service took him to all five theatres of World War II, for which he was rewarded with 21 medals and palms,[65] or alternatively 27 decorations[66] or even 29[67] for his duties under fire.[68] Despite his heroics, Hubbard was not a man who enjoyed war and saw enough killing to last him a lifetime.[69] He resigned his commission rather than assist government research projects and instead published, in 1948, his "original thesis" on his discoveries about the mind.[70] This led in due course to Dianetics and Scientology.

Confused? The Church of Scientology certainly is. This improbable and contradictory account was assembled from over thirty different sources, which were published by the Church of Scientology itself. The Church's own websites have presented at least three different versions of Hubbard's military career since 1996.

As this shows, the Church has been chronically unable to present a coherent picture of what exactly he did. This is hardly surprising. Hubbard did not produce a formal autobiography. However, he often made claims about his life in the dozens of books, hundreds of lectures and thousands of minutes and directives that he produced between 1950 and his death in 1986. He also dictated some biographical notes in the 1970s in answer to questions from his public relations staff. Unfortunately for the Church, he did not keep his story straight. Many of his accounts contradict each other.

Hubbard left his followers with an impossible task in reconciling his different stories. The Church of Scientology has a literalist attitude towards Hubbard's work, regarding him as the unimpeach-able "Source" of its belief system. Everything he wrote and said is deemed to be factually accurate, *even if it is self-contradictory.* The possibility that Hubbard was wrong or, worse, that he was lying is simply not open for discussion. It would be regarded as "invalidating Source", one of the most serious offenses a Scientologist can commit.

A few of Hubbard's works focus directly on his own life, notably the lecture "The Story of Dianetics & Scientology" in 1958 and the essay "My Philosophy" in 1965. To this day, both are regarded as being of key importance in Scientology. It is unclear whether Hubbard wrote the biographical accounts contained in some of the Scientology books and publications quoted earlier in this chapter. Although their copyright was assigned to Hubbard, others likely wrote them on his behalf and the biographical statements were probably compiled from statements that he had made in lectures. Hubbard is also known to have written some biographical state-ments in the third person without claiming attribution.

Whether or not he wrote them, there can be little doubt that Hubbard personally approved most – if not all – of the biographical accounts published before his death. All were published by the Church of Scientology. The draconian penalties that the Church imposes for unauthorized publications would have ensured that its executives sought high-level clearance, probably from Hubbard himself. He would certainly have been the only source for the information on his naval career, as the US Navy's privacy rules meant that until his death in 1986, nobody outside the US Government could obtain his files without his permission. Even the Church of Scientology did not have a copy of the files until it obtained a set in 1979, with Hubbard's permission.

As the compilation of accounts earlier in this chapter illustrates, the Church of Scientology and Hubbard himself were careless about consistency in published biographical accounts. That did not really matter so long as his service records were still being withheld by the Navy. Even writers who were critical about Hubbard and Scientology presented his claims as fact. *Scandal of Scientology* author Paulette Cooper, for instance, wrote in 1971 that "he was severely injured in the war (and in fact was in a lifeboat for many days, badly injuring his body and his eyes in the hot Pacific sun)."[71]

The passage of the Freedom of Information Act in 1973 began to open the floodgates. (Ironically, the Church had campaigned for the Act in order to help it see Government files on Scientology). Although privacy constraints meant that Hubbard's personnel record remained sealed to the general public until his death in 1986, other documents – such as his ships' log books and previously classified Action Reports – became publicly available. An amateur researcher, Michael Shannon, had by 1979 amassed "a mountain of material which included some files that no one else had bothered to get copies of – for example, the log books of the Navy ships that Hubbard had served on, and his father's Navy service file".[72] Some of Hubbard's service file appears to have been released in error to Shannon (to which a handwritten note on the file comments: "What a colossal mess!"[73]). A copy of Shannon's document collection eventually reached Gerry Armstrong, a Canadian Scientologist who was working as L. Ron Hubbard's Archivist and Biography Researcher at the start of the 1980s, in collaboration with the (non-Scientologist) author Omar V. Garrison.

Armstrong became increasingly disillusioned by what he found in Hubbard's personal files. He realized that Hubbard's life story had been grossly misrepresented over the years and urged the church to correct the record before they suffered the embarrassment of Hubbard's falsehoods being exposed publicly. He wrote presciently:

> *If we present inaccuracies, hyperbole or downright lies as fact or truth, it doesn't matter what slant we give them; if disproved, the man will look, to outsiders at least, like a charlatan.*[74]

Armstrong's superiors reacted with hostility to his entreaties. He left Scientology in December 1981 and the Church declared him a "suppressive person" in February 1982. He had earlier provided Garrison with documents from Hubbard's personal files to assist with the production of an official biography of Scientology's founder. After Armstrong was declared a "suppressive" by the Church, Garrison gave him a number of Hubbard's documents, including material from the US Navy and Veterans Administration files, which Armstrong sent to lawyers who had agreed to represent him. This prompted a lawsuit from the Church, which went to trial in Los Angeles Superior Court in 1984.

Armstrong's defence centered on his contention that he was right about the falsity of the Church's version of Hubbard's biography. The Church brought in a former US Navy officer who had served under Hubbard in an attempt to rebut Armstrong's findings in court. The subsequent cross-examination was widely publicized and proved devastating for the Church, which lost the case.[75]

Hubbard's death in January 1986 finally enabled members of the public to obtain his full service record and military medical files. The story told by the files is very different from the many contradictory accounts that the Church of Scientology has published over the years.

CHAPTER 2

The Navy's Account

In stark contrast to the confused and contradictory accounts presented by the Church of Scientology, the US Navy's version of L. Ron Hubbard's naval career is straightforward and consistent. When Hubbard's file was first released to the public in 1986, the Navy compiled a summary of L. Ron Hubbard's service career in response to the many enquiries it had received.

The summary shows that Hubbard was commissioned on July 19, 1941 as a Lieutenant (junior grade) in the U.S. Naval Reserve. He was then on inactive duty until September 21, 1941. He served on active duty for a short period from September 22 to October 6, 1941, when he was "honorably released from temporary active duty". Another period of inactive duty followed between October 7 and November 23, 1941.

Hubbard then returned to active duty from November 24, 1941 to February 16, 1946 before again being "honorably released" from active duty. (The United States entered the war on December 7, 1941; Japan surrendered on August 15, 1945.) He remained on inactive duty from February 17, 1946 to October 30, 1950, when his second letter of resignation from the Navy was accepted and he was honorably discharged from the naval service. He received one promotion during his career, from Lieutenant (junior grade) to Lieutenant.

The Navy summarizes Hubbard's active duty postings as follows:

Ships and stations	Periods	Duties
Hydrographic Office, Bureau of Navigation, Washington, DC	22 Sep 41 – 06 Oct 41	
Headquarters, Third Naval District	24 Nov 41 – 14 Dec 41	Under instruction
District Intelligence Office, Twelfth Naval District	15 Dec 41 – 17 Dec 41	Intelligence Officer
Office of the Naval Attaché, American Legation, Melbourne, Australia	18 Dec 41 – 02 Apr 42	Intelligence Officer
Headquarters, Twelfth Naval District	03 Apr 42 – 30 Apr 42	Intelligence Officer
Office of the Cable Censor, New York, NY	01 May 42 – 24 Jun 42	Intelligence Officer
Lawley and Sons, Shipbuilding, Newport, MA	25 Jun 42 – 28 Jul 42	In connection with conversion of USS *YP-422*
Naval Receiving Station, Long Beach, Long Island, NY	29 Jul 42 – 01 Nov 42	Senior Watch Officer
Submarine Chaser Training Center, Miami, FL	02 Nov 42 – 02 Jan 43	Under instruction
Fleet Sound School, Key West, FL	03 Jan 43 – 16 Jan 43	Student
Supervisor of Ships, Portland, OR	17 Jan 43 – 20 Apr 43	Prospective CO/OINC of fitting out *USS PC-815*
USS *PC-815*	21 Apr 43 – 07 Jul 43	Commanding Officer
Headquarters, Eleventh Naval District	08 Jul 43 – 11 Oct 43	Temporary Duty in the Issuing Office
Naval Small Craft Training Center, Terminal Island, San Pedro, CA	12 Oct 43 – 01 Dec 43	Under instruction

Supervisor of Shipbuilding, Portland, OR	02 Dec 43 – 21 Jul 44	In connection with fitting out USS *Algol* (AKA-54) and Navigator/Training Off.
USS *Algol* (AKA-54)	22 Jul 44 – 28 Sep 44	Navigator/Training Off. Chief Ship's Censor
Naval Training Schools, Princeton, NJ	29 Sep 44 – 27 Jan 45	Under instruction
Naval Civil Affairs, Staging Area, Presidio of Monterey, CA	28 Jun 45 – 04 Sep 15	Under instruction
Naval Hospital, Oakland, CA	05 Sep 45 – 04 Dec 45	Patient
Officer Separation Center, San Francisco, CA	05 Dec 45 – 06 Dec 45	Separation Processing and Detachment

(The repeated instances of "Under Instruction" refer to temporary training assignments.)

According to the Navy's summary, Hubbard was also awarded four medals:

- American Defense Service Medal
- American Campaign Medal
- Asiatic-Pacific Campaign Medal
- World War II Victory Medal

(These are discussed in more detail in Chapter 15.)

The Navy has never changed its account of Hubbard's career; nearly identical versions of this summary have been issued to requesters since 1986 (though there are a few minor corrections between the first and the most recent versions). This presents a marked contrast to the ever-shifting Scientology accounts.

It is immediately obvious from the Navy's summary that large parts of the Scientology version of Hubbard's naval career are contradicted. There is no mention of the USS *Edsall* or Java; no mention of corvettes; only one command, which lasted just 77 days; no mention of combat or war wounds; 1,756 days spent in shore establishments, compared with only 145 days assigned to ships; and only four commonplace medals, not the 21 to 29 medals claimed by the Church of Scientology.

So which version is correct? That question can only be answered by looking in more detail at exactly what Hubbard's naval records say about his wartime career.

CHAPTER 3

Ron the Warrior

L. Ron Hubbard had always expected to have a career in the US Navy. His father, Harry Ross Hubbard, joined the Navy in 1904 as an enlisted man, though he left it in 1909 after he met and married Hubbard's mother. Ron was born two years later on March 13, 1911.

His father rejoined the Naval Reserve in 1917 when the United States entered World War I. After the war, Harry decided to stay in the Navy and transferred from the Naval Reserve to the Navy proper, remaining in the service until April 1946.[1]

During the 1920s the Hubbards experienced an itinerant lifestyle typical of many military families as Harry was posted to different stations around and outside the United States. Ron lived for a while with his grandparents in Helena, Montana but twice travelled to join his parents at the US Naval Base on Guam.

He travelled there in 1928 aboard the cargo auxiliary USS *Gold Star* and returned to the United States on the ammunition ship USS *Nitro* a few months later. He was not too impressed with *Nitro*, noting in his diary: "If this ship is the cream of the naval duty, I'll sure stick to the milk. The officers work about an hour and then sit around and look bored. The enlisted personnel bear the brunt of the work." Nonetheless, he looked forward to going to the US Naval Academy at Annapolis with his friend Dick Derickson.[2]

Harry clearly expected his son to follow in his footsteps, but his hopes were dashed in the fall of 1929. At the time, Ron was studying at Swavely Preparatory School in Manassas, Virginia on a special course for prospective candidates to Annapolis. Ron complained of eyestrain and was tested at the Naval Hospital. He was found to be so short-sighted that he had no chance of passing the Naval Academy's fitness test.[3]

With his prospects for a naval career apparently thwarted, Ron instead turned to the Army. In October 1927, as a 16-year-old schoolboy, he enlisted as a private in the Headquarters Company of 163rd Infantry, Montana Army National Guard, at the State Armory in Helena. His parents were unaware, as they were stationed with his father's unit on Guam, while Hubbard was living with his grandparents in Helena. His record shows that he served for one year and 11 days.[4]

As the minimum age for enlistment was 18, Hubbard should not have been able to join. This issue was raised for an unrecorded reason in April 1941, probably in connection with the pre-employment enquiries made before he joined the US Navy, and prompted him to make a sworn declaration before a New York notary public to explain the circumstances. According to Hubbard, he joined at the request of the unit's commander, a Captain Ferguson, who was a friend of his father. As Hubbard was underage, he needed his parents' consent to enlist. However, as his parents were on Guam, it would have taken four or five months for a request to reach them and a reply to be returned. Captain Ferguson apparently took a short-cut and added two years to Hubbard's age so that he could enlist without needing to wait for parental consent. "This practice," wrote Hubbard, "was quite usual and the company was filled with young men out of High School."[5]

The circumstances of his service are unclear, as very little seems to be recorded about it, and accounts conflict on what he actually did. As Hubbard was at school at the time, it seems likely that his service amounted to little more than training duty. A US Navy form written 20 years later records that Hubbard's active service with the National Guard amounted to 0 years, 0 months and 0 days. It is unclear whether this was an actual record of his service or just a placeholder due to a lack of information.[6] Galaxy Press, the Church of Scientology's imprint for Hubbard's fiction works, claims that Hubbard "rather excelled as a machine gunner" with the National Guard;[7] if so, this would have only been in training practice.

*

The US Marine Corps Reserve in Hubbard's day

The Marine Corps Reserve in 1930 was a very different beast to today's 40,000-strong organization, whose members have seen frequent active service in the Middle East in recent years. Established in August 1916, eight months prior to the US entry into World War I, the USMCR virtually disappeared after the war. By 1925 there were fewer than 700 Marine Reservists.

In February 1925, a new Naval Reserve Act established the USMCR as a permanent component of the Marine Corps. Its unpaid volunteer personnel were required to carry out sixty drill periods of four hours each and fifteen days of field training annually. Active service was limited to wartime or other national emergencies.

The volunteers attended initially as individuals but this changed in late 1929 when the Fleet Marine Corps Reserve was reorganized into homogeneous units. In 1931 the 6th Reserve Marine Brigade was formed with 2,000 members. It was headquartered at Quantico, Virginia and had units dispersed across four reserve areas around the US, with home stations at Philadelphia, New York City, New Orleans, Chicago and San Francisco. [8]

*

The end of his service came about, according to his naval record, "per permanent change of residence" – in other words, he moved away from Helena.[9] He wrote in his April 1941 declaration that he "served only a few months in this company for I was recalled to the tropics by my parents."[10] "Recalled" was not exactly accurate; he dropped out of high school, ran away from his grandparents and took passage on a Navy transport bound for Guam. As he was still enlisted with the National Guard, this technically made him a deserter.

On May 1, 1930, at the age of 19, Hubbard enlisted with the Marine Corps Reserve's 20th Regiment. The 20th was a Fleet Marine Corps Reserve training unit connected with George Washington University in Washington, DC. Hubbard joined the university four months later as an engineering student. For some reason, Hubbard listed his profession prior to joining the Marine Corps Reserve as being a "photographer".[11]

His Marine Corps record shows that once again two years were added to his age. In his April 1941 declaration, he said that his papers were "read in error and because no oath or birth certificate was involved, the error was perpetuated, whether correctly or not I cannot say." [12]

Hubbard was promoted to First Sergeant within only two months, jumping six ranks.[13] His false birth date may have enabled him to leapfrog his contemporaries on the basis of seniority.[14] Hubbard gave a different explanation in a 1951 lecture, attributing his rapid promotion to a lack of experienced personnel (or at least personnel who could *look* experienced). This was quite possibly true, as the entire Marine Corps Reserve had fewer than 2,000 personnel at the time Hubbard signed up. He explained:

When I first got into college, life was pretty dull and I needed a little recreation. This fellow came up to me and he said, "The Marine Reserves are organising a twentieth regiment. Why don't you come down?"...

So I went down and I found out nobody down there knew "to the rear march, to the rear march, to the rear march," and I happened to know "to the rear march, to the rear march, to the rear march." So I went around to the captain and I said, "In view of the fact that I've been an admiral in the Greek navy," or something of the sort – I have forgotten what I told him – "I'll join up if you'll give me a sergeancy." I was nineteen...

The only reason I knew anything about drilling is I had been hanging around with the marines off and on. He couldn't find anybody else who could drill; nobody knew how to drill... So they made me a first sergeant. I figured I might as well cast my act, so I got my hair cut off short so it was sticking up like bristles on a pig's back, and I stood in front of a mirror for a while and got this look on my face, the way I had seen the most successful sergeants look. I cultivated a method of talking tough. I had known a lot of marine sergeants, a lot of marine top kicks – tough boys – and I had seen them handle people, and I just followed a pattern and did what they did.[15]

A Scientology account claims that Hubbard "led his Company G to nineteen out of twenty silver cups in [the] Eastern Seaboard Reserve competition"[16] Despite this success, Hubbard apparently decided that he did not want to continue as a Marine Corps reservist. He requested a discharge on July 18, 1931, stating that "I do not have the time to devote to the welfare of the Regiment."[17] He was discharged on October 22 that same year.

It was a stretch to claim that he had devoted much time to the Regiment in the first place, as he had not met the minimum requirements for duty. He did manage to undertake his two annual compulsory training duties of fifteen days each, which a later record shows took place from June 30 to July 19, 1930 and 23 August to

September 6, 1931.[18] The timing of his discharge request suggests that he was trying to get out of his August 1931 training period. If so, he was evidently unsuccessful.

A later US Navy record shows that out of one year, five months and 22 days of service with the USMCR, he had spent just one month and four days on active service. This corresponds to his training periods, plus four days of drill practice. He was, however, supposed to have done ten days' worth of drill practice each year. His record indicates that he likely only did about a third of the drill practice that was required of him.[19]

On October 22, 1931, he received an honourable discharge from the USMCR and a character reference of "Excellent". In another hand beneath this is written, "Not to be re-enlisted." There is no explanation of either statement, though it followed poor grade reports from the university. The prohibition on re-enlistment permanently disbarred Hubbard from further service with the USMCR. There is no record of him trying to enlist again and no indication that he ever had dealings with the Marine Corps subsequently. In a 1939 letter, Hubbard explained that "at the age of 19, not being old enough for a commission ... I left the service on the advice of my friend Lt-Col. Moriarity USMC."[20]

Hubbard's brief and uneventful stint with the Marine Corps Reserve was nonetheless transformed in his mind into something of far greater significance. Only a few years later, he wrote in a short magazine article, "Most of my life I have been associated with the Corps one way or another in various parts of the world and I should know something about it."[21]

He wrote what he called "leatherneck yarns" for *Adventure* and other pulp fiction magazines, drawing on his supposed experience. In its October 1935 issue he told his readers: "I've known the Corps from Quantico to Peiping, from the South Pacific to the West Indies."[22]

This statement was a gross exaggeration: he visited Peiping –

now Beijing – and the South Pacific at the age of 16, with his parents, and went to the West Indies twice at the age of 21 on a sailing trip and as a hurricane relief volunteer. His trips had nothing to do with the Corps. It is unintentionally ironic that Galaxy Press, the Scientology-owned imprint that publishes Hubbard's fiction, cites his statement as reflecting "the authenticity of his tales."[23]

Indeed, the authenticity of his tales was questioned at the time. A few months after Hubbard's claims in *Adventure*, the magazine printed a letter by a reader who was a serving First Sergeant in the Marine Corps. Noting that the average First Sergeant "has over sixteen years of service", unlike Hubbard, the unnamed reader pointed out numerous errors and inconsistencies in Hubbard's portrayal of the Corps. Hubbard wrote a somewhat defensive response in which he suggested:

> *The sergeant, as he is down there in Washington, might go up to the Navy Department and look up the records of the 20th regiment. He'll find Lafayette Ronald Hubbard duly warranted a first sergeant. If he's got the nerve, he might also call up Major Moriarity, the great Mo, and find out that I've been kicking around with the Corps ever since I was a pup, officially and otherwise.*[24]

Hubbard's next brush with the military was with the US Army Air Corps at the end of the 1930s. He had been a keen glider pilot while at university and enlisted the help of H. Latane Lewis III, who was formerly the Assistant Editor of *National Aeronautics* magazine and had written about Hubbard's gliding exploits. Lewis was a member of the National Aeronautic Association by 1938 and Hubbard appears to have boarded at his house in New York for a while.

Presumably at Hubbard's urging, Lewis wrote to Brigadier General Walter G. Kilner to recommend Hubbard's services as a consultant. He was highly complimentary towards "Captain Hubbard" who, he said, was a member of the Explorers Club, a frequent speaker at Harvard and George Washington Universities and a holder of two aviation records.[25]

Nothing came of this approach. Perhaps the Air Corps found out that Hubbard was not a Captain, not a member of the Explorers Club,[26] not a lecturer, held no flying records and had never addressed Harvard (at least in any official capacity).

The following year, on September 1, 1939 – the day Hitler invaded Poland – Hubbard applied to join the War Department.

Because of the possibility that our nation may, in the near future, find itself at war and because I well know the difficulty of finding trained men at the height of such a crisis, I wish to offer my services to my government in whatever capacity they might be of the greatest use...[27]

Once again, Hubbard was turned down. Two days later President Franklin D. Roosevelt declared that the United States would be neutral in the war that had just been declared by Britain and France against Germany, though in practice the administration's policy tilted increasingly strongly towards supporting Britain's war effort.

In May 1940, Hubbard and his then wife Polly set off on a sailing trip from Oregon to Alaska. As a newly-minted member of the Explorers Club of New York, he was entitled to carry the club's flag on what he termed the "Alaskan Radio-Experimental Expedition". His aunt Marnie Waterbury later recalled that he "dreamed up the trip as a way of outfitting" his 32-foot ketch *Magician*. "His brain was always working and when he was trying to figure out how he could afford to outfit the boat he wrote letters to all these different manufacturers of instruments and equipment offering to test them out."[28]

Hubbard stated the expedition's purpose as "checking data for the US Coast and Geodetic Survey and the US Navy Hydrographic

Office." There is no evidence from the Navy's records that it had any involvement with Hubbard's "expedition". Nonetheless, the tale evidently grew in the telling. The Church of Scientology claims that the expedition was "partially sponsored by the United States Navy"[29] and that Hubbard was given instructions

> ...to photograph all coves and channels capable of harboring enemy submarines, and thence make his way to the Kuril Islands photographing Japanese warships. Along the way, he not only captured an enemy spy and roped a Kodiak bear, but braved seventy-mile-an-hour winds and commensurate seas off the Aleutians.[30]

Far from reaching the Kuril Islands or the Aleutians, Hubbard only just made it to Alaska. His yacht had persistent engine problems and finally broke down in August 1940 at Ketchikan, at the bottom end of the Alaskan panhandle. A shortage of funds for repairs led to Hubbard and his wife being stranded there until December 1940. They did not get any further north than Ketchikan.[31]

There is no evidence that the Navy gave Hubbard any instructions about his expedition. The one piece of evidence that has been published is a letter that Hubbard sent to the Navy's Hydrographic Office from Ketchikan in mid-September 1940, enclosing a package of sailing directions and eleven rolls of film with a note expressing the hope that they would prove of value. He received a letter of acknowledgement from the Navy Hydrographer, thanking him for his contributions.[32]

The Church also claims that the Navy was interested in Hubbard's experiments with nomograms (a type of graphical calculator) for navigation during the trip. According to the Church's account,

Rear Admiral Chester Nimitz, later commander of the United States Pacific Fleet, requested Ron's presence in Washington, D.C., to be fully debriefed regarding his expedition and the details of his navigational experiments. The formula he discovered gave the Navy its first important breakthrough and the basic foundation for the development of LORAN.[33]

LORAN (standing for LOng RAnge Navigation) was a radio navigation system that was developed by the physicist Alfred Lee Loomis in late 1940. There appears to be no independent evidence that Hubbard had anything to do with it, nor has any evidence ever emerged that Hubbard had any dealings with Chester Nimitz.[34]

By the start of 1941, Nazi Germany had occupied most of western Europe and was trying to starve a still-defiant Britain into submission in the Battle of the Atlantic. It was becoming increasingly obvious that the United States would, sooner or later, be drawn into the conflict. In the spring of 1941, Hubbard turned his attention to the US Navy. He later explained to his followers that he volunteered to serve in the knowledge that war was inevitable, in order to avoid being drafted into a position that was not of his choice:

I wasn't drafted, I just knew what inevitably would occur and I'd better have something to do with it. And I remember that I better have something to do with it while I still had some free choice in the matter rather than afterwards when I didn't have any. And I remember very well telling the admiral in charge of the navy yard where I reported in, picked up a commission, "You know, you're going to have a war and I am at least trying to – trying to exercise some discretion as to what part I am playing in this war, and that's the only reason I am here."[35]

Hubbard sought to join the Intelligence Reserve and would have been well aware of the Navy's requirements for applicants, which included the instruction that they were to:

obtain letters of recommendation which positively indicate the qualities which they must have to aspire to a particular activity in the Intelligence Service. Perfunctory letters in the common style of good fellowship are not acceptable. Letters which indicate abilities, application, accomplishment, imagination, conduct, endurance, initiative, intelligence, versatility, loyalty, sound and tested Americanism, and sobriety under strain, give facts of value and are the types of letters desired.[36]

Hubbard enlisted several influential friends to write letters of support for him. Jimmy Britton, the owner of KGBU Radio in Ketchikan, Alaska, was the first to lend his support. Hubbard had befriended Britton the year before on his trip to Alaska and spent several months broadcasting on KGBU Radio while waiting for spare parts to arrive for his yacht's engine.[37]

In a letter sent on March 15, 1941, Britton praised Hubbard as "a man of intelligence, courage and good breeding as well as one of the most versatile personalities I have ever known." He referred to the sterling work which Hubbard had supposedly performed in tracking down "a German saboteur who had devised it to be in his power to cut off Alaska from communication with the United States in time of war through the sabotage of Signal Corps signals."[38] This referred to a claim made by Hubbard in a broadcast for KGBU, though it has never been independently substantiated.

Ten days later Commander W.E. McCain, a friend of the family who had shown the young Hubbard around Manila on a visit in 1927, added his recommendation:

This is to certify that I have personally known Mr L. Ron Hubbard for the past twenty years. I have been associated with him as a boy growing up and observed him closely. I have found him to be of excellent character, honest, ambitious and always very anxious to improve himself to better enable him to become a more useful citizen... I do not hesitate to recommend him to anyone needing the services of a man of his qualifications.[39]

Hubbard also enlisted the help of Robert MacDonald Ford, an old friend from Washington State who was now a State Representative. Ford was evidently not particularly bothered about protocol or propriety when it came to writing letters of recommendation. Decades later, he recalled:

[Hubbard] wanted a letter and I gave him a letterhead and said, "You want a letter? Hell, you're the writer, you write it." I don't know why he wanted it.[40]

Hubbard did not hold back in praising himself:

This will introduce one of the most brilliant men I have ever known: Captain L. Ron Hubbard.

He writes under six names in a diversity of fields from political economy to action fiction and if he would make at least one of his pen names public he would have little difficult entering anywhere. He has published many millions of words and some fourteen movies.

In exploration he has honorably carried the flag of the Explorers Club and has extended geographical and mineralogical knowledge. He is well known in many parts of the world and has considerable influence in the Caribbean and Alaska.

As a key figure in writing organizations he has consider-
able political worth and in the Northwest he is a powerful
influence.

I have known him for many years and have found him
discreet, loyal, honest and without peer in the art of getting
things done swiftly.

If Captain Hubbard requests help, be assured that it will
benefit others more than himself.

For courage and ability I cannot too strongly recommend
him.[41]

Hubbard also obtained help from his Congressman, Warren G. Magnuson, who was a member of the Committee on Naval Affairs and a friend of Ford's. He suggested to Magnuson that the US Navy should set up its own Bureau of Information, both to improve the Navy's public relations and to counter the "defeatist propaganda" about naval affairs that he claimed was "flooding the press".[42] Magnuson was favourably impressed with the proposal and sent President Roosevelt a letter, praising Hubbard in eye-catching terms:

May I recommend to you a gentleman of reputation? L.
Ron Hubbard is a well-known writer under five different
names. He is a respected explorer as Captain Bryan, Navy
Hydrographer, will confirm.

Mr Hubbard was born into the Navy. He has marine
masters papers for more types of vessels than any other
man in the United States.

He has written for Hollywood, radio and newspapers and
has published many millions of words of fact and fiction in
novels and national magazines. In writing organizations he is
a key figure, making him politically potent nationally.

An interesting trait is his distaste for personal publicity.

He is both discreet and resourceful as his record should indicate.

Anything you can do for Mr Hubbard will be appreciated.[43]

The wording of Magnuson's letter was strikingly similar to that which Hubbard wrote for Ford, and it is possible that he may have written it too.

Hubbard's former professor, the Dean of the School of Civil Engineering at George Washington University, chipped in with a generous letter praising Hubbard's leadership, ingenuity, resourcefulness and personality. His failure to graduate and poor grades were an unavoidable issue, but were put down to "the obvious fact that he had started in the wrong career. They do not reflect his great ability."[44]

The legendary science-fiction editor John W. Campbell, a friend and occasional purchaser of Hubbard's short stories, also wrote a letter of recommendation. He largely confined himself to praising Hubbard's ability to turn in a story on time, but added: "In personal relationships, I have the highest opinion of him as a thoroughly American gentleman."[45]

With all of this support it was no doubt a great disappointment to Hubbard when he once again failed his physical examination. His eyesight was still considered unacceptably poor and he was rejected on medical grounds in April 1941.

Despite this setback he did not give up, and time proved to be on his side as the war intensified in Europe. On May 27, 1941, President Roosevelt declared an Unlimited National Emergency. In a radio address, the President told Americans of the threat posed by German submarines to American shipping and the danger that Nazi expansionism posed to the United States. The entry of the US into World War II was now clearly only a matter of time. The country was, however, illprepared to fight; two decade of isolationist policies had left the Navy in a seriously weakened state and in urgent need of manpower, particularly in specialist roles.

A week after the President's declaration, Hubbard's application was re-examined by officers at the Navy Yard at Washington, DC. The Yard's resident Intelligence Officer wrote:

> *Although the subject Applicant is deficient in academic educational background, it is considered that his professional experience in newspaper work and travel compensates for his deficiency in the academic.*[46]

At around this time, Hubbard wrote to the War Department General Staff with a "brief on pre-battle conditioning", perhaps drawing on the "pioneering" psychological theories which he had mentioned in his 1939 letter to the Department. It was received politely but there is no indication that his scheme was ever implemented.

He also wrote to Senator Pat McCarran of Nevada with a plan for a Department of Aviation and a United States Army Air Force (USAAF). These were hardly original suggestions and had already been made by others, but the Senator obligingly made them into a bill, S.1635, with an identical bill introduced in the House of Representatives by William Howard Sutphin, a New Jersey Representative.

Although the bills were not passed, the USAAF was created by the War Department on June 29, 1941. The resolution establishing the USAAF was issued with the intention of avoiding a Congressional vote that would have tied the Administration's hands. Hubbard saw this as a great triumph and later claimed personal credit for the establishment of the USAAF:

> *I went to school in Washington, D.C., and I had a lot of friends up on the Hill during the next few years, and during*

1941 I decided to push a button. A friend of mine (a public-relations man from the Pacific Northwest) and I were sitting over coffee and we decided the government was too calm. We decided we would push a button and see what happened …

We pushed the button on Monday and the autonomous status of the United States Air Force happened on Tuesday. We did it as a little experiment. We didn't care whether the United States Air Force was flying helicopters or digging holes. It was just a point that there was sentiment existing on in some lines. All we had to do was go down and write a bill requesting what we wanted … Then we sent an alarm report that this bill was going through to tear the air force away from the army and the navy and to set up a new department.

So of course this just went along by word of mouth. It was wonderful! Senator's office after senator's office was alerted by the army and the navy, because the army and navy have patrons up on the Hill; they are not orphans. Finally we had collected a long series of names of people who were alarmed that this was going to happen. Then we told them something worse was going to happen – the air force would be set up as an independent department of defense. Then all we had to do was to tell the fellow who was a press relations man for the secretary of war, "Look, boy! You'd better get on the ball because this and this and this." "Huh! I'll see the secretary immediately!" Autonomous status for the United States Air Force was created. That is how it happened.[47]

Hubbard appears to have written to the Senator to inform him that due to his commissioning he would not be in a position to assist him further with the proposal. McCarran wrote to Hubbard on June

30 to thank Hubbard for his proposals, writing: "I have caused your plan ... to be made into a bill which I introduced as S.1635" and said that he regretted but understood Hubbard's withdrawal from the matter.[48]

The Church of Scientology claims that the Navy was "anxious to enlist L. Ron Hubbard" due to his expertise as a navigator.[49] The real reason for Hubbard's acceptance by the Navy was more prosaic: it was desperately short of personnel who could serve in what amounted to an undeclared war. This trumped the normal peacetime physical fitness requirements, so Hubbard's physical defects were set aside. He had applied for a commission as a Lieutenant Senior Grade in the Naval Reserve but, at 30 years old, was under age for this rank.[50] Instead, he was offered – and accepted – a Lieutenant (junior grade) commission. On July 2, 1941, Hubbard received his Articles of Commission issued on behalf of the President and couched in splendidly resonant terms:

Know Ye, that reposing special Trust and Confidence in the Patriotism, Valor, Fidelity and Abilities of LAFAYETTE RONALD HUBBARD, I do appoint him LIEUTENANT (JUNIOR GRADE) in the Naval Reserve of the United States Navy to rank from the TWENTY-FIFTH day of JUNE 1941.[51]

Hubbard's patriotism, valor and fidelity were not in doubt, but the following four years were to tax his abilities to – and beyond – their limits.

CHAPTER 4

Ron the Intelligence Officer

Several of the Church of Scientology's accounts of Hubbard's war years highlight his work for the Office of Naval Intelligence (ONI). His duties are said to have "included counter-intelligence and the organization of relief for beleaguered American forces on Bataan".[1] The account recorded in his US Navy file is considerably more modest.

Hubbard seems to have wished to join ONI from the outset. His old professor at George Washington University wrote, undoubtedly at Hubbard's prompting, to "recommend Mr. Hubbard for a commission in the United States Naval Reserve, for duty in Naval Intelligence." However, this did not mean covert undercover work, as is clear from various pieces of correspondence preserved in Hubbard's file.

On April 21, 1941 the Navy Department notified ONI that "Mr. L. Ron Hubbard is applying at Navy Yard, Washington, for a commission in the Naval Reserve, I-V(S), for assignment to duty in the Public Relations Office."[2] The designation "I-V(S)" stood for "Intelligence Volunteer (Specialist)" and was defined in the *Glossary of U.S. Naval Abbreviations* as denoting "Commissioned Intelligence officers qualified for specialist duties." This classification was abolished in September 1944.[3]

On June 4, the Intelligence Officer at the Navy Yard informed the Yard's Commandant that "[t]he subject Applicant appears to possess qualifications for assignment to the Public Relations Branch, or Foreign Intelligence Branch with particular reference to his familiarity with countries of the Caribbean Area."[4] Hubbard did not in fact have that much familiarity with the Caribbean area. He had organized an expedition for fellow university students aboard a sailing ship in 1932, which went so badly that his shipmates made an effigy of him and hanged it.[5] He subsequently spent up to six months on Puerto Rico. Although he was sent there by his father to help with hurricane relief, he soon found that panning for gold was more exciting.[6]

A month after the Navy decided to accept him, Hubbard received his commission as a Lieutenant (junior grade) in the United States Naval Reserve. He was assigned three days later to the Volunteer Reserve for Special Service (Intelligence duties). As the name suggests, this was part of the Reserve where officers with specialist roles served. A contemporary publication explains:

Procured primarily for shore billets in the mobilization plans of the Navy, they are generally officers and men whose professional qualifications are such that their proposed jobs are self-evident. Herein we find specialists in some form of the general classifications above mentioned and certain others ... Four other groups are really quite simple. C-V(S), I-V(S), L-V(S) and O-V(S) stand, respectively, for communication, intelligence, legal and ordnance officers in the Volunteer Reserve.[7]

In other words, despite his dreams of nautical glory, Hubbard's role was expected to be land-based rather than on a ship. He was not immediately assigned to active duty but was given a correspondence course to familiarize himself with Naval protocols. At the same time, although he was not formally assigned anywhere, he appears to done some work for the US Navy's Public Relations section.

Hubbard wrote on July 21 to his sponsor, Congressman Magnuson, thanking him for his help in obtaining a commission and mentioning that he had already submitted three ideas to accelerate recruiting, all of which were "going into effect". Magnuson replied, "Glad to hear your commission went through. Know you will be right at home in your work with Navy Press Relations." [8]

Hubbard followed up his letter with another a week later, explaining to the Senator that "as Press Relations was getting along well enough" he had offered to write two articles every week for national magazines, with the aim of selling the "American bluejacket" to the public. He had, he said, been given a "free helm" and "because this program will net about three times as much as Navy pay I think it no more than right that I return anything above pay and expenses to Navy Relief. So all goes along swimmingly."[9]

This turned out to be overoptimistic, for not a single article was published. On September 22, he was assigned to active duty and was sent to the Hydrographic Office at the Bureau of Navigation in Washington, D.C. "for the purpose of completing the data on some photographs which he had previously voluntarily submitted to this Office before his commissioning in the Naval Reserve". This was a reference to the images he had produced during his troubled 1940 yacht cruise along the coasts of British Columbia and Alaska.

Hubbard stayed at the Hydrographic Office for two weeks. The Officer-in-Charge described Hubbard's duties in a memorandum of October 22, 1941:

> *During this period he examined the prints of several hundred photographs and selected from them several dozen that were fairly clear possessing some navigational interest. These he mounted and annotated. He also indicated on several charts the position from which the pictures were taken.*
>
> *He also examined the text of the Sailing Directions – H.O. Nos. 175 and 176, British Columbia, Vols. I and II – for the places with which he was familiar as a result of his recent*

yacht cruise in these waters, and submitted several suggested changes or amplifications. These items are all brief, and some are unimportant, but in the aggregate they represent a very definite contribution.[10]

Hubbard referred to this posting in later years, though by 1972 his "brief" and "unimportant" contributions had been transformed in his mind into a recollection that "I rewrote the Hydrographic Office Publications for the US Navy".[11]

After he had completed what must have been a fairly mundane posting, Hubbard's record shows that he was released from active duty on October 6 and remained formally inactive until November 23, 1941, although it appears that he also took an intelligence course between October 21 and November 6.[12] Given his subsequent assignments, it seems likely that this course related to basic training in censorship duties, most likely in New York. From 1939, classes of around 20 Naval Reserve officers at a time were trained in censorship in naval establishments in San Francisco and New York City – America's international communications gateways. About 400 such officers had been trained by December 1941.[13]

On resuming active duty, he spent three weeks under instruction at the Headquarters of the Third Naval District in New York. He was ordered to proceed at the end of his instruction period to San Francisco. From there, he was instructed to board the SS *President Jackson* for transportation on January 8, 1942 to Cavite in the Philippines for duty with the Sixteenth Naval District.[14]

The reasons for Hubbard being posted to the Philippines are not recorded in his file, but it seems likely that it related to his claims to have had knowledge of the region. (In fact, he had only visited briefly during his childhood journeys to see his parents at the US naval base on Guam.) He told an interviewer in 1958 that "because I knew Asia I was thrown into Naval Intelligence".[15]

Hubbard's training and his planned journey to the Philippines were both interrupted by the Japanese surprise attack on Pearl Harbor on December 7, 1941. In a 1951 lecture, he spoke of the moment he heard of the Japanese attack: "I walked out of a little cigar store on Eighth Avenue in New York and a bum was standing there; he had just had access to a radio and he stopped me and said, 'Pearl Harbor is being bombed!'"[16] He received orders a week later to report to the District Intelligence Office of the Twelfth Naval District in San Francisco, and from there to proceed to Cavite on the next available ship. However, circumstances dictated that he would never reach the Philippines.

CHAPTER 5

Ron the Saviour of Australia

If L. Ron Hubbard was to be believed, Australia owes its freedom to his efforts. He wrote in 1965: "In 1942, as a senior US Naval Officer in Northern Australia by fluke of fate, I helped save them from the Japanese."[1] Four years later he told Scientologists that he "once had a big share in saving its bacon from Japan ... A handful of us, months before the coming of US troops, worked like mad to balk the Japs and change their minds."[2] The truth, as ever with Hubbard, was considerably less impressive.

In the days immediately after Pearl Harbor, American, British and Dutch garrisons in the Far East and western Pacific were thrown into confusion by sudden Japanese attacks. Japanese forces seized control of the western Pacific in a series of lightning attacks, landed troops in the Philippines, took Guam and Wake Island, overran Hong Kong, invaded Malaya and moved against the Dutch East Indies. With weak coastal defences and most of her army deployed abroad in support of Britain, Australia had little spare military capacity to defence herself against a territorial threat in her own backyard. A Japanese invasion of the sparsely populated and poorly defended far north of the country seemed to be a terrifyingly real possibility.

The US responded by rushing men and materiel to the western Pacific in a bid to shore up Allied defenses in the region. However, the speed of the Japanese advance hindered American plans. President Roosevelt ordered on December 15, 1941, that fighters, bombers, troops and ammunition were to be sent at once to assist General MacArthur's outnumbered and outgunned garrison in the Philippines.

The transport USS *President Polk* and the liner SS *President Coolidge* were diverted from their planned itineraries and were loaded with equipment, ordnance and troops to be transported to Manila. The *Polk* alone carried 55 P-40E and 4 C-53 aircraft, 20 million .30 caliber, 447,000 .50 caliber, 30,000 three-inch AA and 5,000 75 mm rounds of ammunition, along with five carloads of torpedoes and over 615,000 pounds of rations. 55 pilots were aboard, along with 178 officers and men of the US Navy.[3]

One of them was L. Ron Hubbard. Although the Philippines was a combat zone, he was not assigned to frontline combat duty at his post in the Sixteenth Military District, the naval command covering the Philippines. He later said that he was "a mail officer",[4] in other words, responsible for postal censorship. Military regulations required that outgoing mail written by enlisted men would be opened and read by an officer, who would censor any sensitive content before sealing it and authorizing its delivery. This was an unpopular post, particularly as it seemed demeaning to the enlisted men to have their personal correspondence to wives and girlfriends read by someone else. Many found it particularly galling that officers were allowed to censor their own mail.

Polk and *Coolidge* were originally intended to rendezvous with another convoy, known as the *Pensacola* Convoy, that was already en route to the Philippines. However, the Japanese advance was so rapid that the sea route was effectively blockaded by Christmas 1941. The ships' destination was altered and Hubbard ended up in Brisbane in Queensland, Australia.

After arriving in Brisbane on January 11, 1942, he was granted permission to disembark from the *Polk* to await transportation on another vessel to Manila. He later claimed to have been the "Senior Officer Present of northern Australia, not because I had any rank, but because there wasn't anybody else there."[5]

It was certainly true that there were few other US Navy personnel in Brisbane (which is on Australia's central east coast, not in the north). 178 naval officers and men arrived on *Polk* and *Coolidge* and a previous convoy had brought 2,600 Army Air Force Personnel and 2,000 National Guard personnel, comprising a brigade from the US Army's Field Artillery Corps.

The US Army's first headquarters in Australia had been established at Lennon's Hotel in Brisbane, but by January 1, 1942 it had been moved to Melbourne. Lt. Gen. George H. Brett set about improving logistics by establishing "Base Sections" in port cities on the north and east coasts of Australia. Base Section One was located in Darwin in the Northern Territory; Base Section Two was in Townsville and Base Section Three in Brisbane, both in Queensland; and Base Section Four was in Melbourne, Victoria. Three more were established by April 1942 in Adelaide, Perth and Sydney. They were meant to be staffed by engineer officers but when the initial four were first organized there were not enough qualified personnel to staff them.[6]

In such a situation, roles were likely ill-defined and personnel found themselves doing unfamiliar tasks as the expeditionary force established itself in its first few weeks. The US force's commanders faced a severe shortage of trained officers, men, secretaries and clerks; the Australians were unable to supply adequate numbers to support the US forces.[7] Hubbard's situation was likely even less clearly defined than most: he was at a loose end because of his inability to reach his duty station in Manila and lacked any assigned duty in Brisbane.

There is no record in Hubbard's naval files of what his formal role was in Brisbane, other than that he was nominally attached to the Office of the US Naval Attaché during his stay. It is likely that he was left to his own devices. He appears to have been drafted to work for the commander of Base Section Three, Colonel Alexander L. P. Johnson, while he was waiting for a vessel to take him to Manila. He gave an account in 1959 of how this came about:

[T]he army stopped me and said, "Who are you?" And I gave my name, rank and serial number. And they said, "Do you realize that there's no naval officer in this port or in Northern Australia?" And I said, "Well, I hadn't realized it." Couldn't have cared less, as a matter of fact. I was thinking, "Gosh, it's nice to be alive!"

And — "Well now, in your regulations," the army said, "I'm sure you will find a clause that says, 'By exigencies of service on foreign station, the senior naval officer present shall take command of all naval activities." So I looked at my stripes. I said, "Okay. That's the way it is. I'll sit around and look pretty."[8]

According to Hubbard, his temporary assignment to the US Army Base Section Three was "granted … orally" by Commander Lewis D. Causey, the US Naval Attaché in Melbourne. He also said that he had informed CinC Asiatic Fleet that he had been "assigned for duty on the staff of Base Section Three until further information from the CinC Asiatic".[9]

By his own account, he was given *ad hoc* tasks to perform in the mildly chaotic situation that accompanied the Americans' arrival. He claimed that he had "take[n] command of all naval activities" in Brisbane:

There's 17 merchantmen in Brisbane lower river; they haven't been brought in. There's 4 million dollars worth of jettisoned cargo laying on the docks that nobody has any responsibility for. There are 250 refugees who have just dropped back from Malaysia and Singapore that nobody's taking any responsibility for, and you have about 200 naval personnel drifting through this port that nobody's taking any responsibility for. There are enemy agents all over the place. Nobody's taking charge of naval censorship. Well, here's a sergeant and a girl and there's your office.[10]

He claimed that he had been "the total antiaircraft [defense] of Brisbane, once. One submachine gun. They referred to me as the ack-ack battery!".[11] The weapon in question appears to have been a Thompson submachine gun that was loaned to Hubbard in Brisbane by HQ Coastal Artillery, Australian Military Forces. but which he never gave back. His naval record contains several pieces of correspondence about its non-return, continuing through to the spring of 1944.[12] The details are unclear, as only his superiors' endorsement chits are preserved, rather than the original memos and his replies. His estranged son Ron Jr. alleged in 1982 that his father had "stolen" the weapon and retained it until he was forced to give it back, though this is unproven.

Hubbard alluded to the matter in a 1956 lecture in which he claimed:

> *I myself have been solicited for a Tommy gun. A rather unusual thing to be solicited for, but they knew my name and they knew where I was located. Isn't that terrific? I mean, it's really phenomenal. I mean, they did; they knew my name; they knew the item that was missing and so forth. Of course, it was the wrong navy, but that didn't make any difference at all. It really was the wrong navy. It was "L. R. Hubbard, Royal Australian Navy, Lieutenant Commander," I think it was; something like that. "Please return to the United States Navy the sub-Thompson machine gun which was borrowed from the USS Chicago" – that was the wrong ship, but that didn't matter; it was the Travis – "Please return it," and so on. Now, how they got onto this, I don't know, because the Travis got sunk, you see? And I don't know how they got into this, but somebody keeps a file! That, I'm sure.[13]*

There has never been a USS *Travis*; the only US military ship to bear the name *Travis* was a coastguard cutter which served in the

Atlantic during the war and was sunk by a hurricane off North Carolina in September 1944.[14] The USS *Chicago* did serve in the South Pacific, though she was not stationed in Australia.[15]

Hubbard's claim to have been involved in anti-aircraft defense is likely to have been a typically exaggerated account of a fairly minor role. Base Section Three was located at Somerville House, formerly a private girls' school in a suburb of Brisbane. Contemporary photographs show US Army personnel taking part in anti-aircraft drills, including taking shelter in trenches. (The base's original air raid siren, mounted on a wooden post outside the buildings, is still in place today.)[16] Hubbard would certainly have taken part in these drills and likely carried a weapon in connection with them, though a sub-machine gun with a maximum effective range of 50 yards would have been of very little use against an enemy bomber.

In late January 1941 Hubbard became closely involved in a secret US Army operation to resupply General MacArthur's besieged forces in the Philippines. (The Church of Scientology alludes to this in a reference to Hubbard being involved in "the organization of relief for beleaguered American forces on Bataan".[17]) 11,000 American and Filipino troops were cut off on the heavily fortified island of Corregidor overlooking Manila Bay, under constant attack from the Japanese. Up to 120,000 more troops were being squeezed into a pocket at Bataan on the main island of Luzon. Ammunition and rations were in short supply.

Hubbard's involvement is documented in a five-page report that he wrote on February 3, 1942 after his actions came under scrutiny from his superiors. The operation went drastically wrong as an indirect result of his ship-routing plans and led to the loss of a ship and the deaths of fourteen people. The material losses included hundreds of tons of rations and around 1.7 million rounds of ammunition. Hubbard was subsequently removed from his post and received orders to return to the continental US, amidst strong criticism from his superiors.

MacArthur had requested the Army Chief of Staff, General George C. Marshall, to organize vessels to break the Japanese blockade of the Philippines.[18] The War Department in Washington, D.C. sent Colonel Stephen J. Chamberlin to Australia to manage the effort.[19] When he arrived, Chamberlin was appointed as General MacArthur's Assistant Chief of Staff and Chief of Staff of US Army Forces in Australia (USAFIA)

Chamberlin in Australia and another US Army officer, Colonel John A. Robenson, in the Dutch East Indies, began an intensive effort in early January 1942 to hire or requisition small, fast ships that could resupply MacArthur's forces. It would be a high-risk mission, as escort vessels could not be provided. The ships would have to rely on speed, evasion and a good measure of luck to avoid Japanese aircraft, ships and submarines patrolling the waters of the Philippines and Dutch East Indies.

Hubbard's report names three ships – the MV *Don Isidro*, SS *Coast Farmer* and SS *Admiral Halstead*.[20] All three were involved in an attempt to break the Japanese blockade of the Philippines. *Coast Farmer* and *Admiral Halstead* had been part of the November-December 1941 Pensacola Convoy, in which they had carried largely civilian supplies intended for Guam and Manila. They were unable to reach their destinations due to the Japanese invasion and were unloaded in Brisbane instead. *Don Isidro* was a 3,200-ton steamship with a 68-man crew which had operated before the war as a luxury passenger transport between the Philippine Islands but was sent to Australia when the Japanese invaded.

Don Isidro was selected as the first of the blockade runners and was chartered at Brisbane by Major General Lewis H. Brereton on January 20. Forty enlisted men from the 453d Ordnance (Aviation) Bombardment Company volunteered to travel aboard as armed guards. They had travelled from San Francisco with Hubbard on *Polk* and *Coolidge* the previous December. Fifteen were selected to accompany the ship, and after a coin toss, 2nd Lieutenant Joseph F. Kane was selected to head the detachment.[21]

The ship was armed with five .50-caliber heavy machine guns on *Don Isidro* to serve as anti-aircraft defences, fitted on improvised mounts by the Americans. She was loaded with 700 tons of rations, 4,500 5" anti-aircraft rounds, 1.5 million .30-cal rounds and 200,000 .50-cal rounds, drawn from US and Australian Army stocks in Brisbane.[22]

Hubbard wrote that on Monday January 26, 1942, the "Commanding Officer [i.e. Colonel Johnson of Base Section Three in Brisbane] ordered that a certain vessel be furnished with a route and other needed material to safeguard her voyage. He further ordered that this material and route should be forwarded immediately upon the copying of the route after the despatch of the vessel to one Commander Causey, US Naval Attaché, Australia, member of the Ship Movements Board."[23] The context and subsequent content of the report makes it clear that the order concerned *Don Isidro*, which left Brisbane on a "special mission" at 13:15 on January 27.[24]

However, the text of the routing order was reported to have gone missing *en route* to headquarters in Melbourne. Its sensitivity was such that it was supposed to have been hand-delivered by a courier travelling by plane.

According to Hubbard's report, Chamberlin ordered Hubbard to immediately and personally courier a fresh copy of the routing order to Melbourne on Friday January 30. Hubbard handed it over to Causey and Chamberlin two days later.

He subsequently attended a conference with Major-General Julian F. Barnes (the Commanding General USAFIA), Colonel Van Santvoord Merle-Smith (the US Military Attaché to Australia). Causey, Chamberlin and an aide. The discussion focused on plans to send *Coast Farmer* and *Admiral Halstead* on a "Mission to Luzon", as Hubbard put it, and the order was given to carry out the mission. Chamberlin ordered that Hubbard's commanding officer, Colonel Johnson, was to have "nothing to do with these ships after they leave Brisbane".

Hubbard's handling of the *Don Isidro* came under scrutiny. He was ordered "to show what he had done for the *Don Isidro* 'if anything'". Showing the route selected for the ship, Hubbard said that he had "given the *Don Isidro* additional protection by a set of Japanese answering signals." These were presumably intended to deceive Japanese vessels into thinking that the ship was one of theirs, and had likely been obtained by US naval intelligence. This would have been part of the reason why the matter was handled with such extreme sensitivity.

After the conference, Hubbard sought and obtained an interview with Major-General Barnes "on the grounds that the general must be informed of the folly of sending the *Coast Farmer* and *Admiral Halstead* to Luzon and the further folly of routing them past Thursday Island, New Guinea and past the Japanese land sea and air bases on Ambione [Ambon]". Barnes told Hubbard to relay that information to Chamberlin and asked about the disappearance of the routing order.

Hubbard said that it might have been removed from the aircraft carrying it. He hinted in his report that the responsibility might lie with Sir Thomas Gordon, who was at the time the representative in Australia of the British Ministry of Shipping (War Transport) and was later given charge of all shipping in Australian waters. Hubbard was coy about who exactly brought up Gordon, reporting only that the name "appeared in the conversation". It seems likely, given what transpired the next day, that Hubbard made some insinuations about Gordon's loyalties.

Hubbard was ordered to remain in Melbourne overnight for a further interview the following day. He wrote that he protested to no avail about being made to stay in Melbourne when there was work to be done in Brisbane. According to his report, he was refused access to Chamberlin and Causey ordered him to be silent about his criticism of the blockade-running plans.

At 16:00 on Monday, he met with Commander Causey and Colonel Merle-Smith, the US Military Attaché, but was startled to find himself being "tried" by the Colonel. Hubbard wrote in his report that he was perturbed by the fact that "Commander Causey was a spectator in agreement with Colonel Smith [sic] and saw nothing wrong with a naval officer being disciplined by Colonel Smith while he, Commander Causey, was present". Hubbard's role in Brisbane appears to have come under close scrutiny, along with his views on Sir Thomas Gordon. He wrote that Merle-Smith had engaged in

> *close cross-questioning [of] this officer with regard to the extent of his knowledge of Sir Thomas Gordon. This officer divulged very little. This officer refused to let Colonel Smith have entered into the record words which Colonel Smith said as coming from this officer, "Then you say that you have no knowledge whatsoever that Sir Thomas Gordon is anything but a loyal citizen" (paraphrase). This officer said he admitted no extent of any knowledge whatsoever and would not admit to knowing nothing about Sir Thomas Gordon. This was entered on the record as "Hubbard uncertain".*[25]

The Naval Attaché was also present at the same meeting and accused Hubbard of sending *Don Isidro* "three thousand miles out of her way". The ship had originally been routed directly to the Philippines but was diverted to Fremantle on the opposite side of Australia.[26] Hubbard told Causey that the vessel had been sent south "on the specific orders of Colonel Johnson and that it was only two days further sailing distance and the vessel was less in peril." He justified the route with reference to the "Contact Map in

G-2 [Naval Intelligence]", which showed where enemy forces had been reported in the region but which he claimed neither Causey nor Merle-Smith had ever seen (highly unlikely, given their positions). The order to route *Don Isidro* south was said by Hubbard to have been issued by Colonel Johnson in Brisbane. However, Hubbard's advocacy of the southern route strongly suggests that it was his idea.

According to Hubbard, Causey told him at the end of the meeting:

> *I have sent a message to the CinC Asiatic as of this morning stating that I wish you to be removed from Brisbane, stating that you are making a nuisance of yourself. You have never been under my orders and I consider you as having nothing to do with me. If you wish to serve with Johnson, that is up to you.*[27]

Hubbard evidently took this hard. He admitted that he had walked out of the meeting at that point: "Without taking leave or further addressing either officer, who were now standing in the hall, their conversation and comment overheard widely, this officer put on his cap and left the building."[28] He followed up by writing a five-page account of the situation in which he was critical of the two attachés and implied they were plotting against Johnson.

Despite Hubbard's entreaties the Commander in Chief Asiatic Fleet immediately granted Causey's request for Hubbard to be transferred. On February 11, Causey formally ordered Hubbard back to the continental United States and explained his reasoning in a letter sent three days later:

> *By assuming unauthorized authority and attempting to perform duties for which he has no qualifications, he became the source of much trouble. This, however, was*

made possible by the representative of the U.S. Army at Brisbane [Johnson]...

On February 11, 1942 I sent him dispatch orders to report to the Commanding Officer USS Chaumont for passage to the United States. And upon arrival report to the Commandant 12th Naval District for future assignment. This officer is not satisfactory for independent duty assignment. He is garrulous and tries to give impressions of his importance. He also seems to think that he has unusual ability in most lines. These characteristics indicate that he will require close supervision for satisfactory performance of any intelligence duty.[29]

Causey did not spell out the "unauthorized authority" and duties Hubbard had performed without qualifications, but it seems highly likely that this related to his ship-routing work for Johnson. Hubbard referred in his report to Johnson to using the Contact Map, a Naval Intelligence product, as a factor in deciding where to route *Don Isidro*. Although he was a member of the Office of Naval Intelligence, he had no qualifications to do any work involving intelligence gathering or analysis.

The Church of Scientology has distributed a memorandum said to have been written by Johnson to the Commander of Base Section One in Darwin, dated February 13, 1942. He recommended Hubbard as "an intelligent, resourceful and dependable officer" and asked that an earlier unspecified request should be granted.[30]

The nature of the request is not recorded in Hubbard's naval file, but given its nature and destination, Hubbard may have asked to be transferred to work with the US Army in Darwin. However, the decision was not Johnson's to make and Causey was evidently not willing to let Hubbard stay in Australia.

On February 17, Causey cabled the Bureau of Naval Personnel to inform them that Hubbard was being sent home:

LIEUT. (JG) L.R. HUBBARD IVS USNR ORDERED RETURN US VIA [USS] CHAUMONT AND REPORT TO COM 12 [the 12th Naval District, San Francisco]. HE IS UN-SATISFACTORY FOR ANY AVAILABLE ASSIGNMENT HERE. VIA [SS] PRESIDENT COOLIDGE, A REPORT MAILED.[31]

Hubbard no doubt appealed to Johnson but it would have been of no use, as he was still formally under the command of the Naval Attaché and therefore had to follow Causey's orders. While Johnson certainly seems to have regarded Hubbard well, this did not mitigate the seriousness of his failures. Previous authors of bio-graphical accounts of Hubbard have implied that he fell foul of a personality clash with Causey. Lawrence Wright characterizes it as Hubbard having "got[ten] on the wrong side" of Causey,[32] Jon Atack writes that Causey regarded Hubbard as a "simply a nuisance"[33], and Russell Miller says that Hubbard "antagonized his senior officers".[34]

In fact, as Causey's letter explaining his order and Hubbard's own report on *Don Isidro's* routing makes clear, Causey's criticism was not prompted simply by personality clashes or by inter-service rivalries but by two very serious operational failings. The apparent loss of the routing order represented a major security breach con-cerning a secret operation. It put in jeopardy a vital shipment of supplies for Allied forces who were facing a desperate situation. The circuitous route Hubbard chose for *Don Isidro* delayed the vessel by days at a moment when every day counted. Had it been peacetime, such failures would quite likely have led to a demotion or even a court-martial.

Hubbard evidently exacerbated the situation with what Causey called his "garrulous" nature and attempts at personal aggrandize-ment. The fact that he was sent back to the continental US at a time when the US forces in Australia were short of qualified personnel shows how seriously the matter was taken. In Causey's view, Hubbard clearly needed to be kept far away from any position of independent responsibility.

It was also not only Causey who took a dim view of Hubbard. According to Hubbard's own account, he was "disciplined" by the US Military Attaché, Colonel Merle-Smith. He also does not seem to have been held in high regard by Colonel Chamberlin, General MacArthur's Assistant Chief of Staff, who refused to see him again following the conference on February 1. When the decision was taken to send Hubbard home, his seniors clearly had very little sympathy left for him.

In the meantime, *Don Isidro's* voyage was still underway. Hubbard's mismanagement of her route soon had tragic consequences. Instead of sending the ship by the shortest route through the Torres Strait between Australia and New Guinea, he routed her on a long loop around Australia's southern and western coasts *en route* to Batavia (now Jakarta) on Java, where she was to pick up onward routing orders from the local US Army representatives.

This route was slower and far longer than a Torres Strait passage. The distance from Brisbane to Fremantle is about 2,700 miles, prompting Causey's complaint that Hubbard had sent the vessel "three thousand miles out of her way". (The circuitous routing of *Don Isidro* has been remarked on before by writers – for instance, Walter D. Edmonds noted her "curiously roundabout route" in his 1951 book on the US defensive effort in the South Pacific[35] – but Hubbard had not previously been identified as being responsible for the routing.)

Don Isidro stopped at Fremantle on February 3 to take on fuel and water. She sailed for Batavia (now Jakarta) on Java the following day, where she arrived on February 10. She left two days later with new routing orders that would send her to Gingoog Bay in Mindanao in the southern Philippines. Her course would take her west from Batavia, south through the Sunda Strait, east to the

Timor Sea, north through the Arafura and Banda Seas, and then straight to Mindanao.[36]

On February 18, 1942, the day after Hubbard was ordered home, *Don Isidro* was ambushed by a Japanese bomber about 80 miles off the Australian coast. Evasive action enabled the ship to escape the bombs. Spooked by the attack, the captain decided to head to safety at Darwin. The following day the ship was attacked again at a point about 25 miles north of Bathurst Island, near Darwin. Two waves of Japanese fighter planes and bombers flying from aircraft carriers bombed and strafed *Don Isidro*, setting her on fire.

Eleven of the Filipino crew died in the attacks and all of the ship's lifeboats and life rafts were destroyed. The Philippine-crewed *Florence D,* another blockade-runner heading out from Batavia, picked up *Don Isidro's* SOS calls and attempted to carry out a rescue. However, she was also attacked as she steamed towards *Don Isidro's* position. *Florence D* sank with the loss of three lives, hundreds of tons of rations and millions of rounds of desperately needed ammunition.

Despite the fire, her captain kept *Don Isidro* going in a desperate attempt to reach safety. However, the engines failed three miles offshore, forcing the survivors to jump overboard and swim the rest of the way. They reached the island by 2 or 3 am the next day after spending up to ten hours in the water, and were rescued later in the day by an Australian ship. Several were severely burned. Two of them, a Filipino sailor and the leader of the US Army detachment, Second Lieutenant Joseph F. Kane, subsequently died in hospital in Darwin. Kane sustained severe leg and foot injuries and died of gangrene, while eight of the other Americans were injured, some severely.[37]

Don Isidro drifted until she beached in shallow water. She was left there as a burnt-out hulk, her vital cargo destroyed or rendered unusable. The wreck is today a protected historical site and the casualties are commemorated by a memorial in Darwin.[38]

The ship was probably a target of opportunity for the Japanese, as the main target of the attacking aircraft was the town and port of Darwin. In other words, she was in the wrong place at the wrong time. However, Hubbard bore considerable responsibility for her loss. She would not have gone to Batavia if Hubbard had not routed her there and she would not have been in the vicinity of Darwin on the day of the air raid if she had taken a more direct route to the Philippines. Her loss deprived American and Filipino forces of vital supplies at a time when they were badly needed.

Her fate contrasted with that of *Coast Farmer*, which took a wide-sweeping route past the Solomon Islands and reached the Philippines safely nine days after leaving Brisbane on February 10.[39] *Admiral Halstead*, the third ship mentioned by Hubbard in his February 5 report, safely travelled the Torres Strait route that Hubbard had disdained but was caught in the attack on Darwin while docked there on February 19.

A fourth ship unmentioned by Hubbard, the MV *Don Nati*, left Brisbane on February 18, travelled through the Dutch East Indies, narrowly evading Japanese patrols, and made it to Cebu in the Philippines on March 6.[40] She had been chartered by Colonel Johnson in Brisbane on January 28 on the orders of Colonel Chamberlin.[41] Significantly, on February 11 – the same day that Hubbard was being ordered out of Australia by Causey – Chamberlin issued fresh orders to Johnson instructing him to personally deliver the ship's routing instructions and identification signals. This was likely a response to the fiasco of Hubbard losing the routing instructions for *Don Isidro*.[42]

Whoever was responsible for the other three ships' routing – it seems likely to have also been Hubbard, judging by his later claims of responsibility – had evidently been instructed to use the most direct route available. There seems to have been no further consideration given to using a route around southern Australia.

Despite the disastrous results of his routing order for *Don Isidro*,

Hubbard seems to have remembered his time routing ships in Brisbane as something of a success despite having to deal with superiors whom he regarded as incompetent. Sixteen years later, he told an audience of Scientologists:

> *I'd sent, on my own authority, four cargo ships loaded to the gunwales with machine gun ammunition, rifle ammunition and quinine up to MacArthur ... when Melbourne found out that [my] office was too active for them to do anything about, they went into apathy for a while and then they got reinforced by several admirals, and they finally got brave enough to put the brakes on it.*[43]

He claimed credit for the safe arrival of two ships – probably *Coast Farmer* and *Don Nati* – saying that they "got there just as nice as you please."[44] He did not, however, mention the sinking of *Don Isidro*.

The fallout from the raid on Darwin and the loss of *Don Isidro* may have delayed Hubbard's departure from Australia, as he did not leave on USS *Chaumont* as ordered. His record indicates that while serving in Brisbane, he received secret orders by despatch from the office of COMANZAC, Vice Admiral Herbert F. Leary, who commanded Allied naval forces in the south-west Pacific. Only the despatch's receipt is recorded and not its contents, but it must have been sent at some point between the establishment of COMANZAC on January 27, 1942 and Hubbard's departure from Australia six weeks later. It is the only secret naval despatch recorded as having been received by Hubbard during his time in Australia. The timing suggests that it may have been related to the blockade-running operation, a matter with which COMANZAC almost certainly would have been involved.

Hubbard seems not to have suffered any further consequences from the *Don Isidro* affair beyond his removal from Australia and the criticism he received from Causey. This probably reflected the fact that he was not the sole author of the ship's loss. His routing order was approved by Colonel Johnson, whom Causey explicitly blamed for enabling Hubbard to cause "much trouble". The fateful order that directed *Don Isidro* into the path of the Japanese attack force was issued by the US Army's Colonel John A. Robenson on the advice of Admiral Conrad Helfrich, the commander of Dutch naval forces in the Dutch East Indies. While the ship would likely not have sailed to Java had it not been for Hubbard, the chain of responsibility for her sinking was probably sufficiently attenuated that the blame was deflected away from Hubbard.

There are indications that Hubbard was removed from Base Section Three in mid-February and assigned to a new post for a short time. A record of March 8, 1942 describes Hubbard as a "Naval Observer".[45] When he was being pursued by a Brisbane tailor a month later for non-payment of bills, the complaint was forwarded to the naval authorities in the US by the Office of the United States Naval Observer in Brisbane, based in Australasia Chambers at 406 Queen Street in the city center – significantly, some distance away from Base Section Three.[46] This indicates a likely connection between Hubbard and the office. The complaint was forwarded by the then Naval Observer, Commander Paul S. Slawson, who took up his post with his staff in Brisbane in mid-March 1942, at about the same time that Hubbard left.[47] Slawson had previously been the senior US Naval Attaché in Java,[48] where he had served as one of three Naval Observers to the Dutch East Indies.

Nothing in Hubbard's service record refers to him ever holding the position of Naval Observer and his service record shows him under the Office of the Naval Attaché throughout. He was likely still attached to Base Section Three around February 13, 1942, the date of Colonel Johnson's last known correspondence concerning Hubbard. He left Australia just over three weeks later. If he did serve in the capacity of Naval Observer, it could therefore have been for no longer than about three weeks.

The most likely explanation is that following the *Don Isidro* debacle, the Naval Attaché was anxious to get Hubbard away from the Army base and into a position where he could not cause any more trouble. Equally importantly, the Office of the Naval Observer was under Causey's chain of command and likely answered to another naval officer in Brisbane. The post was not yet staffed but evidently existed, at least on paper, before Slawson's arrival. It is likely that Causey shunted Hubbard into an unoccupied post, located well away from Base Section Three, where he could occupy himself with harmless administrative duties until being relieved by Slawson.

This scenario is supported by Hubbard's own words. In a 1958 lecture, he described how "when naval observers came in there [in Brisbane], by the way, they looked at me in this patched-up office that I was running it from."[49] The arrival of the naval observers in Brisbane corresponds with Slawson's arrival in March; Hubbard's description suggests that there was a brief handover before he left. In a 1963 interview, he said: "I was replaced, I think, by a Captain, a couple of commanders... and about 15 junior officers."[50] (A few years later this was upgraded to "fifteen officers of rank".[51]) The replacements he describes were likely Slawson (who was in fact a Commander) and his colleagues.

Despite the ignominious end of his brief tour in Australia, Hubbard claimed in later years that his stint there had made him famous in the navy:

> [F]or the next two or three years I'd run into officers, and they would say, "Hubbard? Hubbard? Hubbard? Are you Hubbard that was in Australia?" And I'd say, "Yes." And they'd say, "Oh!" Kind of, you know, horrified, like they didn't know whether they should quite talk to me or not, you know? Terrible man.[52]

According to the Church of Scientology, "Hubbard so distinguished himself as an intelligence officer in Australia, he was thereafter known as "that fellow from down under."[53] In reality, Hubbard appears to have been remembered in Australia chiefly for failing to pay his bills.[54]

A letter in Hubbard's file states that he departed Brisbane on March 9, 1942 aboard SS *Pennant*,[55] a Danish flagged vessel that the US government had seized the previous December. She was converted hastily into a troop ship operated for the US Army by American President Lines. Conditions aboard were gruelling. The passengers slept in bunks stacked five high, with officers often taking the top bunk to avoid the vomit showering down on those at the bottom in rough seas.[56]

A medical assessment from 1947 corroborates that Hubbard was aboard *Pennant*, as he claimed to have suffered an injury while aboard the vessel in March 1942.[57] His presence is also attested in the war diary of the heavy cruiser USS *New Orleans*, which was assigned to escort *Pennant* and other vessels travelling in convoy from Brisbane to Nouméa in New Caledonia. The diary's entry for Sunday March 8, 1942 states:

> *The following were reported by Lt. (jg) Hubbard, U.S.N.R., Naval Observer, to be secret agents of Japan or Germany, operating in and around Brisbane: John Leahy, age appx. 29, black mustache, wears horn rimmed glasses; Mrs. Lyell, age appx. 39, heavy features, striking black eyes; Mr. Woodfield, age appx. 40, suave English gentleman; Miss Stephanie Wilkins, age appx. 34, long nose, striking appearance; Dr. Kinston and brother, ages appx. 44 or 45, Germans.*[58]

This was not the first time Hubbard had reported people to the authorities on suspicion of being enemy agents, nor was it the last. He told the FBI in 1940 that a member of staff at a New York hotel might be a Nazi agent,[59] and he reported multiple people – including his estranged wife – to the FBI for supposedly being Communists in the early 1950s.[60] None of his letters appear to have been acted on; indeed, one of them was annotated "Appears mental" by an FBI agent.[61]

There is no indication of why Hubbard suspected that the six people he reported were spies, nor of why he might have reported them to a ship that was about to depart rather than to the authorities on shore. Nor is there any indication of how this was related to any of his duties, particularly as he was in the process of being sent home from Australia. The outcome – if any – of his report is not recorded in his file.

New Orleans and her companion vessel, the destroyer USS *Mugford*, left Brisbane on March 9, 1942 to escort *Pennant* and SS *Perida* to New Caledonia. There they met convoy ZK7 arriving from Melbourne, carrying troops to guard the strategically vital island against the threat of a Japanese invasion. The ships arrived on March 12 at Noumeá on New Caledonia where they unloaded their cargoes and passengers. *Pennant* then continued across the Pacific, most likely bound for Hawaii.[62]

Hubbard later claimed to have been "[flown] in from the South Pacific in the Secretary of the Navy's [personal] plane ... I was the first [US] casualty returned from the South Pacific,"[63] His naval record makes no mention of any air travel from Australia, and his medical record shows no injuries. He said in a 1956 lecture:

> *Most of the guys that were shipped out of there who had been wounded, were shipped out by slow boat. And I didn't, I wasn't that seriously done in. I hooked a ride on the Secretary of Navy's plane; produced the right set of orders (I hope nobody ever kept them on file) and got flown home.*[64]

His followers heard a different version of his return – with no mention of injuries – in a second lecture the same year:

> *I picked up a telephone, called the Secretary of [the] Navy. See, and I said, "I'm tired of this place. I'd like to leave."*
> *And he said, "Yeah."*
> *I said, "Yeah, I've got some important despatches. As a matter of fact, we've got enough despatches here to practically sink the Japanese navy if they had to carry them. There's a lot of traffic and stuff like that, and so forth."*
> *So he sent his plane down and picked me up and flew me home. You think I'm just talking through my hat but that is exactly what happened.*[65]

According to a 1942 medical record, Hubbard returned to San Francisco via Honolulu, Hawaii, where he had presumably arrived by sea on *Pennant*.[66] It is possible that he may have made the journey from Hawaii by air. If so, he most likely made the journey on the *Philippine Clipper*, one of three giant flying boats operated by Pan American Airlines. The US Navy had requisitioned them at the outbreak of the war. It was not "the Secretary of the Navy's plane", though it may well have carried the secretary to Hawaii at some point. Instead, it was used as a general purpose transport which amassed many thousands of hours flying passengers between Pacific destinations.

The aircraft is recorded as arriving in San Francisco from Hawaii on March 23, the same date on which Hubbard's naval record shows him returning to the continental United States. It is unknown whether Hubbard was aboard as no passenger list survives. If he was, it would account for him managing to cross the Pacific in only 14 days, which would have been difficult if air travel had not been involved at some stage.[67]

If Hubbard did manage to secure a place on the *Philippine Clipper*

– which would have been in considerable demand – it raises the question of how he managed to do this given his very junior rank. He implied that he was carrying despatches in his 1956 account of the journey. An alternative possibility is that he persuaded the authorities that he merited a medical evacuation. Immediately after he returned from Australia, Hubbard was briefly hospitalized with a case of "acute catarrhal fever". He told his doctors it had set in "about four days ago", likely corresponding with his arrival in Hawaii, and worsened up to the date of his arrival in San Francisco. Hubbard said he had two such episodes annually;[68] yet, curiously, his medical record shows no such episodes previously.

Catarrhal fever is "an obsolete, nonspecific term once applied to various respiratory and upper respiratory infections, including the common cold, influenza, pneumonia and bronchopneumonia."[69] Following the 1918-1919 influenza epidemic, the Navy adopted the diagnosis of "catarrhal fever, acute" for influenza-like respiratory conditions. In practice, it became a catch-all for a variety of non-influenza complaints, including pneumonia, bronchitis, rubella, tonsillitis, rubella, the common cold with and without fever, which were often misdiagnosed as "acute catarrhal fever".[70]

It was a widespread complaint. In 1942 alone there were over 100,000 admissions of Navy personnel for acute catarrhal fever, with an admission rate of 123.70 cases per 1,000 persons.[71] The cramped conditions aboard *Pennant* would have been an ideal breeding ground for an infectious disease, so it seems likely that he contracted it aboard the ship while in transit from Australia. Although it has been claimed that Hubbard was merely suffering from "a bad cold",[72] naval doctors may well have judged his condition to be more serious than that.

He also complained that while "acting as combat intelligence officer for the Asiatic fleet he exposed his eyes to strong sunlight and has had to wear tinted glasses ever since. Strong light causes pain and tears. He also sprained his left ankle on this duty and he has pain in the longitudinal arch of the left foot while walking."[73] These relatively minor ailments appear to have been the basis for his later claims of being the first returned American casualty of the Pacific war. (This was highly doubtful; the war was already three and a half months old by the time he returned.) He made the claim on a number of occasions, saying one time that he was "one of the first officers back from the upper battle areas"[74] and also:

> I was the first casualty home from the South Pacific. I turned myself in at the hospital, got some adhesive tape glued on me, and I was all set to go home in a hurry and see the wife and kids. But the doctor said, "No, you go to bed." ...
>
> And he said, "Didn't you know?" No, I didn't know. He said, "You are the first casualty home from the South Pacific. Everybody knows that the stress and strain of modern war is such that the human mind can't stand it!"[75]

Hubbard, of course, had been a very long way away from the "stress and strain of modern war". This anecdote suggests a possible reason why he thought he was the first casualty home: a doctor's comment, perhaps made as a joke, which he may have latched onto as a sign of his own privileged status. (He said on another occasion that "I was *supposed to have been* the first casualty who came home from the South Pacific at the beginning of the war."[76]) The story has striking similarities to another distinction that Hubbard repeatedly claimed: to have been the youngest Eagle Scout in America. There, too, he claimed a distinction of which he could not have had personal knowledge, that is not in any known records and which is dubious in any case.

He offered a curious explanation for why he thought people in the rear areas were affected, perhaps thinking of his own situation in Australia:

The people who were carrying forward the war in combat areas had a pretty low percentage of psychotics compared to the people who were standing idle in rear areas, on supply ships and other places. War neurosis came up and slapped those people who had not enough to do, who were merely there being worried. They wanted to do something and nobody would let them.[77]

He was not always consistent about why he left Australia. In a 1958 interview, he said that he had been sent home because "when we lost in the Far Pacific early in the war, they returned nearly everybody who had been involved in it home and they wouldn't send them out there anymore."[78]

He spent ten days in late April and early May 1942 at the US Naval Hospital at Mare Island, Vallejo, California before being discharged. In a 1956 lecture he told his followers that on leaving the hospital, "I was, by the way, walking with a cane. I was in good condition. I couldn't see. I had dark glasses on … they sent me to sea in the North Atlantic the following week."[79]

Although Hubbard somehow forgot to mention his war wounds to his doctors, he did not forget to mention them to his friends. His friend and publisher, John W. Campbell, wrote on May 13, 1942 to the science fiction author Robert Heinlein to tell him:

L. Ron Hubbard's in town—temporarily confined to the Sick Officer's Quarters. He's angry, bitter, and very much afraid—afraid he'll get assigned to some shore job, which he does not want, and kept from going to sea again.

Angry and bitter because, I suspect, he was among those licked. He collected a piece of Jap bomb in his thigh during the Battle of the Java Sea, as far as I can make out. He was aboard ship at the time, apparently, and Allied air power was not giving adequate coverage.

He is a graduate C.E. [Civil Engineer – in reality he dropped out and never graduated], but is also rather competent in several lines. He was barnstorming for a living for a while, and has a private pilot's license. He did some fairly useful mapping along the Alaska coast by a new radio-beam survey method. And he has imagination, of course.

If the guy is hooked for shore duty—he's got a limp; how permanent I don't know, nor how bad—he might be useful. His own feeling is that his direct experience with Jap weapons, methods and tactics might be his prime asset.[80]

Hubbard had, of course, recently arrived from a shore job and had not yet seen sea duty. Also contrary to his later claims, Hubbard did not go to sea in the North Atlantic a week after leaving the hospital. Instead, he was formally assigned back to the Twelfth Naval District on April 3, 1942, where he spent three weeks waiting for a new assignment. Causey's scathing cable about Hubbard's unfitness was added to his file but he managed to avoid disciplinary action. The anger, bitterness and fear that Campbell perceived was certainly not caused by Hubbard having being "licked" by the Japanese, but was much more likely an after-effect of his expulsion from Australia and his lingering concern that the *Don Isidro* affair would mar his career.

No fitness report was written for this period of Hubbard's service, probably because he had spent the entire period working outside of his chain of command. The command to which he was assigned, the Sixteenth Naval District, no longer existed due to the Japanese invasion of the Philippines. The officers who would have written his report were likely either dead or reassigned to other commands. As Causey's reported comments to Hubbard made clear, the Naval Attaché did not regard himself as being responsible for a stray officer in Brisbane.

This may explain why his next fitness report, covering the period May 11, 1942 to June 24, 1942, appears to have been originally intended to cover the period that he served in Australia but no report for that period was ever filed. Erased text is visible in two lines on the report: the first showing the start date and the second listing Hubbard's regular duties. The erased text shows a start date of "Nov. 24, 1941" – the date when he was ordered to the Philippines – and lists his duties as "NY, 3ND, instruction (1/2 mo.); Asiatic Fleet, combat intel. (2 1/2); 12 ND unassigned (3/4 mo); Censor, New York (1 mo.)."[81] The list indicates that the erased text was probably written in late June 1942. However, his commanding officers for the first three assignments do not appear to have provided any reports for his time there.

As the last listed duty indicates, Hubbard was assigned to another censorship role after his abrupt return to the continental United States. The censorship functions of the US Army and Navy had recently been absorbed by the Office of Censorship, a predominantly civilian agency augmented by military reserve personnel. Presumably in response to a query from someone in the personnel department of the 12th Naval District in San Francisco, Captain Herbert K. Fenn, the Chief Cable Censor, advised that "the Subject's qualifications may find a useful outlet in the Office of the Cable Censor, New York." The reference to his qualifications probably related to Hubbard's pre-war career as a writer and sometime broadcaster, which was cited in his service record. Fenn recommended that no disciplinary action should be taken following Causey's criticism of Hubbard's performance in Australia.

The Office of Cable Censorship was an obvious destination for Hubbard, given that he had been trained and assigned as a censor but had not been able to reach his original role in the Philippines. The move also meant that his designation changed from Intelligence Volunteer (Specialist) (I-V(S)) to Deck Volunteer (Specialist) (D-V(S)).[82] He was told that this was "in view of the fact that the Office of Cable Censorship, to which you are attached, is now under the cognizance of the Chief Cable Censor", rather than the Office of Naval Intelligence as before.

Nearly 25 years later, Hubbard claimed falsely that his move from the Office of Naval Intelligence was because "the FBI took over the complete entirety of Naval Intelligence at that time and so those of us who were qualified as Deck Officers were transferred over to the line and I went from there." In reality, nothing of the sort happened.[83] Hubbard did reasonably well in his new job in the Chief Cable Censor's Investigations Department at the International Telephone and Telegraph Company building at 67 Broad Street, New York.

The specific details of his role are not recorded in his naval records. However, the work of the department concerned the investigation of censorship matters, such as attempts to avoid submitting communications to the censors or evading censorship through the use of codes or other methods of concealment. Such activity, if detected, could indicate possible instances of espionage. The Office of Censorship held primary responsibility for such investigations and could ask for assistance from the FBI, though in practice this only happened infrequently. Where military interests were implicated, the armed forces' intelligence offices could become involved.[84]

Years later, this role appears to have been transformed in Hubbard's mind into something much more significant, with the claim that he had been "a B-3 of the Office of Naval Intelligence".[85] In other words, he claimed to have worked in the ONI's investigations department, B-3, which was responsible for uncovering and preventing possible espionage against the navy. There is no evidence of this from his file, but it is quite possible that he had contact with B-3 in his role as a cable censor. On another occasion, he claimed that he had been in this role "in the Asiatic fleet at the beginning of the World War II", which was flatly untrue.[86]

The reality was that his role in the Office of Censorship was only on the margins of counter-espionage. The work of his section might have led to counter-espionage investigations by other agencies, but its focus was on finding breaches of censorship regulations rather than hunting spies. As the Office of Censorship's official history stated, "Censorship held to the view that it was not an investigative agency. It would deliver the raw material [from reporting] to the intelligence agencies and others which had a legitimate war interest, but would not undertake to do intelligence work itself".[87]

One case provides an illustration of the kind of work that Hubbard might have done. It involved a former Pearl Harbor worker sending a cable from Honolulu in which he gave two dates ten days apart. It was intercepted by Cable Censorship, which suspected that the dates represented the dates when the sender would leave Hawaii and arrive in the continental United States (by sea, as the limited air transportation available was effectively limited to government and military use). Such information was regarded as highly sensitive, as the details of shipping movements were closely guarded. The sender was found to have a passenger reservation for the first date stated. The information was passed to Naval Intelligence for action, resulting in the sender being stopped at the dock, brought before a provost judge and fined $200 for breaching censorship regulations.[88]

Hubbard's superior, Commander Andrew Cruise, gave him a positive report, though his performance grades were only just above a passing grade in most areas:

Since reporting to this activity this officer has shown a full realization of the seriousness of an assignment to duty. He has shown an increasing sense of responsibility and displayed a marked improvement in his work. While the period of observation has been short, his work has been entirely satisfactory.[89]

Hubbard was not content with shore duty and still aspired to go to sea rather than being stuck behind a desk. He stated his preference on his reporting form for next duty as "Sea – Patrol" and "Fleet – Pacific (or Caribbean) (Alaska)". On June 10, only a month after joining the Office of Censorship, he sent a memo to the Chief Censor concerning "Sea duty, request for" in which he set out his nautical qualifications. He concluded his request·

I hereby volunteer for patrol torpedo boats or general patrol craft, particularly in the Caribbean Area, the peoples, language and customs of which I know and of which I possess piloting knowledge.[90]

The Navy was desperately short of personnel who were qualified for sea duty. The Office of Censorship was already beginning to make efficiencies by the time Hubbard joined and was able to let him go. Its official history records: "Surplus personnel, particularly the younger officers [Hubbard was 31], were released from Cable Censorship duty from the summer of 1942 onward." The following year, the Navy ordered the office to release all physically-qualified personnel under 30 years of age.[91] Captain Fenn approved Hubbard's request and sent a recommendation of approval to the Chief of Naval Personnel on June 20.[92]

While he was still working for the Office of the Chief Cable Censor, Hubbard began receiving the first of a series of demands from creditors over unpaid bills. The first came from a tailor's shop in Brisbane called Ryders (Employees) Pty. Ltd. of 233a Adelaide Street. The US Naval Liaison Office in Australia forwarded their complaints to his current post in New York, where Hubbard received them on May 30, 1942.

The story was much the same when, in October 1942, the Navy forwarded a complaint to Hubbard from the First National Bank of Ketchikan, Alaska:

Gentlemen,

We are appealing to you, believing that your office might assist us in collecting a promissory note in the amount of $250.00 signed by the above captioned Naval Officer...

Mr. Hubbard has been notified regularly and often, and he has promised to make good the note, always in the near futuro. Wo fool that we have been very lienient [sic] with him, giving him the opportunity to get his affairs in shape, but in our last letter to him addressed care of the Explorers Club, apparently his permanent address, we informed him that we must appeal to his superiors. This notice was on July 10th. 1942, since which time we have heard nothing...

We are sorry to have to take this step and it is difficult to believe that he would put us in this position.[93]

Hubbard's response was to pay only the $15 interest owed on his debt. He informed the bank that "[t]he reason of non-payment of this note is the sharp decrease in pay which I was willing to take to help my country. Until this war is ended and I can resume my former profession I can make only small and irregular payments."[94]

In fact, Hubbard was earning considerably more money as a Naval officer than he ever had as a pulp fiction writer. Like many of the other pulp writers of the time, he had eked out a frugal existence in cheap hotels and down-at-heel boarding houses; writing penny-a-word fiction was not an effective road to riches. During his 1940 yachting trip, he and his wife had been stranded for several months in Ketchikan after a mechanical breakdown. Short of funds, he borrowed $250 from the town's First National Bank to pay for supplies and repairs. He had still not paid it back two years later, prompting a stream of correspondence demanding restitution.

On June 22, 1942 he received a signal informing him that his request for sea duty had been granted:

*LTJG LAFAYETTE R HUBBARD D V(S) USNR HEREBY
DETACHED PROCEED IMMEDIATELY NEPONSET MASS
REPORT BY LTR COMONE DUTY CONNECTION CON-
VERSION YP422 AT GEORGE LAWLEY AND SONS AND
AS CO OF THAT VESSEL WHEN PLACED IN FULL COM-
MISSION.* [95]

His instructions required him to go to the shipyard of George
Lawley and Sons in Neponset, Massachusetts and take charge of
the conversion for military use of a vessel designated USS *YP-422*.
When the conversion was completed, he was to take command of
it. Hubbard was also temporarily promoted to full Lieutenant to
reflect his new responsibilities, though his substantive grade
remained Lieutenant (jg). For the first time, he now had the
prospect of being able to go to sea in command of his own vessel.

CHAPTER 6

Ron in the Atlantic

When the United States entered the war on December 7, 1941, decades of neglect of its small vessel fleet had left it with only a dozen or so anti-submarine craft that were any smaller than destroyer size. The Navy's entire defensive force on the Eastern Sea Frontier – an area stretching from the St. Lawrence River to North Carolina – consisted of only four yard patrol boats, four subchasers, one Coast Guard cutter, three World War I patrol boats and five combat-ready aircraft. The Gulf of Mexico and the Caribbean were equally unprotected.[1]

To make matters worse, the country had virtually no experience of a submarine conflict such as that in which it now abruptly found itself engaged. Defensive measures that had been standard in Britain for two years were completely lacking in the US. Coastal towns refused to dim their lights for fear of harming tourism.[2] Merchant ships in US coastal waters travelled without escorts and kept their navigation lights on. Radio discipline was non-existent and shore stations continued to broadcast time signals and weather forecasts.[3]

The result was a massacre. German U-boats had free access to North American coastal waters, sinking ships in New York harbor, in the waters off Long Island, and far down the St. Lawrence River. Up and down the Atlantic coast, from Newfoundland to Bermuda, hundreds of vessels were sunk, many of them brightly lit despite the U-boat threat or silhouetted against the undimmed lights of coastal towns. It was no wonder that the U-boat commanders called this period "The Happy Time".

Britain had found itself in a similar situation at the outbreak of war in 1939. The British were slightly luckier in that they had already begun production of small anti-submarine ships in anticipation of a repeat of the submarine warfare of World War I. They dubbed these vessels corvettes, reviving a term used in the 17th and 18th centuries for a class of small sailing warships.[4]

Civilian vessels such as trawlers and yachts were also requisitioned and converted into gunboats to provide additional security in the waters around ports and naval facilities.

The US adopted a similar solution, converting civilian craft and also loaning ten corvettes and 22 anti-submarine trawlers from the Royal Navy. The latter were manned with British crews. Depending on size, converted vessels were classed as Patrol Gunboats (PG), Patrol Yachts (PY) or Patrol Yacht, coastal (PYc). Trawlers were among the smallest vessels converted and were usually designated as coastal patrol yachts or yard patrol vessels. They were given the task of patrolling a designated sector of coastal waters to keep U-boats away from key ports and coastal installations. Such vessels were typically armed with machine guns and obsolescent naval weapons.

When Hubbard arrived at George Lawley's shipyard on June 25, 1942, he was put to work as a Conversion Officer, overseeing the conversion of a vessel called the *Mist* into the US Navy gunboat *YP-422*. Built by the American Ship Building Co. of Cleveland, Ohio in 1941, she was acquired by the US Navy on June 4, 1942.[5] The vessel was never given a name in naval service (there was no "USS *Mist*" – the name has not been used for any 20th century US Navy vessel). The Church of Scientology has claimed in recent years that *YP-422* was a "hastily fitted subchaser"[6] or, alternatively, an anti-submarine convoy escort vessel.[7] In fact, she was a heavy beam trawler. Nor was she a British vessel, despite later claims by the Church. The only Royal Navy vessel to bear the name *Mist* was an Admiralty drifter built in Aberdeen in 1918.

The conversion work went smoothly. *YP-422's* engine was tuned and her deck strengthened to accommodate her new armament, a 3" .50 caliber (76 mm) dual purpose gun mounted on the forward deck and two .30 caliber (7.62 mm) machine guns. These were intended to counter enemy aircraft and surfaced submarines, though they were not very effective in that role, as German submarines had much more firepower. In June 1942 the identically-armed USS *YP-389* was chased down and sunk off Cape Hatteras by a U-boat using its 88 mm deck gun and 20 mm anti-aircraft gun.

Exactly one month after arriving Hubbard was able to take *YP-422* out of her dock for a trial trip in the harbor which was recorded by a naval photographer. Engines were revved up and down, controls were tested and the compasses were adjusted – a tedious task for which several hours were needed. The trial was successful and on July 28 at 11:00, *YP-422* was formally commissioned.[8]

The following month, *YP-422* put to sea for a short test cruise, for the first and only time that Hubbard was aboard her on the open ocean. During her shakedown cruise the vessel conducted 27 hours of training exercises. A few practice rounds were fired to test the deck gun. There was no suggestion that any enemy vessels had been involved. According to a former crewman, Eugene LaMere, "the *YP-422* never saw combat".[9]

The Church of Scientology claims that Hubbard "did see action in the North Atlantic, but aboard a different vessel".[10] This claim cannot be substantiated. There is no record of Hubbard serving aboard any other North Atlantic vessel, and the Church has never given details of when or where this happened or of what this other vessel might have been.

Hubbard received an "above average" rating for his work on the conversion of *YP-422*.[11] However, he still seems to have been not entirely happy with his posting and he continued to express a preference for "patrol vessels" in "Caribbean waters". He also appears to have attempted to continue his pulp fiction writing, though apparently with substandard results. He wrote in 1946:

> *You love to write. The Navy had no influence upon your*
> *writing. The Navy never stopped you writing. On the 422*
> *what you wrote were not stories.*[12]

Hubbard would have known that a yard patrol vessel such as *YP-422* would be expected to spend most of its time in the coastal waters of the continental US, though in *YP-422's* case it was to have a much more eventful – though short – career than most yard patrol vessels.

By September 9, Hubbard was confident enough about his vessel to send a message to the Commandant of the Boston Navy Yard reporting that *YP-422* was in excellent condition, crew training was "approaching efficiency" and morale was high. "As soon as a few deficiencies are remedied," he added, "this vessel will be in all respects ready for sea and is very eager to be on her way to her assigned station or task force."[13]

YP-422 embarked on her shakedown cruise in October 1942. Her prospective Commanding Officer, however, was not on board. He had become involved in a dispute with the Commandant of the Boston Navy Yard, Commander J. H. Keefe. Tense relations had developed between the officers in charge of the conversion work and those assigned to crew the ten YPs being converted at the Neponset shipyard. This culminated in an order from the Commandant prohibiting YP officers from approaching the conversion office or even speaking to any of the shipyard workers.[14]

Hubbard fired off a memorandum to the Vice-Chief of Naval Operations (VC OPNAV) in Washington. He named the officer that he held responsible for the dispute and claimed that the prospective YP Commanding Officers were all "startled" by the order.[15] Perhaps not surprisingly, this got Hubbard into trouble. On September 25, the Commandant requested that Hubbard be relieved of command:

LT L RON HUBBARD IS IN COMMAND OF YP 422 COMPLETING CONVERSION AND FITTING OUT AT BOSTON. IN THE OPINION OF THE COMMANDANT HE IS NOT TEMPERAMENTALLY FITTED FOR INDEPENDENT COMMAND. IT IS THEREFORE URGENTLY REQUESTED THAT HE BE DETACHED AND THAT ORDER FOR RELIEF BE EXPEDITED IN VIEW OF EXPECTED EARLY DEPARTURE OF VESSEL. BELIEVE HUBBARD CAPABLE OF USEFUL SERVICE IF ORDERED TO OTHER DUTY UNDER IMMEDIATE SUPERVISION OF A MORE SENIOR OFFICER.[16]

Hubbard was determined not to go down fighting and sent a telegram to VC OPNAV protesting his removal:

BECAUSE OF MY REPRESENTATIONS MADE TO THE VICE CHIEF OPNAV 12 SEPT 1942 COMMANDANT NAVY YARD BOSTON RECOMMENDING MY REMOVAL FROM COMMAND TO BUPERS. RESPECTFULLY REQUEST INTERCESSION MY VESSEL IN CONDITION SUPERIOR TO ANY OTHER IN DIVISION.[17]

His plea was ignored. On October 1, 1942, the Commandant of the First Naval District, Captain H. G. Copeland, sent Hubbard a memo detaching him from command of *YP-422* and ordering him to report to the Commandant of the Third Naval District "for such duty as he may assign you."[18]

Hubbard later made an extraordinary series of claims about his brief service aboard *YP-422*. They are detailed in the Church of Scientology's publication *Ron: Humanitarian – Restoring Honor and Self-Respect*. We are informed that having returned from "hard action in the South Pacific," Hubbard was given command of "a hastily fitted subchaser." There is no doubt that this is meant to refer specifically to *YP-422*, as the vessel is mentioned by name and is shown in an accompanying photograph. But Hubbard's biggest problem was the crew:

... Unofficial naval policy was to man [such vessels] with only expendable crews. Consequently, upon entering the Boston Navy Yard, Ron found himself facing a hundred or so enlisted men, fresh from the Portsmouth Naval Prison in New Hampshire. A murderous looking lot, was Ron's initial impression... While on further investigation, he discovered not one among them had stepped aboard except to save himself a prison term.[19]

This claim is a good illustration of how Scientology takes literally Hubbard's anecdotes in his lectures and uses them as the basis of its account of his life. The source is a 1961 lecture in which he said:

[I have] governed a ship of criminals one time. A whole ship. A hundred percent. They were on their way to Portsmouth Naval Prison and they took them off the prison train and shipped them to me. Combat vessel needed a crew. They didn't have any crews. They had a lot of people in uniform, but didn't have people they wanted to send out into the teeth of the North Atlantic in 1942. A hundred percent criminals these fellows were. I governed them by throwing away their service record books. I just told them, "well, I'm not going to make any marks in your service records." I saw them come aboard with their braid dirty and their hammocks black with grime and they stood there slouched, and that was the first intimation I had that this was the crew. There they were. More than a hundred men lined up on the deck.[20]

Hubbard's claim was somewhat undermined by the fact that *YP-422* only had 33 men in her crew (plus Hubbard and his second-in-command), not a hundred. There is no indication from the ship's muster rolls that any of them were transferred from a prison.[21]

According to Hubbard, after only six weeks under his instruction they had been transformed from criminals to superb seamen. A Scientology account claims that they became the finest in the fleet, "with some seventy depth charge runs to their credit and not a single casualty".[22] The author of that account appears to have gotten somewhat confused at this point, as Hubbard's depth charge runs were actually made aboard a completely different ship in a different ocean at a different time, the Pacific-based subchaser USS *PC-815* in May 1943.

Hubbard made the same claim to have commanded a crew of criminals in two lectures given in August 1951 and April 1954. In the latter lecture, he told an audience of Scientologists:

I reported to Boston in the very early part of the war to take command of a corvette. They had emptied Portsmouth and that was my crew. Anybody who even vaguely could be let off from serving seven years and accessories, which is to say denial of citizenship. Anybody who had any vaguest idea that he might not immediately kill an officer, you know he might wait for a few days, why, they had scraped together and thrown together one corvette crew. Oh, dear.

It was quite amusing. I saw them come aboard and they were dirty and they were ragged and their hammocks were all muddy and, ooh boy, this was a real foul bunch. Well, I looked through their service records. Summary court-martial, court-martial, summary court-martial, general court-martial, general court-martial, summary court-martial and sentence suspended. Sentence suspended in view of the fact that he has volunteered for sea duty.

Well, you'd have thought that'd been the crummiest ship in the navy. Funny part of it was that individually these people were terrible, but collectively they presented a front which could be very dangerous to an environment. You see that? All they had to do was simply look around and recognize in themselves that we had a social group here that might, because of its numerical superiority, have a chance. They had to recognize that. When they recognized that they straightened up and you never saw such a crew in your life.[23]

*

The USS YP-422 After Hubbard

Hubbard's first command, YP-422 (ex-Mist), was one of three sister trawlers acquired by the US Navy and converted into military vessels – the others were Surge, converted as USS YP-417, and Calm. After Hubbard left the vessel, YP-422 had an unexpectedly adventurous career despite her diminutive size and weak armament. Perhaps due to a shortage of better equipped vessels, YP-422 was used in a fully-fledged escort role along the length of the US East Coast, roaming as far south as Key West in Florida.

In the spring of 1943, she was sent to a new post in the South Pacific but never reached it. As she was approaching Noumea in New Caledonia in the early evening of April 24, 1943, she struck Tumbo Reef, three miles southeast of the entrance to North Bulari Passage, and went aground.

The destroyer USS Perkins received an urgent distress call at 7.10 pm: "Am aground sinking fast and may capsize send help immediately." The local US naval force, Destroyer Squadron Five, immediately mounted a rescue effort. The crew was taken off the stricken YP-422 but the vessel did not sink and remained stuck on the reef.[24]

The stores and equipment of YP-422 were subsequently offloaded to lighten the stranded vessel. Repeated efforts were made over the following months to pull her off the reef. However, these were unsuccessful, and on June 13, 1944, the Navy declared YP-422 to be "a total loss".[25]

Following his removal from command of *YP-422*, Hubbard was sent to the Naval Receiving Station at Long Beach, Long Island, New York. Part of the giant Long Beach Naval Base, the receiving station was responsible for processing personnel who were entering or leaving the Navy. He remained at there for some months, working as the establishment's Senior Watch Officer in what would have been an essentially administrative capacity.

The fitness report covering Hubbard's tour at the Receiving Station shows that he still wanted to serve on "PC Boats, patrol" in "Caribbean or Gulf". On October 8, 1942 he wrote to the Chief of Naval Personnel requesting a transfer to the Submarine Chaser Training Center (SCTC), which he referred to as "PC School", in Miami, Florida. He noted that "study at this school of new anti-submarine equipment and tactics will increase any value I may have as a naval officer."[26]

His request was approved by the Commandant of the Third Naval District and his request was approved on the same day.[27] He reported to the SCTC on November 9, 1942, and quickly made friends with a young lieutenant named Thomas Moulton. In a later lecture, Hubbard gave an account of how he had obtained his transfer, falsely claiming that he had been detached from command of a corvette squadron. He also said he had been slated to return to Australia, which was highly improbable after his failures there:

> *I myself got a set of orders and it said, "You are hereby detached as commander of the squadron and you will proceed to the training center in Florida for preparation to take command of a new war vessel." Reason, you see... there actually weren't many people got home from the Asiatic fleet. Maybe you noticed that. There was a few casualties around. And so I got detached and I went to Florida, not Melbourne.*[28]

Hubbard fitted in well at the SCTC, though he seems to have regarded his posting there as something of a vacation despite the rigorous schedule. He recalled his time there in a 1964 Scientology lecture, commenting that "it was a lovely, lovely warm classroom, and I was shipped for a very short time down into the south of Florida... and, boy was I able to catch up on some sleep."[29]

His friend Thomas Moulton later recalled under cross-examination during the 1984 Armstrong trial that Hubbard had presented himself as an authority on destroyers:

> *Q: And to your knowledge had [Hubbard] any previous naval experience before attending the Sub Chaser School?*
>
> *A: It was common knowledge that he had been in destroyers for some time before that.*
>
> *Q: You don't have the exact details?*
>
> *A: Other than hearing the instructors in the classrooms refer to it. He was used as something of an authority in the classroom.*
>
> *Q: Do you know what his position was on these destroyers?*
>
> *A: I am told he was gunnery officer on the Edsall. I don't know about the others.*[30]

In fact, Hubbard had never served aboard any destroyers and there is no record of him having anything to do with the USS *Edsall*.

*

The Submarine Chaser Training Center and the 'Donald Duck Navy'

The Submarine Chaser Training Center (SCTC) was established in March 1942 by Cdr. Eugene F. McDaniel, a veteran destroyer officer. He had seen the horrors of the Battle of the Atlantic first-hand and was fiercely anti-Nazi and anti-

Japanese as a result. The school initially occupied a building overlooking Biscayne Bay on a pier that had formerly been used by the Clyde-Mallory Line's steamships.

The six-week training course was intensive, with students permitted only alternate Sunday afternoons off. A typical weekly schedule included training in anti-submarine warfare, medical instruction (subchaser captains were usually expected to also serve as the ship's doctor), sonar, communications, radar instruction, gunnery, ship handling and navigation instruction, with frequent examinations. Ordnance training alone took a full week to cover the range of weapons available to subchasers. On at least three days a week, including all day on Saturdays, students trained aboard a subchaser to practice drills, docking, seamanship and "tentative command".

One of the final stages of the training program comprised a cruise lasting between three and five days in which the student officers took on the roles of the enlisted personnel they would be commanding. These included standing watch, operating the sound gear, serving as quartermaster or engineer, manning the helm and training the guns.

The SCTC adopted as its mascot an unofficial cartoon showing Donald Duck with a depth charge projector, known as a Y-gun, and a depth charge. The subchaser fleet thus gained the nickname of the "Donald Duck Navy",[31] a term of derision for some of those who served on the bigger ships of the "Tin Can Navy" but remembered fondly by the nearly 50,000 officers and men who served on subchasers in World War II.

*

Hubbard came near the bottom of his class, ranking 20th in a class of 25. Nonetheless he was rated "Qualified for command of 173' Submarine Chaser".[32] It must have been with some satisfaction that, at the end of the 60-day course, he received news that he was being put in charge of his own subchaser: the USS *PC-815*, then under construction in Portland, Oregon. This was a big step forward for him, but it was overshadowed by worries about his health. He later noted in a personal record, written in his handwriting and entered into the record in the Armstrong case:

> *In 1942 – December 17th or thereabouts – while training in Miami, Florida, I met a girl named Ginger who excited me. She was a very loose person but pretended a great love for me. From her I received an infection of gonnohorea (sp?). I was terrified by it, the consequences of being discovered by my wife, the navy, my friends. I went to a private doctor who treated me with sulfa-thiazole and so forth. I thought I was cured but on a plane headed to Portland, Ore. I found I was not. I took to dosing myself with sulfa in such quantities that I was afraid I had affected my brain.[33]*

Hubbard's gonorrhea is not mentioned in his naval medical records. He evidently concealed it from the Navy's doctors, perhaps fearing disciplinary action (though in fact, the Navy's policy was to treat venereal diseases as a medical rather than a disciplinary matter.[34]) Many years later, he told Scientologists that he had "got interested" in venereal diseases,

> *because we had innumerous – numerous cases of VD – a very unlovely subject. And of course, these cases would sort of wind up on my docket as something I had to do something about.*
> *And when you're working in expeditions or corvettes, or*

something like this, you seldom have a doctor. Or the doctor is dead drunk or something.

You sail out of a port and you've got seven out of a crew of a hundred men totally incapacitated. That can be very serious when you're already shorthanded, you see? VD. So of course, you break out the knockout drops and the sulfathiazole and the penicillin and so on and you let them have it.[35]

CHAPTER 7

Ron the Sub Hunter

L. Ron Hubbard's second and last command was aboard the USS *PC 815*, a Pacific Ocean subchaser. His command of *PC-815* lasted just 78 days, between April 21 and July 7, 1943; its disastrous conclusion ruined any chance Hubbard might have had of commanding another vessel.

News of Hubbard's posting reached him while he was still at the Submarine Chaser Training Center (SCTC) in Miami, Florida, at the start of January 1943. The Chief of Naval Personnel informed Hubbard that he was to be detached to Portland, Oregon, for "duty in connection with the fitting out of the USS *PC-815* at the Albina Engine and Machine Works, and for duty as commanding officer of that vessel when placed in commission".[1]

This must have been a happy moment for Hubbard. Following the debacle of his month-long post to oversee the conversion of the USS *YP-422*, he must have relished the prospect of another chance at command and a renewed opportunity to demonstrate his worth.

*

The Albina Engine & Machine Works
The Albina Engine & Machine Works in Portland, Oregon, where Hubbard's subchaser was built, was located on N. River Street, in the Albina section of Portland, on the east bank of the Willamette River upstream of the Fremont Bridge. It was founded by Scottish immigrant William Cornfoot in 1904 to serve as a repair yard. Covering an

area of 13½ acres, it had six open slipways and four outfitting docks. Ships of up to 319 feet (97 m) long and 50 feet (15 m) wide could be accommodated in the docks, while the slipways could take vessels up to 150 feet (45 m) long and 50 feet (15 m) wide.

The Albina yard was overshadowed by Portland's two far larger Kaiser Corporation yards. It nonetheless played an important part in supplying the US Navy with vessels during the war as well as continuing its original role as a repair yard. Its workforce of 150 in early 1941 increased to 4,400 before the war's end, two-thirds of whom were involved in new construction and most of the remainder in repair work.

The first of Albina's naval contracts, for the delivery of four 173-foot subchasers, was awarded in April 1941. Over the next four years, the yard built 139 more vessels and delivered another 42 constructed by subcontractors. The yard specialized in smaller types including patrol craft escort (PCE), small tankers (YO), degaussing units (YDG), gasoline tankers (YOG), self-propelled water barges (YW) and various types of landing craft. It was one of only three US shipyards to produce landing craft support, large (LCI(L)), and also built landing craft control (LCC) and landing craft infantry (LCI) vessels.[2]

The yard was an assiduous booster of its vessels; a contemporary magazine article calls its subchasers "the fastest, cockiest, fightingest war craft afloat". Albina dubbed its subchasers "Hellships" and its landing craft support vessels "Slaughter Sloops", giving appropriately infernal nicknames to each, such as "Hell Hurricane", "Hell Hornet" and the somewhat unfortunate "Hell Holocaust".[3] Hubbard's PC-815 was dubbed the "Hell Howler".

Albina was sold around 1971 to Dillingham Corporation

*and was renamed as Dillingham Ship Repair. It closed in
1986 under a new owner, Cascade General, which moved
its operations to Swan Island.*[4]

*

Hubbard's original candidate for executive officer (XO) was unavail
able, leaving him with two inexperienced ensigns. He asked his friend
at the SCTC, Lt Thomas S. Moulton, to be his executive officer for a
short time until a permanent candidate could be found. Although
Moulton wanted (and was soon to get) his own command, he agreed
as a favor to serve temporarily as Hubbard's XO. Due to the small
number of officers aboard, Moulton also had to double up as medical
officer, communications officer and engineering officer.[5] Hubbard
too had to double up, serving as morale, welfare, medical and ship's
service officer.[6]

Hubbard reported to the Fleet Sound School, Key West, Florida,
for training in the use of sonar equipment. According to his own
account, he was trained "under a British instructor"[7] (which is quite
plausible, as British sonar technology had been exported to the
United States as early as 1940). He concluded the 13-day course with
an "average" rating but was ranked near the bottom of the class, only
achieving 20th place out of a total of 25.

By January 18, Hubbard had reported to the Navy's Supervisor
of Shipbuilding in Portland, Oregon. It was conveniently close to
Hubbard's old home at Bremerton, only 150 miles to the north, and
his wife Polly was able to visit for dinner parties with the Moultons.

What Hubbard did at the shipyard is not recorded, but it is
possible to reconstruct the scene. *PC-815* was the first of six sequen-
tially-numbered subchasers constructed by the yard and launched
between January and September 1943.[8] Her sister ship, *PC-816*,
was under construction at the same time in an adjoining dock. The
British writer Nicholas Monsarrat (who served in the Royal Navy

during the war) described the scene at the fitting-out of the corvette HMS *Campanula,* on which he served as First Lieutenant, in 1940:

> [We] toured the ship together, as green as grass. Neither of us had seen a corvette before, though there were certainly enough of them around...
>
> Ours was afloat, almost finished, and jammed with workmen: the chief noise was supplied by some last-minute riveting going on on the after-gun platform, but there were several minor performers of note among the welders, caulkers, joiners, carpenters and plain crash-and-bangers employed on board.
>
> We were an hour on our tour, mostly climbing over obstacles and avoiding paintwork, but examining every discoverable corner and going over the ground from bridge to magazine to fore-peak to tiller-flat: we liked the look of her, though she was as yet more like an unfinished factory than a ship.[9]

Only a few days into his stint at Portland, Hubbard was again being pursued for unpaid debts. This time Dave Margolis of 22nd and G Streets, Washington, DC, wrote to the Navy requesting that it make Hubbard pay his unpaid bill of $120.75 and enclosing the previous (presumably fruitless) correspondence with Hubbard. The letter was forwarded to Hubbard with an instruction that he was to attend to the matter.[10] The Navy informed Margolis that it could not legally control or direct the financial affairs of its officers. Unfortunately, neither the original letter from Margolis nor Hubbard's reply is preserved in his file.

PC-815's Prospective Commanding Officer remained otherwise untroubled during the rest of the ship's precommissioning period, during which Hubbard oversaw the ship being fitted out and made ready. The process did not go entirely smoothly, as *PC-815* hit a mudbank during trials and damaged her propeller, necessitating an unscheduled drydocking to carry out repairs.[11] Nonetheless, Hubbard was given an approving report by Commander Leland D. Whitgrove, the Supervisor of Shipbuilding at Portland:

> *This officer has performed his duties as Prospective Commanding Officer during the precommissioning period in a highly satisfactory manner. He has taken a commendable interest in his ship and undertaken his work conscientiously and energetically. No comment is submitted regarding his fitness for promotion as he has not been under my observation while on sea duty.*[12]

At 10 a.m. on Tuesday April 20, 1943, *PC-815* was formally commissioned. Hubbard and the rest of the crew signed the logbook to register that they had reported aboard for duty.

Two days later, as the ship was being tested and readied for sea, the Albina Engine and Machine Works held a photo-opportunity for the *Oregon Journal*. Moulton and Hubbard were photographed in their sea jackets, Hubbard posing with a suitably nautical pipe rather than his usual Kools cigarettes. The article was certainly entertaining, if more than a little inaccurate:

Ex-Portlander Hunts U-Boats
Guides New 'Hell Howler'

Lieutenant Commander Ron ("Red") Hubbard, former Portlander, veteran sub hunter of the battles of the Pacific and Atlantic has been given a birthday present for Herr Hitler by Albina Hellshipyard and instructed to deliver it with a nasty blast "right in Der Fuerher's face".

Hubbard, an old hand at knocking tails off enemy subs, is typical of the high type naval officers commanding Albina subchasers, which have been nicknamed Hellships.

Men like Hubbard and Lieutenant Roy [sic] Moulton, his executive officer are the ones instructed to defeat America's greatest menace – the undersea craft.

Hubbard is an active member of the Explorers Club, New York City. He has commanded three internationally important expeditions for that organization. In 1934 Hubbard had charge of the Caribbean Motion Picture Expedition and took the first underwater films. He was the first to use the now famous bathosphere [sic] or diving ball [sic] for this work. In 1935 Hubbard headed a cartographic survey in West Indian waters and in 1939 and 1940, for the navy hydrographic office, led the noted Alaska Radio Experimental Expedition.

Hubbard comes from a long line of naval men. His father is Lieutenant H.R. Hubbard; his grandfather, Captain Lafayette Waterbury; his great grandfather, Captain I. C. De Wolfe, all of whom helped to make American naval history.

Hubbard, although he spent his youth in Portland, has left little of the world's 39 seas and seven oceans unexplored. Of Albina Hellships, he says:

"Those little sweethearts are tough. They could lick the pants off anything Nelson or Farragut ever sailed. They put up a sizzling fight and are the only answer to the submarine menace. I state emphatically that the future of America rests with just such escort vessels."

Executive Officer Moulton said in taking over the Hell Howler, "We have a crew of 60 of the toughest, smartest sailors I ever saw. We may not end this war single-handed, but the Hell Howler will clip a few days off it. Our ship is a trim and deadly man-of-war."

Moulton, like Hubbard, comes from a sea-faring family. Reared on the Gloucester Banks, his uncle was first mate *on the Thomas Lawson, only seven-masted schooner ever built. Three of his uncles held master's papers. His family at one time owned a fleet of seven vessels. Moulton also is a shipfitter. He learned the craft in the Bath iron works in Maine.*[13]

There can be no doubt that the source of the personal information on Hubbard was Hubbard himself. Some strange inaccuracies appeared to have crept in, however.

Hubbard was not even a full Lieutenant, let alone a Lieutenant Commander. Having only been temporarily promoted, his substantive rank at the time was still Lieutenant (junior grade). His father was a Lieutenant Commander but was demoted to lesser rank in the article. His grandfather "Captain" Waterbury had been a small-time vet and coal merchant and had never served afloat. "I.C. De Wolfe" was in fact the maiden name of Hubbard's grandmother, Ida Corinne, not his great-grandfather, John DeWolfe, who had been a wealthy banker.

Hubbard had not participated in either the Battle of the Atlantic or the Pacific. His youth was spent not in Portland, but mostly in Helena, Montana, Washington, D.C. and Bremerton, Washington State. He had never visited most of the world's seas and oceans (nor did he in later life). There is no record of any underwater films having been taken on his Caribbean expedition and he did not take a bathysphere or diving bell.

He did not become a member of the Explorers Club until 19 February 1940 and had, by April 1943, undertaken only one expedition (to Alaska) under the Club's auspices. The Navy Hydrographic Office had had no involvement; on his own initiative, in mid-September 1940 Hubbard had forwarded a package of films and sailing directions to the Office in the hope that they might prove useful. His "cartographic survey of West Indian waters" in 1935 never took place; at the time, he was writing pulp fiction stories in New York and Los Angeles. Nor did he embark on an expedition in 1939, though he did sail to Alaska in 1940 with his wife Polly.

*

The Corvette Conundrum

The Church of Scientology has claimed, and continues to claim, that L. Ron Hubbard's service in the North Atlantic was aboard one or more "corvettes" or "an antisubmarine escort vessel with Atlantic convoys". It has also claimed that he commanded British corvettes, leading the "Fourth British Corvette Squadron".[14] The Church has continued to claim in a television advertising campaign launched in 2011 that Hubbard "commanded corvettes during World War II", even though this was debunked as long ago as 1987.[15]

This claim originates with Hubbard himself, who stated that one week after being admitted to hospital in Vallejo, California in the spring of 1942, "they ordered this casualty to duty in command of a corvette in the North Atlantic."[16] In another version of Hubbard's story, he told Australian Scientologists that "they shipped me home [from Australia] and within a week gave me corvettes, North Atlantic. And I went on fighting submarines in the North Atlantic and doing other things and so on. And I finally got a set of orders for the ship. By that time I had the squadron."[17] Yet another version came from Hubbard in a 1954 lecture in which he said that he "reported to Boston in the very early part of the war to take command of a corvette."[18]

The term "corvette" refers specifically to a class of small anti-submarine warships, the first of which were built in British yards in 1939. Their design was based on a type of whale-catcher developed in the UK in the mid-1930s. A number were transferred to the US Navy and were referred to as Temptress-class vessels.

Neither of Hubbard's two commands, YP-422 or PC-815, were corvettes, despite his later claims. Hubbard's naval record shows that he knew this perfectly well. It includes a memorandum that he wrote on October 19, 1943 in which he correctly described his vessel YP-422 as a "heavy-beam trawler". Likewise he consistently and correctly referred to PC-815 as a subchaser. This shows that he knew exactly what type of ships they were: he knew better than to call them corvettes at the time.[19]

Real corvettes were not referred to as subchasers. Their hull nomenclature was quite different from the PC- and SC- designated subchasers. The 38 corvettes lend-leased to or built for the US Navy were designated as PG- (for Patrol Gunboat). They varied considerably in size, with displacements of anything from 700 to 1,500 tonnes, but even the smallest corvette still had more than twice the displacement of PC-815.

Although Hubbard claimed on a number of occasions to have commanded a "corvette squadron", speaking on one occasion of the "six other ships in my squadron",[20] *in reality "corvette squadrons" did not exist. In the Royal Navy corvettes were assigned to numerically designated Escort Groups, tasked with protecting transatlantic convoys, or to Support Groups, which chased down U-boats that had tried to attack a convoy.*[21] *No "Fourth British Corvette Squadron" ever existed.*

*

PC-815 remained in Portland until the end of April, outfitting and conducting trials. Her departure was delayed for another week by damage caused to the propeller during the trials, which necessitated a brief period in dry dock. In the second week of May, *PC-815* got underway down the Columbia River, headed for the naval yard at the Pacific coastal port of Astoria. She arrived around May 17, 1943 and took aboard a small quantity of ammunition for structural firing tests. These were to be used to test the ship's weapons – the guns and depth charge launchers – which, for obvious reasons, could not be done in the river.

On May 18, 1943, *PC-815* left Astoria for Seattle to have radar and Mousetrap depth charge launchers fitted at the Bremerton shipyards. Her journey was interrupted almost immediately when a Navy aircraft crashed offshore and the ship, along with others in the vicinity, was ordered to undertake a search and rescue operation. After a day's searching, *PC-815* received new orders: progress south to San Diego, pick up radar equipment there and undertake a shake-down cruise. But the ship had barely left the search area when, at 3.40 a.m. on May 19, about fourteen miles off Cape Meares, her sonar equipment detected a return echo. Hubbard was immediately convinced that it could only mean one thing – the presence of an enemy submarine.

*

US Navy Subchasers at War

PC-815 was one of 317 173-foot steel-hulled subchasers built by the United States during World War II. Along with the smaller 110-foot wooden-hulled SC subchasers, they were the brainchild of President Franklin D. Roosevelt. He had been the Assistant Secretary of the Navy during World War I and was himself a keen sailor. As Admiral Royal Ingersoll later put it, "they were one of Mr. Roosevelt's fads: he was a small-boat seaman himself and loved to cruise on little things like the [165-foot presidential yacht] Potomac and he liked small ships."[22]

Subchasers had the advantage of being easy and relatively cheap to mass-produce. In military terms, however, as Ingersoll noted they were "not very good ... the submarine-chaser was no craft to combat the submarine on the high seas." The Navy's fixation on building sub-chasers delayed the introduction of more capable destroyers and convoy escort vessels capable of anti-submarine warfare in the open ocean. Their inadequacies were recognized at the time; Roosevelt's Secretary of the Navy, Frank Knox, wrote in a letter that the president's focus on small ships was "Blind Folly".[23]

The weak armament of PCs made them fairly ineffective at sinking submarines. Only three submarines were sunk by the entire PC fleet in the course of the war – all, curiously, within a single eight-week period.[24] Their useful-ness lay more in the deterrent effect which they had upon enemy submarines and in the support which they were able to provide to larger warships. For the most part, they were confined to operating in inshore waters along the east and west coasts of the United States.

A typical PC had a crew of around five officers and sixty enlisted men. Most were recruited, like Hubbard, from the US Naval Reserve. Regular Navy officers had a reputation for looking down on the subchaser fleet, fearing that serving aboard would take them away from combat and damage their career prospects. Nonetheless, tens of thousands served on them with pride.

CHAPTER 8

Ron's Battle

Although Germany's U-boats were perhaps the most famous submarines of World War II, the Japanese had a far more varied and in some respects more innovative submarine force. It was not used very effectively, however, as the Japanese High Command stuck rigidly to the view that submarines should be used as an adjunct of the surface fleet, rather than as a separate striking force. The small numbers of Japanese submarines in service further diminished their impact. Nonetheless the Japanese had the biggest and fastest submarines in the world, with the longest range, the most advanced torpedoes, and the only submarines with the capability of being able to carry and launch aircraft.

The threat of Japanese submarines on the west coast of the United States was not a theoretical one, despite the distance of over 5,000 miles separating the US and Japan. In February 1942 the Japanese submarine *I-17* had caused panic in southern California when it surfaced off Santa Barbara and shelled an oil refinery. In September that same year, a plane launched from *I-25* carried out the first and still the only aerial bombing attack on the continental United States, dropping four bombs near Brookings, Oregon. *I-25* subsequently sank two freighters and a Soviet submarine which was heading for the Panama Canal (which the Soviets blamed on a sneak attack by an American submarine). There had been no attacks since then but in May 1943, vessels off the west coast were still wary of possible Japanese threats.

Naval vessels relied on sonar to detect submerged enemy submarines. The system was housed in a streamlined retractable dome that projected beneath the ship's bottom but was operative only at moderate speeds – at this time, up to 18 knots – due to water friction. It could work in active and passive modes, echo-ranging with a series of sharp pings or listening for the noise of a submarine's propellers or machinery.

The echo-ranging mechanism aboard *PC-815* sent out a focused beam of sound which was directed through the water by the operator. An echo would be heard if the beam was interrupted by an object in the water. A return did not necessarily have to mean the presence of a submarine, as unwary or inexperienced soundmen found. Schools of fish, whales, wrecks, coral reefs and even water layers of a different temperature and density can reflect echoes which could only be distinguished from a "live" contact by an expert – and even then, not always reliably. The use of sonar equipment was and remains a fine art, not only for the soundman but for the commander who has to decide how to respond to an ambiguous contact.

The sonar equipment on *PC-815* was connected to a chemical recorder. This was a device invented by the British to record sonar readings and plot attacks. The recorder was a small metal box with a glass top, underneath which was a constantly moving roll of chemically treated paper. A small stylus moved back and forth across the paper, giving the range element on an underwater target. When an echo was received, a trace was made on the paper by the stylus. From the angle established by a series of these traces, an adjustable plotter bar indicated the rate at which the range was closing, and also gave the correct time to release depth charges.

When *PC-815's* sonar pinged in the early hours of the morning of Tuesday, May 19, 1943, the ship's crew immediately took action. Hubbard's subsequent account of the incident was set out in a secret Action Report addressed to the Commander in Chief, Pacific Fleet (CINCPAC). It was couched in distinctly unmilitary language – reading more like one of Hubbard's pulp fiction stories – for which he was later chided by the Commander Northwest Sea Frontier (COMNORWESTSEAFRON).

> *Proceeding southward just inside the steamer track an echo-ranging contact was made by the soundman then on duty... The Commanding Officer had the conn and immediately slowed all engines to ahead one third to better echo-ranging conditions, and placed the contact dead ahead, 500 yards away.*
>
> *The first contact was very good. The target was moving left and away. The bearing was clear. The night was moonlit and the sea was flat calm... The USS PC-815 closed in to 360 yards, meanwhile sounding general quarters... Contact was regained at 800 yards and was held on the starboard beam while further investigation was made. Screws were present and distinct as before. The bearing was still clear. Smoke signal identification was watched for closely and when none appeared it was concluded the target must not be a friendly submarine. All engines were brought up to speed 15 knots and the target was brought dead ahead...*

At this point, Hubbard's military terseness slipped completely:

> *The ship, sleepy and sceptical, had come to their guns swiftly and without error. No one, including the Commanding Officer, could readily credit the existence of an enemy submarine here on the steamer track and all soundmen, now on the bridge, were attempting to argue the echo-ranging equipment and chemical recorder out of such a fantastic idea...*

At 04:50, a target on the surface was spotted and Hubbard gave the order to open fire on it. His crew responded with "astonishing accuracy, bursts and shells converging on the target." It turned out to be no more than a floating log, but Hubbard thought it was good for the morale of the gunners to ensure that the newly-installed guns worked. *PC-815* mounted four further attacks on the elusive submarine in the hope of forcing it to the surface, without success. At the end of the sixth attack the ship's supply of depth charges was exhausted. Urgent signals requesting more ammunition at first met with no response.

At 08:15 and 09:30, two US Navy blimps, *K-39* and *K-33*, appeared on the scene to help with the search. *PC-815* made "intermittent sound contacts throughout the morning".[1]

By noon, Hubbard believed that the enemy submarine was disabled in some way, or at least unable to launch its torpedoes. *PC-815* was lying to in a smooth sea and presented an easy target but had not been attacked. A second subchaser, *SC-536*, arrived at 12:15 but was unable to make contact with the target.

On the bridge of *PC-815*, Hubbard led the other ship on an attack run, blowing a whistle to signal when to use its depth charges. *SC-536* dropped two depth charges at 14:30 and the blimp *K-39* dropped another one nine minutes later, "using sound ranges and bearings transmitted over scene of action circuit, together with signals from aircraft's MAD [Magnetic Anomaly Detection] equipment".[2]

At least four attack runs were carried out by the surface vessels, of which the second, according to *K-39*, was the only one that "indicated any results". Hubbard was encouraged by what this attack produced:

> *The observation blimps began to sight oil and air bubbles in the vicinity of the last attack, and finally a periscope. This ship also sighted air bubbles... At 16:06 oil was reported again and*

this ship saw oil. Great air boils were seen and the sound of blowing tanks was reported by the soundman... All guns were now manned with great attention as it was supposed that the sub was trying to surface. Everyone was very calm, gunners joking about who would get in the first shot.

Hubbard's observations were not wholly supported by the crew of *K-33*, which had taken over aerial duties when *K-39* returned to base. *K-33* reported:

About 15 seconds after the explosion disturbance reached the surface and 20 feet astern of it, an air bubble 15 feet in diameter broke surface. Air continued to surface at this spot for about 15 seconds, but no oil or debris were evident.[3]

PC-815 now made a startling discovery: there appeared to be not just one submarine but two. Hubbard reported that a second contact was made with a target at a distance of 420 yards, drawing away at about four knots. Another subchaser, *SC-537*, arrived at the scene at about 14:30.

At 16:46, a Coast Guard patrol boat brought in further supplies of ammunition. Twenty-seven depth charges were transferred on to *PC-815* and made ready for firing. Not long afterwards, a second Coast Guard patrol boat, USCGC *Bonham*, arrived. There was now a total of five ships and two observation blimps involved in the search for the supposed enemy submarines.

As his vessel was leading the attack, Hubbard likely assumed tactical command of the other units present. He later described this small flotilla as his "squadron". This was apparently the origin of his claim to have commanded a "corvette squadron" during the war. Although he did not identify the period when he commanded the "squadron", the fact that he referred to a submarine hunt with six other units present leaves little doubt that he was describing the May 1943 incident off Cape Meares, which fits that description exactly.[4] He did not mention to his followers that his temporary command lasted for less than three days.

At 18:00, *K-33* reported seeing a periscope while investigating a sound contact of *PC-815*. The fleet war diary recorded:

> *[O]ne competent observer in the K-33 and another reliable man saw a periscope emerge for about 8 seconds and then disappear. The periscope wake was abeam to starboard, about 100 yards distant. Surface craft were advised, a flare dropped, and MAD search began. Half an hour later, surface craft established a sound contact and made a three charge attack without visible results.[5]*

PC-815 and *SC-536* subsequently dropped another two depth charges apiece on sound contacts.[6] The flotilla continued searching throughout the night and into the following day. The attacks continued, but still no there was no sign of either submarine having been damaged or destroyed. Hubbard was not discouraged, even after 34 fruitless hours:

> *Because we had three times found two sub targets on the previous day, we considered from her failure to surface that she had gone down in 90 fathoms. The other still had batteries well up for it made good speed in subsequent attacks (three to six knots).*

A report that the submarine had surfaced caused the vessels to begin "flying north," but they turned back after the contact turned out to be a fishing boat. *SC-537* was detached to investigate but, complained Hubbard, "for some time the *SC-537* was remote from us and it has not been established why she had difficulty with this ordered patrol".

Bonham was assigned another search area "where she would be out of the way." Hubbard ordered his own ship to return to the original search area to resume the hunt. Suddenly, at 07:00, he spotted what he thought was the submarine attempting to surface:

> *Suddenly a boil of orange colored oil, very thick, came to the surface immediately on our port bow... The Commanding Officer came forward on the double and saw a second boil of orange oil rising on the other side of the first. The soundman was loudly reporting that he heard tanks being blown on the port bow.*
>
> *Every man on the bridge and flying bridge then saw the periscope, moving from right to left, rising up through the first oil boil to a height of about two feet. The barrel and lens of the instrument were unmistakable... On the appearance of the periscope, both gunners fired straight into the periscope, range about 50 yards. The periscope vanished in an explosion of 20mm bullets.*

According to the fleet airship war diary, *SC-536* "made depth charge attack on oil slick without apparent results". Three hours later *K-39* made a "strong magnetic contact" 12 miles west-north-west of Cape Lookout. *PC-815* made sound contact in the same area and carried out an attack at 13:10, but *K-39* was unable to observe any results through visual observation or MAD readings.[7] Sound contact was made again at 13:45, prompting another attack by *PC-815*, but with the same lack of results. Then, at 19:45, *K-33* reported that it had identified a target:

> *K-33 made a sequence of excellent MAD contacts, which PC-815 confirmed with sound contact, verified with propeller noise, and attacked. K-33 followed up by dropping four bombs, two set for 125 foot depth and two for 50 foot depth,*

spaced so as to extend surface track pattern in direction of
estimated target track. There were no apparent results.[8]

More attacks were carried out by *SC-537*, *Bonham* and *K-39*, which
reported seeing "an air bubble about 12 feet in diameter [that]
broke the surface one thousand yards northwest of the location of
the last attack." The spot where the air bubble appeared was duly
attacked, but no sound or MAD searches were able to reestablish
contact. Instead, the monitoring blimp observed that the attacks
had "destroyed a large school of fish."[9]

The submarine hunt continued for a second evening. By this
time, *PC-815* and *SC-536* had exhausted their last depth charges.
As the ships continued to search for the elusive submarine, another
subchaser, *PC-788*, was sighted and cajoled into joining the search,
although her captain "protested very strongly against helping, ...
requesting continually to be allowed to be secured." By this time,
the commanders of two of the other vessels had evidently decided
they were on a wild goose chase. Hubbard subsequently complained in his action report:

During the night of the 21st when this vessel was attempt-
ing to make a routine sweep and search in the standard
sweep formation, neither the SC-537 nor the USCGC
Bonham showed any understanding whatever and refused
by their actions to cooperate. It is later understood that the
Bonham had a top speed of 9.2 although she reported her
speed to us as 12 and that she was under the supposition
that she would blow herself up if she dropped charges. The
SC-537 had one contact which she reported during the
following day and failed to prosecute it. The SC-537 left the
scene with her racks full of charges although the SC-536
and the PC-815 had exhausted all theirs. Echo range was
never more than about 900 yards in this shallow water and

despite orders neither vessel would close in to this with one exception, as noted in the attacks as of the following morning.

Hubbard later alluded in a Scientology lecture to his disagreement with the other commanders, telling his audience:

I had the officers of six other ships in my squadron come aboard, and only one of them stood alongside of me, and the other five were trying to convince me that if I kept this up I was going to get everybody killed. I said, "Kept what up?"

"You keep attacking these submarines."

I said, "What are we supposed to be doing, gentlemen?"

And they said, "Well, every time a submarine shows up, you needn't signal attack! It's stupid! You're going to get somebody hurt!"[10]

Frustratingly for Hubbard, the sonar contact continued to be present but stationery on the sea bottom even after *PC-815* and *SC-536* had dropped around a hundred depth charges. *PC-536's* regular commanding officer arrived on the scene and, taking over from his executive officer, promptly curtailed his ship's involvement in Hubbard's search. There was also a marked reluctance onshore to provide more support for the sub hunt. Moulton recalled that he sent

quite a nasty message asking why in thunder we couldn't get any help out there and get some ammunition. I coated this and sent it with a carbon copy so it would be equivalent to full copies to everybody on the coast, I guess.

I did see the message that came back immediately from the commander in chief of the Pacific Fleet, Admiral King,

*with a carbon copy to me asking Admiral Fletcher what
was going on out there and why he had not been told of an
action taking place.*

*I saw the carbon copy that went back from Admiral
Fletcher to him where he said there was no submarine. I
think he said "there were no submarines, repeat, no submarines in the area."*[11]

K-33 reported a "strong MAD contact" at 07:15. Observers on *PC-
815* reported seeing a periscope and opened fire with machine guns
at the point beneath the blimp, which also dropped several depth
charges. According to Moulton, the object turned out to be a
floating log.[12] Afterwards, contact was lost and no further contacts
were made. At 17:00 the Commander Northwest Sea Frontier,
Admiral Fletcher, ordered the search to be discontinued.

Seven hours later *PC-815* received orders to return to Astoria
naval station, having been in action for some 68 hours. Hubbard
noted that they were welcomed "with considerable skepticism. Her
records had not been examined, her crew had not been questioned
and no qualified report had been made." His ship had expended 37
depth charges and had maintained "contact with submarines" for
over 55 hours. Three minor casualties were suffered, probably as a
result of tiredness affecting the crew's performance.

Hubbard did not mention that his executive officer Thomas
Moulton was nearly shot when the starboard 20 mm gun accidentally
fired off an entire magazine, without anyone being at the trigger. The
gun had been assembled incorrectly by an exhausted gunner and a
key part had been put in backwards. Moulton was on the mast of *PC-
815* when the gun went off, firing until its entire ammunition drum
was empty, missing him by a few inches and shooting off the ship's
radio antenna. He later recalled: "I was making love to the mast and
was almost out to the other side. Looking down the barrel, it looked
like it was coming right toward me."[13]

In concluding his Battle Report, Hubbard was unequivocal about his achievements:

It is specifically claimed that one submarine, presumably Japanese, possibly a mine-layer, was damaged beyond ability to leave the scene and that one submarine, presumably Japanese, possibly a mine layer, was damaged beyond ability to return to its base...

This vessel wishes no credit for itself. It was built to hunt submarines. Its people were trained to hunt submarines. Although exceeding its orders in originally attacking the first contact, this vessel feels only that it has done the job for which it was intended and stands ready to do that job again.

He was supported by Moulton, who in his own action report (attached to Hubbard's) stated:

From listening to sound gear, with which the Executive Officer has had considerable experience, from surface evidences seen personally, such as boils produced by blowing of tanks, quantities of oil, and the general character of the action itself, the following conclusions are drawn:

(1) During the period from 03:00, Tuesday, April 18, 1943, until 24:00, Friday, April 21, 1943, the U.S.S. P.C. 815 fought two submarines, presumably Japanese.

(2) That one of them was definitely sunk, beyond doubt.

(3) That the second was damaged beyond repair and may therefore be considered as not capable of returning to Japanese territory.

Despite the skepticism with which Hubbard had been met on arrival at Astoria, his claims were taken seriously. Vice Admiral

Fletcher personally took charge of the investigation. He ordered Hubbard to report to him for an interview and examined the hundred-page-plus Battle Report which Hubbard submitted. The Commanding Officers of *SC-536* and *-537*, CGCs *Bonham* and *78302*, and blimps *K-33* and *K-39* were also ordered to report. Lieutenant Commander E. J. Sullivan U.S.N., Commander Airship Squadron 33, submitted an oral report after having visited the area during the search on one of the blimps.

In a secret memorandum addressed to the Commander-in-Chief, Pacific Fleet, Fletcher stated:

> *An analysis of all reports convinces me that there was no submarine in the area. Lieutenant Commander Sullivan states that he was unable to obtain any evidence of a submarine except one bubble of air which is unexplained except by turbulence of water due to a depth charge explosion. The Commanding Officers of all ships except the PC-815 state they had no evidence of a submarine and do not think a submarine was in the area.*[14]

Fletcher added that there was "a known magnetic deposit in the area in which depth charges were dropped". The implication was obvious: *PC-815* had fought a three-day battle with an underwater lump of magnetized rock.

Hubbard never accepted this. He claimed (but was not awarded) two battle stars for his American Campaign Medal and, to this day, the Church of Scientology claims that he sunk up to two enemy submarines. After the "battle", Hubbard wrote melodramatically:

> *I, as a sailor, have sinned with the rest it is true. On the bottom of the North Pacific there probably lie two 2,000 ton Japanese submarines, worth perchance a score of million*

dollars to the enemy before my depth charges sunk them. Perhaps not less than three hundred enemy lives struggled wetly out to Soldier Heaven. But it is better not to dwell upon these things. They should be dedicated to DUTY and recorded in files which are seldom opened. But the small voice cries (that inevitable small voice) and wonders if among them any could paint or appreciate the india ink sketches of a bamboo tree wherein the strokes must go as the tree must grow.[15]

CHAPTER 9

The Mystery of the Missing Submarines

The crew of the *PC-815*, Hubbard and the Church of Scientology consistently claimed that two submarines were present and both were sunk or fatally damaged. The US Navy has been equally consistent in denying that. Which is likely to be right?

Looking first at the testimony of the seven commanding officers involved, it is clear that Hubbard was the only one who believed that a submarine was present. He himself noted that the other vessels were reluctant to join in the hunt, or refused outright – a clear sign that their commanders thought that he was engaged on a wild goose chase.

Hubbard did not attempt to explain their behaviour but implied that it was due to "inexperience or unwillingness". He commented that he had been handicapped by a lack of outside officers trained in anti-submarine warfare and claimed that the blimps had "showed a deep blank on the usual knowledge of ASW one might expect of them." One can only guess at what Admiral Fletcher thought of this, considering that it came from an officer who had never served on a subchaser before and whose only experience of anti-submarine warfare was a shore-based course in Florida.

A major point against Hubbard's case is the lack of any physical evidence. The British writer Nicholas Monsarrat, who served aboard three Royal Navy corvettes during the war and rose to command his own, described what he saw at the moment HMS *Campanula* sank a submerged German U-boat:

One more run, one more series of thunderous cracks – and then the sea, spouting and boiling, threw up what we were waiting for: oil in a spreading stain, bits of wreckage, woodwork, clothing, scraps of humanity... . Contact failed after that, and though we waited till dusk, nothing else worth collecting made its appearance. We had enough, in any case.[1]

Anti-submarine vessels were required to collect and return such debris to shore for confirmation of a kill. It was rumoured that German U-boats kept a torpedo tube filled with debris to eject as a way of fooling the hunters. Human body parts tended to be regarded as clinching evidence, as there was no way to fake that (though British mariners joked darkly that U-boats kept a Jew or a Pole in the torpedo tube just in case).[2] On Royal Navy ships, body parts were collected from the water, put in a bucket and stored in the ship's refrigerator for later analysis.

Hubbard was certainly aware of the need to collect such evidence. He reported having seen an oil slick on the night of May 20–21 but found that it was "too thin for samples". On several subsequent occasions he reported having seen large quantities of oil – "a ball of orange colored oil, very thick". However, it seems he did not collect any of it, despite having earlier highlighted the density needed for samples.

He also described how he had tried, on the morning of May 21, to take aboard "a strange object, a small round ball laced with a line netting, which was floating here". He evidently felt that it was a submarine's emergency buoy, used to mark the position of a submarine in distress so that surface vessels could come to the rescue, and he referred to it as a "marker". (It was probably a fisherman's float). However, he did not mention it again in his report and it is not clear what became of the object.

All of the other commanding officers stated definitively that they "had no evidence of a submarine". This would seem to rule out any of the other vessels having spotted oil on the surface, which could only have come from a damaged vessel underwater. This immediately undermines one of Hubbard's key pieces of evidence. As he had not returned any samples, he was unable to physically substantiate his eyewitness reports.

The instrumental evidence provides another telling point. Hubbard's report provides some details on this. He commented on several occasions that the other ships had only been able to acquire a "poor" contact or none at all, though he laid the blame for this on faulty instrumentation or poor tactics by the commanding officers.

The strongest instrumental evidence he cited, other than that from his own ship, was not sonar at all, but was produced by the magnetic anomaly detectors (MAD) aboard the Navy blimps. MAD was not a very accurate or effective system, sensitive only to a few hundred yards, and some regarded the airships as worse than useless in anti-submarine work. But Hubbard acknowledged his dependence on it:

> *No attack was made, after the arrival of the blimps, without verification of sound contact by magnetic or magnetic contact by sound. Because her sound gear was not working properly (which fact she reported to us several times) the SC-536 stood by for us to verify. This teamwork, the blimp's smoke flares, and the use of echo ranging gear saved us many times from losing contact.*

The blimps evidently did detect something, which Fletcher explained as a "known magnetic deposit". It may also be significant that he did not comment on Hubbard's claim that "inoperative sound gear" had prevented the other vessels from detecting his submarines.

The PC-815's sonar system provided further information which was saved in an attack recorder, a device that made a reading of a contact's type of echo, strength, general characteristics, distance and direction. The recording was reviewed at least twice, by a staff officer working for Fletcher, and by Rear Admiral Frank A. Braisted, Commander of the Fleet Operational Training Command, Pacific. Braisted's verdict was that the contacts recorded on "some of these attack runs were mushy; the echos were mushy and could have been due to fish or knuckles in the water, bubbles, but that two may have been submarines."[3] The sonar evidence thus pointed to a small but mostly ambiguous possibility that a submarine had been present.

Hubbard's former colleagues in US Naval Intelligence would have provided strong evidence against his claims, though Hubbard himself was probably never aware of this. The United States repeatedly broke the Imperial Japanese Navy's signals code during the war. This enabled major successes such as the ambushing of the Japanese Navy at Midway in June 1942 and the shooting down of Admiral Yamamoto's aircraft on Bougainville Island in April 1943.

The US had a good idea of where the Japanese submarine force was at the time – it was principally engaged in the South Pacific, the Indian Ocean and the Aleutians – and was able to use this knowledge to intercept enemy submarines. It is likely that Admiral Fletcher had access to this intelligence. In March 1943, for instance, the encrypted radio communications of the Japanese submarine *I-6* were intercepted, deciphered and used to send three US submarines to ambush it in the western Pacific (though they were unsuccessful). There was no indication that there was one, let alone two, Japanese submarines operating in continental US waters.

This combination of factors likely persuaded Admiral Fletcher that there had been no submarines. Viewed objectively, Hubbard's report was very thinly supported. There was no physical evidence and the instrumental evidence was, at best, ambiguous; only the *PC-815* claimed to have had strong sonar contacts, whereas as Hubbard himself noted, all the other vessels had poor or no contacts with the supposed targets. Although the blimps did have contacts with their magnetic detectors, this was readily explained by the known magnetic deposit in the area.

The evidence gathered at the time was strong enough to indicate that there was *probably* no submarine in the area, but the Navy could not be sure that this was *definitely* the case until after Japan had been defeated. In January 1943, the United States Army and Navy set up a Joint Army-Navy Assessment Committee (JANAC) to catalog enemy Naval and merchant shipping losses during the war. (The Air Force was part of the Army at the time, but had its own representative on JANAC.) Using PoW reports, intelligence sources and bombing reports it put together a comprehensive index of enemy war losses. The US Navy and British Admiralty subsequently conducted a joint survey of the Japanese Navy to assess its losses.

Both eventually produced reports on enemy losses, the Admiralty in June 1946 and the Navy Department in February 1947.[4] The two reports overlapped considerably but each published different levels of detail. Both reports identify the vessels sunk and the date. The British report gives the identity of the ship(s) or aircraft responsible for the sinking, but only a vague location. The American report gives a precise latitude/longitude location but only a general category of sinking agent (e.g. "ship", "aircraft", etc.) By cross-referencing the two, it is possible to identify who sank which submarines, with exact details of where and when.

In Hubbard's case, no vessel is recorded by either the British or American naval authorities as having been sunk off the West Coast of the United States at any time during the war. Almost every Japanese submarine was accounted for. Of the 130 Japanese submarines destroyed during World War II, the cause of destruction of only five was never determined, and of those, the location of only one remained unknown.[5] The files of the Imperial Japanese Navy also revealed that no submarines had been present off Oregon and only one submarine had lost in the whole of May 1943 – the *RO.137*, sunk by the USS *SC-669* in the New Hebrides.

Indeed, there was no good reason why any Japanese submarines would have been in the Oregon area at the time. The US coast was near the limits of their range and would have necessitated a long and extremely hazardous journey across an ocean dominated by the US Navy. When Hubbard fought his "battle" in May 1943, the Japanese Navy's main attention was on the battle for the Aleutians. Occupied by Japanese forces at the start of the war, the Aleutian islands of Attu and Kiska – administratively part of Alaska – were the only part of the United States to be have been occupied by the enemy. The Japanese submarine force was ordered to carry out an evacuation of their garrison on the islands. It proved to be a very costly task, with three Japanese submarines destroyed in only two weeks. Ironically, one of these submarines, the *I-9*, was the only confirmed Japanese casualty of a PC-class subchaser – the *PC-487*, on June 10, 1943, only a week after the conclusion of Hubbard's own phantom battle.[6]

A final piece of evidence is perhaps the most obvious of all. If one, or possibly two, Japanese submarines were sunk by Hubbard, where are they? No wrecked Japanese submarines have been found off the US West Coast. People have looked for them, including the Church of Scientology, which is said to have mounted a costly expedition in the early 1980s. But nobody has ever found them. Hubbard's submarines, in fact, seem remarkably elusive. Certainly nobody has been able to identify which vessels they were or where they presently lie.[7] This has not deterred the Church of Scientology from claiming that Hubbard sunk them.

During the 1984 trial of Hubbard's former biographical researcher, Gerry Armstrong, Thomas Moulton provided an alternative explanation of the US Navy's non-recognition of Hubbard's "achievement".

Q: Now, you had mentioned earlier that there was some aspect of the political climate which I believe influenced Admiral Fletcher's conclusion; what was that?

A: Well, I am sure that – without that it would have been – at about that time either just before this action or just after, I think it was just after, you had the shelling of a refinery here somewhere in the Los Angeles area, I believe just up the coast. It was written up in Reader's Digest a couple of months ago, three months ago.

At that time it caused quite a local panic, so I am told, and the press so indicated, and everybody on the West Coast apparently started a bunch of rumors, became quite upset about it.

I know that the commanders of the various areas received a lot of inquiries from shoreside people. It wasn't a panic, but it was getting into that stage.

It got so bad that I remember in Oregon that the papers there, there were several articles. I saw one of them asking people to keep quiet, not start rumors and so forth, and I am quite sure that this was well known to all the commanders up and down the coast, and it was to their advantage, at least publicly, not to admit that there were submarines in the area and, of course, once Admiral Fletcher had sent this message to Admiral King, knowing how the Navy works, I am sure he wouldn't back down from it.[8]

This has been accepted and reiterated by the Church of Scientology in recent years. In a 1998 briefing document distributed to its members, the Church claimed:

[Vice Admiral] Fletcher had recently lost two fully loaded carriers at the Battle of Midway and had assured his superiors that the waters within his command were

submarine-free. He could not afford an incident such as an encounter with Japanese submarines as it would have sounded the death-knell to his hopes of regaining a decisive command. Consequently Fletcher tried to bury the whole affair. Nevertheless, the crew members all received combat honors after the war.[9]

This highly speculative explanation does not stand up to scrutiny (nor is it accurate; only one American carrier, the USS *Yorktown*, was lost at Midway). The Church of Scientology has not provided any evidence that Fletcher had promised his superiors that "the waters within his command were submarine-free" and there was no reason why Fletcher would or could have made such a risky promise, as there was no way he could have guaranteed it. At the same time as Hubbard was fighting his "submarines", there were no fewer than thirteen real Japanese submarines active in the waters around Attu and Kiska in the Aleutians, within the area of the Northwest Sea Frontier. Fletcher would have been very well aware that there were enemy submarines in the geographical area which he commanded.

The Church of Scientology is also incorrect in saying that the crew of the *PC-815* received engagement honors for their involvement in the "battle." Hubbard's record shows that he did not receive engagement honors at any point in his career and the *PC-815* is not recorded as having received any engagement stars. This was as might have been expected, given that the Navy determined that no actual combat had occurred. Hubbard did manage to give the crew one reward, though: after they returned to Astoria on May 22, the *PC-815* took aboard a rare consignment of ice cream to share between the crew. It was not much, but it was better than nothing.

CHAPTER 10

The Coronados Affair

The USS *PC-815's* delayed journey to San Diego resumed on May 28, 1943. On that same day, Hubbard received new orders to call in first at the port of Alameda, across the bay from San Francisco. On May 30, *PC-815* joined up at Alameda with the USS *Croatan*, a recently-commissioned escort aircraft carrier, which she was to escort the following day to San Diego. The two ships arrived at the southern Californian port on June 2.

Hubbard's second-in-command, Lt Thomas Moulton, left at this point to return to Seattle, where he was soon to get his own command. Although he did not realize it, Hubbard's own command was about to come to a sudden end.

San Diego was to be *PC-815's* new base for the next two and a half years. New equipment was fitted including a "Mousetrap" forward-firing depth charge launcher to replace its old depth charge racks. Hold-ups at the San Diego Naval Base meant that the ship's crew had had little time to conduct a shakedown to ensure that everything was functioning correctly. At the end of June 1943, the Fleet Operational Training Command ordered *PC-815* to join other vessels in conducting anti-submarine training exercises in the waters off San Diego.

On June 28, the day's exercises came to an early end at only 4 pm. Hubbard decided to use the opportunity to hold an unscheduled gunnery drill with *PC-815's* 3" gun, firing four rounds of practice ammunition. A drifting target employed during the day's earlier exercises was used as an aiming point. The ship then headed for an island a few miles south of San Diego and anchored in seven fathoms of water to sit out the night. A small arms drill was also conducted, consuming an estimated 120 rounds of .30 (rifle) and .45 (pistol) ammunition. The crew fished for food before turning in for the night. At 7 am the following morning, *PC-815* returned to San Diego, where Hubbard learned how much trouble he had just gotten himself into.

The island off which *PC-815* had anchored was called Coronado del Sur (South Coronado), the largest of four small rocky islands about 13 miles south of San Diego. Unfortunately for Hubbard, the Coronodo Islands are Mexican territory, located about five miles south of the US-Mexican maritime border and seven miles off the coast of the Mexican state of Baja California. The islands have never been permanently settled, as they are inhospitably arid and have no harbors, bays or protected anchorages.

During Prohibition, an American-run casino hotel, bar and seafood restaurant was built on Coronado del Sur to cater for Americans seeking forbidden pursuits such as drinking alcohol, gambling and prostitution. The resort's trade was decimated after Prohibition was repealed in 1933 and Mexico outlawed gambling in 1934. The "Coronado Islands Yacht Club" went bankrupt the following year and the hotel was taken over by the Mexican state, which used it to accommodate a small guard force from the Mexican Navy.[1]

The Mexican detachment on Coronado del Sur apparently saw *PC-815* at anchor off the island, firing shells and small arms. A formal complaint was made to the US authorities, and less than 48 hours after returning to San Diego, Hubbard and his crew were ordered before a tribunal to explain themselves. The tribunal was chaired by Rear Admiral Frank A. Braisted. It was the second time in only two months that their paths had crossed. Braisted had reviewed the sonar recordings of Hubbard's submarine "battle" in May and was almost certainly aware of Admiral Fletcher's findings on that incident.

The facts of the case were indisputable – nobody attempted to deny that what had been reported had actually happened. Instead, as Hubbard's opening statement to the Board of Investigation shows, he pleaded a mixture of ignorance and innocence:

Q. Relate the movements and operations of the PC 815 from 1500 to 1700 on 28 June 1943.

A. The operation during that period to the best of my knowledge and belief is, that at 1600 or thereabouts, this ship received permission from OTC to secure from exercises. In view of the fact that it was only 1600 and in view of the fact that this ship had been informed that it must make every effort to complete its shakedown, of which it had had very little, due to the delay in repairs at the Destroyer Base, San Diego, California, I ordered general quarters and exercises at general quarters. The ship came to general quarters and as there was a target in the vicinity used by air-craft for bombing practice I ordered that four rounds of target ammunition be expended when I observed the range was clear of ships. The order to commence fire was given. The exercises having been concluded and the night appearing foggy and this vessel being without accurate calibrations, and in that I had had a very arduous day and have not yet been able to train my officers to dependability in piloting, I proceeded to the bank at the East side of South Coronado Island and anchored there in 7 fathoms of water after the ship had been veered, heading 182 degrees on the South Point, 336 degrees on the North Point of South Coronado Island – degrees are gyro.

The ship secured and the men at dusk fished for whatever they could catch. The gunner's mates and other people of the landing party fired small arms from the starboard side of the fan tail at a target thrown over from the ship. The

*firing was to the Eastward and no shots could have possibly
ricocheted into the Coronados as I supervised it personally.
A very small quantity of ammunition was expended for I
was trying to teach my officers to safely handle a .45.*

*At no time was I aware of invading Mexican Territorial
waters, and had no intention whatsoever of causing any
damage to Mexican property, or to frighten the Mexican
population.*

*During the night a skiff approached the ship, evidently
from shore, and the men in it requested of us 10 gallons of
gas to get to the mainland, which gas my Executive Officer
did not see fit to expend. There were several fishing vessels,
names not recorded, lying well inside us close to shore and
in communication with it. At no time did anyone even
casually refer to the Island being shelled.*

*My actions during this period were based upon: (1) the
necessity of training the gun crews at every possible chance
(2) the unofficial statements to me at the Saturday conference by Commander Ferguson that it would be all right for
me to arrange for planes which I took to include as permission to hold non-scheduled firing practice; and, (3) an
attempt to obtain enough rest for myself so that I could
competently instruct my officers on the following day in
Mousetrap firing and anti-submarine warfare training.*

*That is the answer to the Board's questions to the best of
my knowledge and belief.*[2]

A succession of witnesses from *PC-815's* crew were called to give
evidence. The Navigation Officer admitted that this was the second
time that *PC-815* had anchored off the Coronados, that he thought
the Coronados belonged to the United States and that he had not
consulted the navigational guides before the ship's anchoring.

The other witnesses were cross-examined in detail about the circumstances of the firing itself. The conduct of the exercise and the question of whether the shells had actually hit land were examined in particular detail. The evidence on the latter point was inconclusive – some said that all four shells fired had fallen in the water, but others reported seeing impacts on land.

One of the most damaging points to emerge, from Hubbard's point of view, was that his orders had not granted him permission to anchor at discretion, especially not in Mexican territory:

Exercise 54-2. Vessels schedule [sic, should be "scheduled"] for Sound School the following day will remain at sea. Operating in Sound School areas plus 4626, 4726, 4826, 4825, 4725, 4625 [apparently map grid references] unless given other areas for night steaming and exercises. Other vessels, unless scheduled for other exercises, upon completion of Sound School work will return to port prior dark.[3]

In other words, Hubbard was explicitly confined to a specific area off San Diego. His new second-in-command, Lt (jg) George Asmann, admitted that the orders did not include authority to anchor if desired. He also admitted that while he knew that the Coronados Islands were Mexican territory, "it did not particularly come to my mind that they were Mexican islands" and that he had assumed that they were included in the Sound School operating areas. When pressed by the investigating officers, Asmann admitted that he was in the pilot house of *PC-815* during the firing "because it was cold and wet outside and that [he] wanted to be warm and dry."

Hubbard attempted to pin the blame for the incident on the inexperience of his crew:

Q. Captain, why did you anchor at the Coronados Islands in the position shown by the testimony on the 28th of June?

119

A. Because I have no officer with more than three and one-half months total officer of the deck experience aboard naval vessels and because it was foggy and there were kelp beds and menaces to navigation in my designated operating area, which I did not leave. By so entering I would have had to spend the entire night on the bridge – a thing which I have done on the ship many times before. On three separate occasions when leaving my officers in charge of the bridge they have become lost, a fact which was dangerous to the safety of the ship. I am attempting to remedy their lack of experience as rapidly as possible but at the time in question I do not think any commanding officer sensible of his responsibilities would have guaranteed the safety of his ship unless he utilized an existing anchorage. There was no reason to continue steaming in these waters through the night.[4]

After hearing thirteen hours of evidence, the board concluded its hearings on Saturday 3 July, 1943 and produced eighteen findings of fact:

1. That the U.S.S. PC 815 fired 4 rounds of 3"/50 caliber turret ammunition at about 1619 on 28 June 1943, from the one 3"/50 caliber gun mounted on board.

2. That no navigational data was available to determine the position or course of the PC-815 at the time the shots were fired at about 1619 on 28 June, 1943.

3. That the position of the ship was in general, Northeast of South Coronados Island at an undetermined distance.

4. That land was in the line of sight at the time of firing and that this land was some part of the Coronados Island [sic].

5. That neither a safety officer nor a check-sight observer was stationed at the gun.

6. That all of the fall of shot of the 4 shots fired from the 3"/50 caliber gun were not observed by any officer on the ship.

7. That an undetermined number of splashes were observed in the water in the direction of land during the firing.

8. That evidence of shells hitting land or rocks on the Northern end of South Coronados Island was observed on two separate instances during the conduct of firing.

9. That evidence of a shell hitting land or rocks on the Northern end of South Coronados Island or on land behind the Northeastern end of South Coronados Island in the line of fire was observed on a third instance during the conduct of firing.

10. That the ship was underway at the time of firing making one-third engine speed, about 9 knots.

11. That there was no U.S. Naval directive prescribing that the PC-815 fire guns of any caliber in any area on 28 June, 1943.

12. That upon completion of firing of the 3"/50 caliber gun the PC-815 proceeded on various courses and speeds and at about 1706 on 28 June, 1943, anchored about 500 yards off the Eastern shore of South Coronados Islands in 7 fathoms of water with 65 fathoms of chain to the starboard anchor with the lighthouse structure on the Northeast sector of South Coronados Island bearing about 326 degrees true and the left tangent of South Coronados Island bearing about 185 degrees true.

13. That after anchoring on the afternoon of 28 June 1943, firing of .30 caliber and .45 caliber weapons was conducted from the port and starboard quarters of the PC-815 by certain officers and members of the crew during the period from about 1730 until sometime after sunset.

14. That approximately 80 rounds of .30 and 40 rounds of .45 caliber ammunition was expended, some of which were fired into the water in the direction of South Coronados Island.

15. That shots from the small arms firing were not observed to hit the South Coronados Island.

16. That the ship remained at anchor throughout the night of 28-29 June, 1943.

17. That the ship remained in the vicinity of South Coronados Island on the afternoon of 27 June and remained overnight in approximately the same position as the ship was anchored on 23 June, 1943.

18. That there was no U.S. Naval directive authorizing the PC-815 to anchor in the vicinity of the Coronados Islands on 27 and 28 June, 1943.[5]

Braisted approved the findings of the investigation and pronounced his verdict on the culprits. Hubbard was deemed primarily responsible and was relieved of command as well as being given a formal letter of admonition. George Asmann, his executive officer, was also given a letter of admonition. Braisted informed Hubbard:

1. The facts and testimony ... indicate that on June 28, 1943, while serving as Commanding Officer of the U.S.S. PC 815, you:

(a) Disregarded orders by having the vessel under your command conduct a gunnery practice without proper authority; and

(b) Disregarded orders by anchoring in Mexican Territorial waters without proper authority.

2. The above led to the receipt of a complaint against the vessel under your command from Mexican Authorities.

3. Because of the short time that you have been in

command and the exigencies of the service, this letter of admonition is written in lieu of other more drastic disciplinary action which would have been taken under normal and peacetime conditions.[6]

As Braisted made clear, the needs of the wartime Navy and Hubbard's own inexperience saved him from more severe disciplinary action. In peacetime, the offences committed would certainly have entailed a court-martial that would have resulted in a demotion or possibly even dismissal.

The loss of his command was the very least that could have been expected, however, and so it was that on July 7, 1943, after less than eighty days in command, Hubbard made his last entry in *PC-815's* log book: "1345, Signed on Detachment, L. R. Hubbard".

*

The USS PC-815 After Hubbard

After Hubbard left PC-815 she continued to be stationed at San Diego and performed occasional patrol, escort and training duties off the southern California coast. Her Movement Card indicates that she was inactive for much of this period but was reactivated on September 2, 1945.

Early on the morning of September 11, 1945, her career came to an abrupt and tragic end just outside San Diego harbor. A thick but short-lived fog bank formed ahead of the subchaser as she was escorting the submarine USS Apogon into the port. Visibility was down to 300 yards as PC-815 entered the fog bank at a speed of seven knots.

At 6:47 am, at a point about one and a half miles south of Point Loma, a ship was sighted dead ahead of PC-815. Her commander attempted to take evasive action but it was too late to avoid a collision. The USS Laffey, a veteran of D-

Day and the Battle of Okinawa, struck PC-815 "just abaft the PC's bridge, target angle about 340°". PC-815 burst into flames and began to sink bow-first as the destroyer backed away. She was rapidly submerged within two minutes and sank only five minutes later.[7]

Laffey and Apogon rescued all but one of PC-815's crew, who was recorded as missing, presumed dead. Another PC-815 crewman was seriously injured. Although Laffey suffered significant damage, with the fire from PC-815 spreading into one of the destroyer's compartments before being extinguished, her crew sustained no casualties. Her captain radioed the shore at 7.15 am to give them the bad news: "We have just collided with the PC-815 and she has sunk."[8]

PC-815's wreck came to rest in one of the harbor's shipping channels. Because it constituted a navigational hazard, Navy divers demolished it in early November 1945. The remains of the wreck still lie in about 90 feet (27 m) of water and are diveable.

*

Hubbard was posted to temporary duty onshore at the Issuing Office, Headquarters, Eleventh Naval District in San Diego, whilst waiting for another assignment, which he hoped would be in the South Pacific. He was not demoted but in practice his new post represented an enormous downgrade. As an officer in a Registered Publications Issuing Office, his role would have been related to the distribution of classified publications and identification documents to units in the south-western United States.[9] Compared to commanding a fighting vessel, this would have seemed an extremely menial role.

One final consequence of this affair was that Hubbard received a stinging fitness report from Rear Admiral Braisted. The Admiral noted that he would "prefer not to have" Hubbard under his command. He rated Hubbard "below average" overall and marked his view of Hubbard's judgment as being that he "frequently draws wrong conclusions". In his concluding remarks Braisted declared:

Consider this officer lacking in the essential qualities of judgement, leadership and cooperation. He acts without forethought as to probable results. He is believed to have been sincere in his efforts to make his ship efficient and ready. Not considered qualified for command or promotion at this time. Recommend duty on a large vessel where he can be properly supervised.[10]

Similar recommendations had been made previously by the US Naval Attaché in Australia and the Commandant of the Boston Navy Yard but had not been acted on. This time, notice was taken. Braisted was the most senior officer to report on Hubbard during his entire Naval career. Reports on the Coronados affair went all the way up to the Secretary of the Navy and the Judge Advocate General, casting a permanent blight on Hubbard's naval career.

Hubbard evidently found Braisted's criticism hard to take. Three years later, he wrote in a personal record: "I can forget such things as Admiral Braystead [*sic*]. Such people are unworthy of my notice … My service record was not too glorious. I must be convinced that I suffer no reaction from any minor disciplinary action, that all such were minor. My service was honorable, my initiative and ability high."[11] However, the damage to his career was permanent. In his remaining seven years of service in the United States Naval Reserve, L. Ron Hubbard never commanded another vessel.

CHAPTER 11

"Mister Roberts" and the USS *Algol*

Almost as soon as Hubbard was relieved of command, he reported sick. On July 15, 1943 – the same day as Rear Admiral Braisted issued a letter of admonition concerning the USS *PC-815's* shelling of Mexico's Coronado Islands – Hubbard was put on the sick list in San Diego. He complained of a variety of problems, ranging from epigastric pains to back pains to malaria.

Hubbard remained on the sick list for seventy-seven days, with one complain confirmed: a duodenal ulcer.[1] He later blamed his ailment on the stress he had suffered over the Coronado incident:

> *I was reprimanded in San Diego in mid-43 for firing on the Mexican coast and was removed from command of my ship. This on top of having sunk two Jap subs without credit, the way my crew lied for me at the Court of Inquiry, the insults of the High Command, all combined to put me in the hospital with ulcers.[2]*

He may well have exaggerated the effect it had on him, as he later wrote:

> *Your stomach trouble you used as an excuse to keep the Navy from punishing you. You are free of the Navy. You have no further reason to have a weak stomach. Your ulcers are all well and never bother you. You can eat anything.[3]*

The treatment for the ulcers had an unfortunate side-effect; he wrote:

Sexual feeling has been depressed by several things amounting to a major impasse. To cure ulcers of the stomach I was given testosterone and stilbesterol. These reduced my libido to nothing.[4]

In later years he told an improbable story about his stay at the hospital:

I had earlier, in the San Diego Hospital where I had been for some back injuries, helped them with their problems with what is called "filoriasis" of which they knew nothing. As I had been in the South Pacific and knew something of it, they were very glad of any data concerning it. They were unaware of a French serum which existed for it and did not know that it did not make people impotent or sterile, and did not know that a spell in a cold country was all it really needed. They had a regiment of Marines there in San Diego who had all contracted the disease and had been shipped ashore. They then sent these to Alaska where I am sure they all recovered in the cold.[5]

While he was still in San Diego, the navy decided that he would be assigned to the Small Craft Training Center in San Pedro, California. This may have been an attempt by his superiors to remedy the failings exposed during his stint on *PC-815*. Hubbard later gave two rather different accounts of how he left *PC-815*. According to Hubbard's son, he wrote home to inform his family that he was in hospital because he had been injured when he picked up an unexploded shell from the deck of his ship; it had exploded in mid-air as he threw it over the side.[6] He gave an alternative account in a 1952 lecture in which he told his audience:

They took me off the ship [PC-815] and hospitalized me, and then they let me out of the hospital. And I got out of the hospital and the ship had gone. And so they sent me over to the officer's pool, and there was nobody over at the officer's pool to amount to anything, and by this time they'd lost all their – all their navigators were at sea and things like that.[7]

Hubbard said that he was sent to the "naval operating base down in San Pedro" and that by this time, two or three years into the war, "I really was bored with it." He claimed that he was ordered by the Commanding Officer at San Pedro to take out a "YMS" (an auxiliary motor minesweeper) and said that he was given "a job operating the nucleus crew training program". Finally, he said, he "wound up with the Commanding Officer hysterically wiring Washington to get me put on duty at that base."[8]

The Church of Scientology's account claims that his duties "were variable, and involved both direct instruction of skippers and crews, as well as the redrafting of instructional materials for some fifteen thousand others." The Church claims that Hubbard was "for all intents and purposes, [the] first to address ... the instruction of military personnel during the Second World War."[9] It does not explain how the nine million personnel recruited up to that point somehow managed to be instructed.

While Hubbard's claims were clearly exaggerated – he only spent seven weeks at San Pedro – there is evidence that he played some sort of training role. He was principally a student "under instruction" at the SCTC but while waiting for further orders to sea duty, he is also recorded as having performed the additional duties of a "Staff Assistant, Sea Training".[10] The details of these duties are not recorded.

Due to his long stay in the naval hospital, he did not report to the SCTC until 16 October, by which time he already wanted a change of scenery. Only three days after arriving, he sent a letter to the Chief of Naval Personnel requesting a reassignment:

1. It is requested that I be given orders to landing vessels such as LST's [Landing Ships, Tank], destined for any combat area.

2. It is believed that my services may be of greater use in the amphibious forces, although Commander McDaniel of the Sub-Chaser Training Center, Miami, has again recently recommended that I be given another command such as a PCE or PC, it appears to me that officers with sea experience are more urgently needed in landing vessels.[11]

He provided a somewhat exaggerated resumé of his own career, claiming that he had been "commander of three expeditions" and had acquired "a resultant understanding of the waters and beaches of various parts of the world". His claims about his brief service in the US Marine Corps Reserve would have surprised his former superiors: "infantry training and understanding of landing tactics gained as 1st sergeant, USMCR, 1930/31 as well as in National Guard. Qualified in nearly all small arms and infantry weapons. Experience in thus handling up to a battalion of men."[12]

Hubbard was well aware that the débacle in the Coronado Islands would count against him. He attached a statement seeking to justify his actions, saying that most of the crew of *PC-815* had asked to return to his command. He claimed to have been given permission to fire at his own discretion, and complained that other vessels had not been censured for anchoring off the islands. Hubbard added a somewhat unconvincing excuse – that he was in the grip of a throat infection and "dull from sulfa-thiazole" at the time, which he said "may serve to explain in part an apparent lapse of judgment".

The commanding officer of the SCTC recommended approving Hubbard's request. He wrote that he considered Hubbard to have "latent ability" and to be "capable of doing good work if properly directed."[13] However, the letter was passed via Rear Admiral Braisted, Hubbard's nemesis in the Coronados affair. Braisted did not make any specific recommendations but drew the Chief of Naval Personnel's attention to the proceedings of the Board which had investigated Hubbard's case.

The result was a foregone conclusion. The note came back annotated with the comment: "No action – past record indicated not qualified to command."[14] Braisted had earlier recommended that Hubbard serve on a large vessel "where he can be properly supervised." Perhaps thus reminded, the naval authorities now moved to implement this recommendation by assigning Hubbard to duty in connection with the conversion of the attack cargo ship USS *Algol* in Portland, Oregon.[15] He served as Navigator and Training Officer (also, later, Chief Ship's Censor). His duties involved overseeing the training of *Algol's* crew, as well as his old role of mail censorship.

*

Attack cargo ships

Attack cargo ships were a class of vessel used by the United States in World War II to land amphibious assault troops and keep them supplied with combat cargo, using the ship's boats. They could carry landing craft and were equipped with numerous rapid-firing guns to provide anti-aircraft defences and support shore bombardments. The US built 108 such vessels between 1943 and 1945. Some were purpose-built but many others were converted from non-military vessels or from existing cargo ships.

The USS Algol was typical of her kind. She had originally been a Type C2 cargo ship, laid down at Oakland, California in 1942 and launched in February 1943 as the SS James Barnes. She was decommissioned at the Willamette Shipyard in Portland, Oregon on December 3, 1943 prior to her conversion into an attack cargo ship.

This work would have entailed fitting weapons and larger hatches and booms, as well as reconfiguring her hold for combat loading. This enabled the ship's embarked forces to have immediate access to weapons, ammunition and other supplies needed for an amphibious landing. Cargo needed later in the operation would be stored further down in the hold. This approach contrusted with peacetime cargo loading, which emphasizes the most efficient use of space. In wartime, the priority was to make the cargo available in the order required to support an operation.

Some World War II attack cargo ships continued to be used until as late as the Vietnam War in the 1960s. New vessels of similar design, redesignated as amphibious cargo ships, continued in service with the US Navy until 1994. This class of ship was eventually superseded by a new type of vessel, the amphibious transport dock, which can carry aircraft as well as vehicles and landing craft. Ten such vessels are currently in service with the US Navy.

*

Judging from his own words, Hubbard was not an especially keen crew member. He appears to have become depressed about the faltering trajectory of his career. "My salvation is to let this roll over me," he wrote glumly in his diary on January 6, 1944, "to write, write and write some more. To hammer keys until I am finger worn to the second joint and then to hammer keys some more. To pile up copy, stack up stories, roll the wordage and generally conduct my life along the one line of success I have ever had."[16]

Hubbard remained with *Algol* for the next nine months. His time with the ship was interrupted only by a week-long course on amphibious operations, which he attended in April 1944 at the Operational Training School of the Twelfth Naval District at the

Naval Station Treasure Island, in San Francisco. His performance was rated as satisfactory by the Supervisor of Ships at the Willamette Shipyard. Hubbard was described as "conscientious and energetic" and was stated to "have the necessary qualifications for promotion to the next higher rank [i.e. Lieutenant Commander] and his promotion when due is recommended." Mysteriously, Hubbard's Fitness Reports aboard *Algol* reveal a previously unrecorded proficiency in Japanese.

As the date of *Algol's* commissioning approached, however, Hubbard's preference for combat duties appears to have waned. Rather than subchasers or LSTs, he now stated a preference for serving on auxiliary vessels – *Algol* was classified as an amphibious ship, not an auxiliary – or with the Hydrographic Office on shore.

The news from the Pacific theatre may have had something to do with this. Throughout 1943 and 1944, fierce fighting had raged across the western Pacific as Allied forces fought their way from island to island. At the landings on Tarawa in November 1943, more than a thousand Americans were killed and two thousand wounded. The Gilbert Islands were assaulted in November 1943 and January 1944 saw landings on the Marshall Islands. The reconquest of New Guinea began in April 1944, while on 15 June, two divisions of US Marines began an assault on Saipan in the southern Marianas, and in the battle that followed 16,500 Americans were killed or wounded. Shortly afterwards, in the Battle of the Philippine Sea, the Japanese made a determined attempt to destroy the American fleet but were repulsed.

For the first time, military censorship of US casualties was relaxed to bring home to the American public the deadly seriousness of the struggle in which the nation was engaged. Shocking pictures showing blazing ships and beaches strewn with dead Marines were splashed on the front pages of newspapers across the United States. Front-line duty in the US Pacific Fleet was becoming increasingly hazardous. *Algol*, as an attack cargo ship, was expected to operate close inshore to support amphibious landings – and so would not only be right in the front line, but would be a prime target for enemy attacks. Only a few months later, *Algol's* sister ships were to face the threat of kamikaze attacks.

On April 21, 1944, *Algol* was commissioned and immediately put to sea for trials. Through August and most of September she conducted exercises at sea. As Navigating Officer, Hubbard signed the ship's deck log daily, but there was little to report except "under way, as before".

He later claimed that while aboard *Algol*, he "wrote a textbook for his crew, not only greatly simplifying the technology of navigation and its terms, but making navigators out of men who would have otherwise floundered."[17] In a 1957 lecture, he claimed that the crew were "a lot of interesting psychos" who had "had gone mad in the process of amphibious warfare, just lying off islands, you see, and doing nothing." He said that he had scared the crew by telling them what the ship's name meant:

The sailors on that ship when I went aboard were very horrified to find out (because I did not omit telling them) that they were sailing on a ship called, in Arabic, The Evil Eye.[18]

(He was incorrect; the name comes from the Arabic *ra's al-ghūl*, meaning "head of the ogre".)

Algol's shakedown concluded on September 3, 1944 and she put into Oakland, CA to load cargo for transport to Saipan, the scene of a recent battle. Hubbard, however, did not want to go there. On September 9, 1944 he wrote to the Chief of Naval Personnel requesting a transfer to the Naval School of Military Government, following a general Navy request for applicants "for intensive training with eventual assignment to foreign duty as civil affairs officers in occupied areas." He claimed to have been "educated as a civil engineer", though he did not mention that he had only completed two out of three years of his course and had failed to graduate. He also claimed to be conversant in "Japanese, Spanish, Chamorro, Tagalog, Pekin [sic] Pidgin, Shanghai Pidgin", which would have been no mean feat considering that he had been in Japan and China for only a few days, as a teenager, in the late 1920s. In addition, he claimed that he was "familiar with the sociology and governments of North China, Japan, the Philippines", and claimed that he was "experienced in handling natives, all classes, in various parts of world, as laboring crews, students or business associates".

Hubbard's request was supported by his commanding officer, Lieutenant Commander Axton T. Jones. He gave Hubbard a generally favourable Fitness Report for his service aboard *Algol*, stating that he was "an above average navigator and is to be trusted. This officer is of excellent personal and military character. Recommended for promotion when due". Jones noted that he had "improved impressively", but added a caveat: "Lieutenant Hubbard is a capable and energetic officer, but is very temperamental and often has his feelings hurt."[19]

On September 15, Hubbard was informed that he had been accepted on the Military Government Program. But just before he departed from *Algol*, a very curious incident occurred. On Wednesday, September 27, at 4:30 p.m., *Algol's* Deck Log records:

> *[T]he navigating officer reported to the OOD [Officer on Deck] that an attempt at sabatage [sic] had been made sometime between 1530-1600. A Coke bottle filled with gasoline with a cloth wick inserted had been concealed among cargo which was to be hoisted aboard and stored in No. 1 hold. It was discovered before being taken on board. ONI [Office of Naval Intelligence], FBI and NSD [Naval Security Detail] authorities reported on the scene and in-vestigations were started.*[20]

The log entry is signed by the navigating officer, L. Ron Hubbard. However, the log makes no further mention of the incident and no record has been yet discovered of the outcome of the investigations. Nor is there any explanation of what Hubbard was doing searching the cargo or how he managed to find this "gasoline bomb". There is not even any confirmation that the bottle was some sort of improvised incendiary device; the only known record of the incident is that entered in the *Algol's* logbook.

Shortly after 10 pm the same evening a signal was received stating that "Lt Lafayette Ron Hubbard, D-V(S), USNR 113392, is this date detached from duty." Years later, Hubbard seems to have transformed this incident into something much more dramatic, which he claimed involved

> the discovery of a sodium bomb in a box of torpedo detonators. A sodium bomb soaks up water from the air and explodes when the ship is at sea. I asked that the cargo be unloaded and was refused. They said it really wasn't a sodium bomb. But when I offered to throw it in the water you never saw G-men scatter so fast.[21]

Hubbard's son L. Ron Hubbard Jr. claimed in an affidavit that his father was relieved of duty after he had "apparently concealed a gasoline bomb on board the USS *Algol* in order to avoid combat." Other critics have echoed this claim. The Church of Scientology's official biographer of Hubbard, Dan Sherman, has rejected it, pointing out:

> L. Ron Hubbard was never relieved of duty from a Pacific-based USS Algol... Not only is the statement false – for Mr. Hubbard discovered a concealed gasoline bomb aboard the Algol – but his services aboard the Algol terminated with a promotion to the United States School of Military Government at Princeton University.[22]

Leaving to one side the inaccurate statement about the terms of Hubbard's transfer – he was not promoted, his rank remaining unchanged – the Church's statement is, for once, not inconsistent with Hubbard's service record. His file contains no suggestion that he was relieved of duty aboard *Algol* or that he was disciplined for any matter resulting from the discovery of the "gasoline bomb". Planting it would have been extremely risky and would have gained nothing. Hubbard's posting to the School of Military Government was imminent and his Captain had consistently given him satisfactory reports, recommending him for promotion. It is still unclear what happened aboard *Algol* that night, but there seems to be no hard evidence to support the claim that Hubbard was responsible for the incident.

Hubbard later claimed that the Broadway show *Mister Roberts*, which became a popular movie of the same name, was based on his own experiences aboard the *Algol*. He said in a lecture in 1956 – the year after the film was released – that "There was a story made about that vessel, by the way. It was called *Mister Roberts*. You may have seen this picture or read the book."[23]

When his staff asked Hubbard in June 1972 about how he had supposedly become connected with the play and film, he said:

> *I frankly don't know how this came about. Many of my friends in New York were playwrights and when I was there after my return from the South Pacific in the middle of 1942, and as there were very few people who had been in the War so far, the story must have been passed around amongst playwright friends. Later, in 1944, I was again on the playwright beat and entertained my friends with the fabulous story of "The Bucket". Sometime later some of them told me I had been immortalized. I didn't know what they were talking about. This is all the connection I know of, and of course there may be no connection at all.*[24]

There is no record of Hubbard associating with playwrights. Instead, at the times that he mentioned – mid-1942, when he was in Brooklyn and late 1944, when he was on a course at Princeton – he was visiting friends in the science fiction world, some of whom wrote about their interactions with Hubbard. None of them are known to have been involved with Mister Roberts.

Hubbard told his Scientologist followers that he was the prototype for the Mister Roberts character, played by Henry Fonda, and that the *Algol's* Lt Cdr Axton T. Jones had inspired the vicious commanding officer played in the film by James Cagney. The tale was faithfully relayed by Hubbard's Public Relations staff:

> *At the end of the war, having been relegated because of his physical condition to the amphibious forces in the Pacific, he had the adventures which are reported on the screen in "Mister Roberts". "The Bucket" of that motion picture, stage play, and the novel is actually the A.K.A. 54, the U.S.S. Algol. The captain so brutally characterized in the picture is actually Lieutenant Commander Axton P. [sic] Jones. L. Ron Hubbard as "Mister Roberts" was with the ship less than a year, however, and contrary to the script, was not killed at Okinawa.*[25]

Hubbard had a history of making unverified claims of involvement in various successful films of the time. He had already claimed to have written the screenplays of John Ford's legendary films *Stagecoach* and *The Plainsman*, starring Gary Cooper.[26] His claim to be the inspiration for *Mister Roberts* seems equally unfounded.

The film was based on a popular 1946 novel written by Thomas Heggen, and subsequently adapted for Broadway by Heggen and Joshua Logan. Heggen based the story on his own experiences aboard the attack transport USS *Virgo* in 1944–45. The character of Mister Roberts is said to have been an amalgam of Heggen himself and another officer called Don House, an assistant gunnery officer aboard the USS *Rotanin*. There is no indication that Hubbard and Heggen ever crossed paths; Heggen was still serving aboard *Virgo* when Hubbard claimed to be "on the playwright beat."[27]

*

The USS Algol After Hubbard

The USS Algol had a long and eventful career after Hubbard's departure. She participated in the Battles of Luzon and Okinawa in 1945 and earned a service star for each of the two operations. She survived the war unscathed, avoiding any combat damage or casualties. During the first three years of the Korean War, she transported UN troops to various places in Korea, notably Incheon during the September 1950 battle, and earned a further five service stars.

Algol was transferred to Atlantic service in the 1960s after a few years in mothballs and supported the 1962 American blockade of Cuba during the missile crisis. For much of the rest of the decade, she supported amphibious training by the US Marine Corps on the US East Coast and in the West Indies. She was eventually decommissioned in 1970 and was struck from the Navy list in 1977. She was sunk off New Jersey's Shark River in 1991 to create an artificial reef.

CHAPTER 12

"Crippled and blinded"

Hubbard's last active post with the US Navy took him, at his request, to Princeton, New Jersey in late September 1944. He was one of hundreds of officers from all arms of the US Armed Forces who underwent training at the School of Military Government at Princeton. This prompted later claims that he had "attended Princeton University", perhaps even as a postgraduate.[1] As usual, the truth was far less impressive: the US Government had taken over some of the buildings on Princeton's campus and used them for military training.

The US Government faced a huge problem in the territories it was liberating in the Pacific and East Asia. Unlike the European countries occupied by the Nazis, many of the lands occupied by the Japanese had little or no experience of independent self-government before the war. Territories such as the Dutch East Indies (now Indonesia) and many of the Pacific islands were run as colonies of Western powers such as France, the Netherlands and the United States. Other territories, such as New Guinea or the Philippines, were dependencies of Allied powers.

Unlike in occupied Western Europe, where local administrators continued in office under Nazi stewardship, the colonial administrations in Japanese-occupied territories were completely uprooted. The Japanese pursued an ostensibly anti-colonialist agenda (exemplified by their term for their overseas empire: the "Greater East Asia Co-Prosperity Sphere"), so a swift and forceful "decolonization" program accompanied their invasions. While this was supposedly liberation from Western control, in practice

Western administrators were simply replaced by Japanese administrators who imposed a brutal regime of forced labour and virtual enslavement.

The eradication of Western administrations was so complete that in some territories the Americans had to rely on Japanese administrators and the Imperial Japanese Army to maintain order well after the end of the war. The United States recognized that it needed a corps of trained administrators, ready to take charge of the newly liberated territories – and ultimately, of Japan itself.

The military government training programs of the US Army and Navy divided the Pacific between them – the Army focusing narrowly on Japan and the Navy more broadly on Formosa (Taiwan), Indonesia, Korea, the Philippines, Okinawa and Japan. Schools of military government were established at Columbia University in New York City and at Princeton University.[2]

The training consisted of a series of crash courses in the geography, history, culture, economy and government of the areas that were to be occupied. The topics studied included international law, psychology, civil administration, political science and languages.[3] As a contemporary journal put it, the goal was to enable the trainee administrators:

[T]o handle such contacts with the civilian populations of the western and southwestern Pacific as might be expected to develop in connection with naval operations in that area. They were to be trained as officers capable of handling liaison activities with the Army, with such civilian agencies as may impinge upon the Navy, with our allies, and with the native populations of the area, and also as civil affairs officers equipped to participate in the administration of such military governments as might in the course of events be established under naval control.[4]

Hubbard was among those undergoing training for duty as a military administrator, though a later Scientology account implies that he was actually a tutor, claiming that he gave lessons on "Oriental Justice and law enforcement."[5] There is no evidence of this from his service record. Hubbard's friend John W. Campbell wrote warmly of Hubbard's move to Princeton, which he seemed to think would be a combat role: "He'll go in with the first wave of landing craft, unarmed, but in navy officer's uniform, to take charge of civilians trapped in the newly formed beachhead."[6] In reality, he would have worked well behind the front lines to implement the military occupation of reconquered territories. Many of the trainee administrators were in fact conscientious objectors.[7]

It is unclear why Hubbard wanted this duty. Throughout the war he had consistently expressed a preference for deck duty aboard combat vessels. Even after his removal from the USS *PC-815* in July 1943, he continued to lobby for a new command. In the Fitness Report covering the period immediately before his posting to Princeton, he expressed a desire for duty aboard auxiliary vessels or shore duty at the Hydrographic Office. The letter which he wrote requesting assignment to the Military Government course represents the only record of him expressing a preference for administrative duties. There is no obvious reason why he should have chosen such a radically different assignment, but it was likely rooted in his claims of expertise in Asian culture. He told Scientologists a few years later:

> At the end of the war I was educated at Princeton for a while in civil affairs. The Navy had found that you couldn't take an area and knock apart all of man's works in it and then expect to operate in that area. They didn't state it in those terms; they just said, "It gets to be a mess and we have got to have somebody to take care of it." So they tried to find officers who had had experience in Asia, and they brought

them into Princeton and ran them through an assembly line
of what happens to have been a very fine school. Hoping
that their past experience was enough to carry them
through with the job, the Navy jammed down the throats
of these officers enough knowledge for them to go out and
set up governments and to set up units that could handle
people, to square things around after the military had been
at work.[8]

Hubbard's claimed "experience in Asia" was in reality very limited: he spent a few months on Guam with his parents in two separate visits when he was between the ages of 16 and 18. He taught English to local children in a Navy-run school for a few weeks but otherwise occupied himself with home-schooling and his first efforts at writing pulp fiction stories. He also visited China, Japan and the Philippines on tourist excursions. Nonetheless, he claimed in another lecture:

Anybody who had experience with Asia was welcome as the
flowers of spring up at Princeton where they were being
trained, so they pulled me out of the Pacific and I went to
Princeton in the last few months of the war.[9]

While he was at Princeton, he was invited to join a group of science-fiction writers who met every weekend at Robert Heinlein's apartment in Philadelphia to discuss possible ways of countering the kamikaze menace in the Pacific. They were semi-official, brain-storming sessions that Heinlein had been asked to organize by the Navy, in the faint hope of coming up with a defence against the kamikazes. "I had been ordered to round up science fiction writers for this crash project," Heinlein later recalled, "the wildest brains I find."[10]

According to Heinlein, Hubbard told him that both his feet had been broken when his last ship was bombed: "Ron had had a busy war – sunk four times and wounded again and again." As a result, Heinlein tried to avoid asking Hubbard to walk down the street to spare him from his apparent pain.[11] L. Sprague de Camp managed to annoy Hubbard by appearing in the uniform of a lieutenant commander (he was working at the Philadelphia Navy Yard at the time): "When Lieutenant Hubbard appeared in Philadelphia in the winter of 1944, the Heinleins, the Asimovs, and the de Camps made a night of it with him. I cannot blame him for showing slight vexation at my having half a stripe on him, since he had at least been at sea, while I had been navigating a desk."[12]

Another of the group, Jack Williamson, then a Sergeant in the US Army, held a dinner on December 2, 1944 for his fellow writers and their wives. Hubbard told his colleagues of his adventures earlier that year. "Hubbard was just back from the Aleutians then," said Williamson, "hinting of desperate action aboard a Navy destroyer, adventures he couldn't say much about because of military security ... I recall his eyes, the wary, light-blue eyes that I somehow associate with the gunmen of the old West, watching me sharply as he talked as if to see how much I believed. Not much."[13]

John W. Campbell also recorded Hubbard's tall stories, telling a friend: "He was in command of an attack cargo carrier that helped at Saipan just before he was assigned to his present job. He's been sunk five times, wounded four". The USS *Algol* had indeed gone to Saipan, but Hubbard had departed from the ship before she had even left California and he had, of course, not been in command. Hubbard's lingering bitterness over his treatment in Australia had evidently dissipated by this time, as he boasted about the (still secret) mission to Campbell: "He was *the* naval officer in charge of sending ships through to MacArthur on Bataan".[14]

Hubbard recalled his time at Princeton after the war, complaining about the effect it had on his health:

During my Princeton sojourn I was very tired and harrassed (sp?) and spent week-ends with a writer friend in Philadelphia [i.e. Heinlein]. He almost forced me to sleep with his wife. Meanwhile I had a affair with a woman named Ferne. Somehow, perhaps because I had constantly wet feet and no sleep at Princeton, I contracted a staphloceus infection. I mistook it for gonnhorea (sic) and until I arrived at Monterey, believed my old illness had returned. I consulted a doctor there who reassured me. This affair again depressed my libido. The staphloceus infection has not entirely vanished, appearing as rheumatism which only small doses of stilbestrol will remove. The hormone further reduces my libido and I am nearly impotent.[15]

His depression came through in a diary entry that he wrote around this time:

The Great Era of Adventure is over. I feel a little like a child who tries to see romance in an attic and holds tenaciously as long as he can to his conception, though he well recognizes the substance of object as a disinteresting tangle of old cloth and dust. I am already in possession of some of this coin — the malaria and the ulcers. I have also multiplied and squared my desire to scratch my feet on far soil. I know that the process of going and the reward of arriving are the one uncomfortable and the other disappointing. It is the horizon one never sees which lures him. And I have come to that state of mind, that supreme disillusion of knowing that nothing waits, that the horizon never seen does not exist. I am restless still.[16]

January 27, 1945, marked the end of Hubbard's time at Princeton. He achieved a respectable score (though, oddly, he later claimed to

144

have "failed my overseas examination"[17]) and earned a satisfactory
fitness report:

> *This officer has completed the course in Military
> Government at Princeton University standing about
> midway in the class of three hundred. He is forceful, re-
> sourceful, alert and wellpoised. He has a very good
> personal and above average military character. He is well
> fitted for promotion and is so recommended.*[18]

Hubbard again expressed a preference for deck service aboard aux-
iliaries in the Pacific. He now also saw himself as a potential
Navigation Instructor at the Submarine Chaser Training Center in
Miami, Florida – no doubt harking back to his days there in 1942
when he was regarded as "something of an authority".

Together with four other officers, he was ordered to proceed to
the Naval Civil Affairs Staging Area at the Presidio of Monterey, CA.
On April 2, 1945, he and his colleagues were assigned to duty with
a civil affairs team outside the continental limits of the United
States, which would most probably have been in the Pacific or
south-east Asia. But just one week later Hubbard turned up at Oak
Knoll Naval Hospital complaining of stomach pains. He was
promptly hospitalized for examinations.

*

Oak Knoll Naval Hospital

*Hubbard's last posting before he was mustered out of the
US Navy took him to Oak Knoll Naval Hospital, also known
as Naval Hospital Oakland. The hospital was built in 1942
on the site of a former golf and country club near Oakland,
California, east of San Francisco Bay. By the end of the war,
the 220-acre site accommodated a sprawling complex of*

*135 buildings. 6,000 patients were cared for by a 3,000-
strong staff of military and civilian personnel.*

*Its usage and population declined sharply after the war
but the facility gained fresh importance during the Korean
and Vietnam wars of the 1950s through to the 1970s. The
temporary wartime buildings were replaced in 1965 with
a new permanent hospital providing 597 beds. It was closed
in 1996 following defense cuts and was demolished in 2011.
The site has been acquired by developers with the intention
of transforming it into a residential community.*[19, 20]

*

Every official biography of L. Ron Hubbard has included, without
fail, the claim that Hubbard ended World War II at Oak Knoll Naval
Hospital, crippled and blinded with serious war wounds. The
Church of Scientology claims that "eventual combat wounds would
finally preclude him from serving with American occupation
forces."[21] Hubbard himself said:

*Blinded with injured optic nerves, and lame with physical
injuries to hip and back, at the end of World War II, I faced an
almost non-existent future. My service record states: "This
officer has no neurotic or psychotic tendencies of any kind whatsoever," but it also states "permanently disabled physically."*

*And so there came a further blow – I was abandoned by
family and friends as a supposedly hopeless cripple and a
probable burden upon them for the rest of my days. Yet I worked
my way back to fitness and strength in less than two years,
using only what I knew about Man and his relationship to the
universe. I had no one to help me; what I had to know I had to
find out. And it's quite a trick studying when you cannot see.*

I became used to being told it was all impossible, that

146

there was no way, no hope. Yet I came to see again and walk again.[22]

There is no doubt that this claim came from Hubbard himself. The original text, written in Hubbard's own handwriting, was admitted as evidence in the 1984 trial of his former biographical researcher, Gerry Armstrong. Today, it is reported to be on display at Hubbard's former home, Saint Hill Manor in Sussex, England. Copies are still frequently disseminated by the Church of Scientology. According to the Church, "in alluding to injuries suffered through the Second World War, he is referencing wounds sustained in combat on the island of Java and aboard a corvette in the North Atlantic."[23] There is no record of Hubbard having been anywhere near Java, nor of Hubbard having served aboard a corvette in any ocean, nor of him sustaining any wounds in combat at any time (or indeed seeing ever combat in the first place).

Hubbard himself told a different story on several occasions. He told Scientologists in a 1958 interview that when he was at Oak Knoll he "wasn't sick, I was just banged up."[24] In a 1960s interview he stated that he had spent "the last year of my naval career in a naval hospital. Not very ill, but I had a couple of holes in me – they wouldn't heal. So they just kept me."[25] It is hard to reconcile "crippled and blinded" with "not very ill" and "just banged up".

What were these supposed injuries and where and when were they sustained? This question went unanswered until 1997, when the Church of Scientology published a volume entitled *Ron – Letters and Journals*. In it we learn that:

> *the muzzle flash of a deck gun had left him legally blind, while shrapnel fragments in hip and back had left him all but lame. In consequence, he could barely seat himself at a typewriter, could not focus on a printed page and, for that matter, could not discern the pages of his own books.*[26]

Hubbard's official Scientologist biographer, Dan Sherman, told a worldwide audience of Scientologists in 1997 about "the slivers of shrapnel [Hubbard] took in the chest."[27] But Hubbard's extensive medical records show a very different story.

Hubbard's Active Duty Fitness Reports span the full range of his active service with the US Navy, from his preliminary examination in March 1941 through to his final active service assessment on December 6, 1945. It is perhaps worth noting the results of his first examination, on April 18, 1941. He was found to be entirely physically normal save for four missing teeth and poor vision – 17/20 in his right eye and 15/20 in his left, corrected to 20/20 with glasses. He was initially rated as "NOT physically qualified for appointment as an officer Class I-V(S)". Later that same year his eyesight was rated as having deteriorated to 12/20. The US Navy's desperate need for manpower following the declaration of an Unlimited National Emergency led to this particular requirement being waived, which allowed Hubbard to join the US Naval Reserve despite having physical deficiencies which would have barred him from the peacetime navy.

Skipping forward another year to June 1942, four months after his supposed exploits on Java, we find that Hubbard had suffered from "active conjunctivitis in Asiatics since January – receding" and his eyesight in his left eye had deteriorated further to only 8/20. He had also developed hemorrhoids and later suffered from urethral discharges, which are a classic symptom of venereal disease. Sulfa drugs were used in treatment but in excess could cause bloody urine, something which Hubbard's shipmate Thomas Moulton recalled seeing him passing on at least one occasion. Hubbard himself later complained about the amount of sulfa he had been fed in the Navy. Hubbard recorded in his private papers that he had caught gonorrhea from a "very loose" girl named Ginger, which forced him to take sulfa to treat the infection.[28]

There is no mention in Hubbard's files of the broken ankle he claimed to have suffered in 1942[29], nor the bullet wounds Hubbard said had been inflicted by the Japanese.[30] The eye injury resulting from a muzzle flash was supposedly sustained while he was serving as Gunnery Officer aboard the USS *Edsall* prior to its sinking off Java.[31] There are several problems with this claim: there is no record of Hubbard having either trained or served as a Gunnery Officer aboard any vessel, there is no record of him having had any association with the ill-fated *Edsall*, and none of his medical reports attributed his eye problems to gunfire.

Hubbard's and Scientology's accounts claim that he sustained injuries in naval combat. Where could this have happened? His service aboard the USS *YP-422* lasted barely a month before he was relieved of command and it took him no further than the waters immediately off Boston Harbor. The most warlike activity committed by *YP-422* under Hubbard's guidance was a 27-hour series of training exercises, during which a few practice rounds were fired to test the gun. There was no suggestion of enemy action, nor any reports of injuries sustained by any of the crew. At no point in the vessel's career, under Hubbard's command or that of his successors, did it see combat. So he could not possibly have received those "slivers of shrapnel in the chest" aboard *YP-422*.

He did conduct what he believed was a lengthy action against two Japanese submarines – or a likely underwater magnetic deposit, according to the US Navy – when commanding the USS *PC-815* the following year. In his own subsequent Battle Report, however, he stated that the crew had suffered "total casualties, 3, all very minor". (He did not specify the type of injuries, but they were likely cuts and bruises resulting from operating the ship's weapons). He did not include himself among the casualties. There was no suggestion from any of the vessels involved in the "battle" that they had received any enemy fire, or had been the victims of friendly fire. So he could not possibly have received shrapnel injuries aboard *PC-815*, either.

The USS *Algol* did travel to combat zones and received commendations, but this was well after Hubbard had left the ship. His service with the vessel was again quite brief, comprising nine months in a dockyard working on its conversion or undertaking sea trials subsequently. At no time during Hubbard's service with *Algol* did the vessel see combat, nor was Hubbard ever recorded as having sustained an injury while aboard.

In fact, there is no evidence anywhere in Hubbard's records that at any time in the war he took part in a combat action or sustained injuries resulting from combat. Nor is Hubbard recorded as having made any claim through official channels relating to such injuries. He later claimed, "my service record states: 'This officer has no neurotic or psychotic tendencies of any kind whatsoever,' but it also states 'permanently disabled physically.'" No such statement appears anywhere in his medical records.

Hubbard's supposed "blindness" is also not recorded in his medical records. They did record a deterioration in his eyesight, which dropped by up to five points in the first year of his service in the US Navy. Nonetheless, with the aid of glasses he remained 20/20 in both eyes until the start of 1945. After he decided to apply for a disability pension, his eyesight was reported to have deteriorated rapidly. At the time of his last report on December 12, 1945, he was rated at only 5/20 in both eyes (which glasses corrected to 12/20 and 14/20 in right and left respectively). This certainly counted as poor eyesight but it was a long way from blindness. There is also no record in his file of him having been declared "legally blind".

The tests performed at Oak Knoll Naval Hospital revealed that he suffered from a duodenal ulcer – the same problem for which he had been hospitalized in San Diego in July 1943. He was given a month's convalescent leave from July 31, 1945 to August 30, before being re-admitted to hospital. A report sent to the Commanding Officer of Oak Knoll Naval Hospital on September 10, 1945 gives a concise summary of Hubbard's medical problems. There is no hint of any injuries, sustained in combat or otherwise:

This officer patient was admitted to the sick list at Naval Affairs Staging Area, Presidio of Monterey, Monterey, Calif., on 10 Apr 1945, with Ulcer, Duodenum. He was transferred to this hospital on the same day.

Review of the current health record reveals that on 15 July 1943, he was hospitalized at USNH [US Naval Hospital], San Diego, Calif., for epigastric pain and vomiting. X-ray examination at the time revealed a duodenal ulcer. The diagnosis was changed to Ulcer, Duodenum, on 24 July 1943, and he was returned to duty on 8 Oct 1943.

On admission here he complained of epigastric distress with a feeling of fullness and of nausea and vomiting, which was relieved by food. Gastro-intestinal examination by x-ray on 19 May 1945, and 16 June 1945, revealed a duodenal ulcer with slight deformity of the duodenal cap. Treatment has consisted of bland diet, belladonna, and pheno-barbitol 7 with continuation of symptoms. The gastro-intestinal series on 31 Aug 1945 was reported as: "Esophagus and stomach negative. Duodenal ulcer with deformity of duodenal cap. Deformity has not increased since the last examination. There is some scarring of the micosa but there is no demonstrable crater. No obstruction."

According to the history obtained from the patient his symptoms first began in April 1943, at which time he held his present commissioned rank of Lt. There is noting in the current health record or history to rebut the presumption of soundness prior to that time.

In view of the recurrence of a duodenal ulcer, and its persistence as demonstrated by x-ray evidence while under

treatment, it is the opinion of the Board that this officer is
not physically fit to perform all the duties of his rank, and
that he should ordered to appear before a retiring board.[32]

The hospital's Commanding Officer forwarded the Board's report to the Chief of the Bureau of Medicine and Surgery, R. T. McIntire, recommending approval of the Board's opinion. However, McIntire did not agree. On October 3, 1945, he disapproved the Board's recommendation and rated Hubbard "physically qualified to perform duty ashore, preferably within the continental U.S."

In other words, Hubbard's ailment was inconvenient rather than disabling and it would not stop him from performing a desk job. The restriction to shore duty in the continental US would enable him to have access to a hospital if his ulcer flared up again. In later years, Scientology claimed that the finding that he was physically qualified for duty was "[t]hanks in great part to the unusual discoveries that L. Ron Hubbard made while at Oak Knoll in 1944, [which meant] he recovered so fully that he was reclassified for full combat duty."[33]

The Chief of Naval Personnel supported McIntire's verdict but added that "since his services are not required in this limited capacity, he will be processed for release from active duty in accordance with the provisions of AlStaCon 282200, September, 1945".

The Church of Scientology, predictably, has a very different view of Hubbard's medical problems and the Navy's verdict on Hubbard's health status. When a TV documentary on L. Ron Hubbard was screened by Britain's Channel 4 Television in November 1997, which related the story of Hubbard's career as documented in his naval file, the Church responded with a fierce counterblast:

[T]he fact is, L. Ron Hubbard very definitely suffered
blinding and crippling injuries through the course of

combat in the Second World War, and that fact is perfectly
clear in his naval medical records.

One medical report describes a severe bone infection in
the hip and back, forcing him to walk with a cane. Another
shows his vision was registered at 20/100 – which,
according to medical review, meant that he could not dis-
tinguish facial features until three or four feet away, could
not make out a street sign beyond ten yards and could not
read a newspaper.[34]

Hubbard's file shows that he complained in 1946 of a "chronic
infection in my right hip [that] has lamed me."[35] Instead of being
an injury sustained "through the course of combat", as Scientology
claims, Hubbard was very clear about where and when it it
occurred: "This infection was contracted at Princeton University in
1945, January, according to record. Sudden transition from the
tropics to the slush and icy cold of Princeton caused rheumatic
chills."[36] The claim that he was forced to use a cane appears to have
come not from the Navy, but from one of Hubbard's lectures in
which he claimed he was "walking with a cane" after returning from
Australia – not at the end of the war.[37]

Furthermore, his records specifically state that he did not suffer
any combat injuries. Yet, according to *What is Scientology,*

So complete was his recovery that officers from the Naval
Retiring Board reviewing Lt. Hubbard's case were actually
upset. After all, they reasoned, how could a man physically
shot to pieces at the end of the war pass his full physical ex-
amination? The only answer, they concluded, was that L.
Ron Hubbard must be somebody else. And when they found
that all was in order, they designated him fit for active
duty. [38]

While at Oak Knoll, Hubbard appears to have gotten involved in a serious fist-fight – a remarkable feat for a man who had supposedly been "physically shot to pieces". In two lectures delivered in the 1950s, Hubbard claimed that while on convalescent leave in Hollywood in July 1945, when he was still undergoing treatment at Oak Knoll Naval Hospital, he was attacked by three enlisted men who were causing a disruption outside the hotel where he was staying as an outpatient. Because of his knowledge of judo, Hubbard was able to fight them off:[39]

> I said, "The shore patrol has been called, and if you boys are very smart you will get out of here quick." I started to pass them and go on down the street, and one of them grabbed me by the arm and started poking me with his finger. Then one of them picked up a beer bottle, the other one swung me around with my back to the one with the beer bottle and the guy swung the beer bottle, aiming at my head. One of the things that I had been doing in trying to rehabilitate myself was carrying on with judo. I had gotten training in judo in 1941 before I went into the service, but up at the hospital it was just regular exercise. The judo instructor and I had had quite a bit of fun.
>
> It was very instinctive to duck underneath this beer bottle as it was coming down, and that made the fellow with the beer bottle come over to the side with his wrist in reach, so what I did was break his arm automatically and throw him over his head into the man who was holding me. That guy went into a bumper and cut his face open and the fellow with the bottle went into him with a broken arm. The beer bottle fell on the pavement, and the third guy got up off the running board of the car where he had been sitting and came at me, so I just caught up the beer bottle and shoved it in his face.

They made me go before a court martial, and it was very funny but the court martial, looking at these three men and the fact that I had been in Oak Knoll hospital, wouldn't believe me. They were sure that four or five other officers and myself had caught these men one by one and beaten them up, and that this was a cooked story. I almost got in a lot of trouble with this one ... I am not trying to tell you what a great warrior I am, but that what that did for my morale was fantastic. I don't think I would be alive today if I hadn't handled those three men.[40]

This would have been an impressive – not to say impossible – feat for a blinded cripple. However, there are indications that the fight really happened, although probably not in the way that Hubbard later described. An order in his file shows that on October 6, 1945, he was summoned as a prosecution witness to a general court-martial scheduled for October 10 at the US Naval Receiving Station, San Pedro. He was to testify in a case involving Carpenter's Mate Third Class Edmond Fain and Shipfitter Second Class Jacob J. Lauff.[41] The details are not recorded on his file, but it is likely that the two men were involved in the fight. A later medical note records that he remained in San Pedro for over six weeks, presumably attending the military judicial authorities. He subsequently returned Oak Knoll for further treatment, although no injuries from the fight are mentioned.[42]

Nearly a decade later, Hubbard put a rather different spin on his participation in the court martial. He now claimed to have participated in it as the counsel for one of the accused:

One time I was at a court martial. I was a summary court's counsel for an enlisted man while I was in the hospital. And this summary court's – was meeting and convening upon – in fact, I think he'd been found without an ID card or

something of the sort. But he had really messed himself up.
He'd started to fight the Shore Patrol. And he'd – oh, mopery
and dopery on the high seas, strictly. They had him. They had
practically thrown the book at him and I was his counsel ...
I got him off on the basis that he'd been returned from a
combat zone and probably was not quite right in the head.[43]

The fight's outcome may have been rather different from how
Hubbard later portrayed it. His "Affirmations" of 1946 imply that
he lost badly:

You are not a coward. Fist fighting had no bearing on your
courage. You were ill when you were fought before. You did
not understand the rules. You can whip anyone now and
have no physical fear of hand to hand fighting. They who
fought you before were knaves and fools. You would be
merciless to them now. Nothing can stand up to your
fighting now. You are strong and wonderful in combat. You
never know fear or defeat. You refrain from fighting
because you are too powerful.[44]

Hubbard claimed that his stay at Oak Knoll Naval Hospital had
enabled him to test and develop a revolutionary medical-psycho-
logical approach which, in the 1950s, became Dianetics and then
Scientology. He later claimed that this was a pivotal juncture in his
life and related it in considerable detail, as in an autobiographical
account recorded in 1972:

As the Captain of Oak Knoll Naval Hospital was an intimate
friend of my father's, and as the War was obviously all over
for me, I was very pampered and had the run of the place. I
knew of course many Naval doctors and some of them had
not only known [Commander] Thompson [a friend from the

1920s] but also knew me. They were engaged at that time in trying to do something for the Japanese prisoners of war who had been returned and who were in terrible physical condition from starvation and other causes. They had considerable research projects going and they were only too happy to hand out data and listen to any suggestions.

I was basically researching in the field of endocrinology to determine whether or not structure monitors function or function monitors structure. I had the run of the medical library and the doctors were very pleasant concerning my examination of their records on Japanese war prisoners. It was obvious that the ex-prisoners of war had damaged endocrine systems ... using nothing but Freudian Psychoanalysis and using a park bench as a consulting room. I set out to find out whether or not those who would not assimilate hormones had mental blocks.

There was a sufficient number of these done to make it very plain that those who could assimilate hormones did not have severe mental trauma, and those who could not assimilate it did have mental traumas.

It was in this way that I put together guidelines for further research. I was not interested in endocrinology but in resolving whether or not function monitored structure or structure monitored function.[45]

This was, and remains, the philosophical basis of Scientology: that the mind controls the body and (if properly developed) can exercise control over "matter, energy, space and time", enabling such feats as telekinesis, clairvoyance and out-of-body travel. Hubbard's key claim in relation to his "endocrinological research" was that he had used his discoveries to heal his war wounds, to the astonishment of his superiors. However, his record shows that he had no war wounds to heal in the first place.

He claimed in later years that he had posed as a doctor to get access to medical texts in the hospital's library and to patients, some of whom were American former prisoners of war who were recovering from their mistreatment at the hands of the Japanese.[46]

While staying at the Eleanor Hotel in Hollywood, he was informed that he was to be mustered off the active duty list. It was evidently not welcome news, for understandable reasons; as well as fulfilling his own personal ambitions, the Navy had provided the only regular income which Hubbard had ever had in his adult life. He sent an anxious telegram, playing down the seriousness of his ulcer:

> *Respectfully submit willingness to serve in full duty status 6 months. Require Form Y waiver for duodenal ulcer not acute. Desire sea duty as navigator full construction. Regular duty station USN Hospital Oakland awaiting results of medical survey now in Bureau. Have served at sea with present symptoms much worse as navigator large auxiliary without prejudice to duty and did not leave that duty because of present diagnosis.[47]*

(It may be noted that he submitted this appeal at a time when he was supposedly "physically shot to pieces", according to the Church of Scientology.)

It was likely a sign of his anxiety that he followed this up with another telegram sent the next day. This was evidently the result of hasty consultations with friendly colleagues, who had apparently suggested that Hubbard should transfer out of the Naval Reserve if he wanted to stay with the Navy:

> *Supplementing my wire of yesterday on further advices here, if I can avail myself of October first promotion my desire is to transfer to regular Navy.[48]*

Hubbard's hopes were soon dashed. The Bureau of Naval Personnel quickly sent a letter of rejection back to Hubbard:

In view of your general service classification and since reference (c) [the Report of Medical Survey] found you physically qualified for limited shore duty only, you are not considered physically qualified for promotion and the authority for your appointment to the rank of Lieutenant Commander under the terms of reference (d) [Alnav 317-45] has terminated.

By endorsement to reference (c) this Bureau modified the recommendations of the Board of Medical Survey and the Bureau of Medicine and Surgery, and you are to be released from active duty since your services are not required in your limited capacity.

Therefore, no action will be taken to effect your promotion prior to your release from active duty.[49]

That was the end of the matter, as Hubbard had no further recourse. On December 5, 1945, he was discharged from Oak Knoll Naval Hospital and was ordered to report to his final active duty station, the Officer Separation Center in San Francisco. His posting there lasted only for the one day during which the formalities of separation were conducted. He was then detached, albeit still on active duty, from which he was released on February 16, 1946.

Perhaps the clearest overview of Hubbard's ailments was presented in a letter that he wrote on December 6, 1945, as part of a claim for a pension and disability benefits. He listed a catalog of problems, none of which could be described as a combat-related injury:

Malaria, Feb 42, Recurrent;
Left Knee, Sprain, March 1942;
Conjunctivitis, Actinic Mar 42 (eyesight Failing)

Sporad. Pain Left side and back, undiagnosed, July 42;
Ulcer Duodenum, Chronic, Spring 43;
Arthritis, Rt Hip, Shoulder, Jan 45.[50]

The dates he provided for the onset of each malady can be correlated with what he was doing at the time:

- Hubbard's "recurrent malaria" correlates with the end of his stay in Brisbane. There is no record from that time of him suffering from malaria, but this claim likely refers to the "acute catarrhal fever" for which he was hospitalized at the end of March 1942, and which he also claimed was a recurring ailment.[51] A report of July 15, 1943 states that he had three attacks of catarrhal fever in the previous 12 months. The same report states that he had "malaria about 16 months [ago] in combat area", which would correspond with his time in Brisbane, but there is no record from that time of any malaria and he did not report it to his doctors the year before. The source for this claim was probably Hubbard himself.[52]

- The onset of his "actinic conjunctivitis" correlates with his voyage from Brisbane to Hawaii on the SS *Pennant*. In an assessment conducted during his hospitalization in March 1943, he told the examining doctor that "while acting as combat intelligence officer for the Asiatic fleet he exposed his eyes to strong sunlight".[53]

- His left knee sprain also correlates with his voyage on the SS *Pennant*. The record of his March 1943 medical examination states that Hubbard claimed to have "also sprained his left ankle on this duty and he has pain in the longitudinal arch of the left foot while walking,"[54] and in a 1947 examination Hubbard said specifically that he had injured himself by falling off a ladder aboard the *Pennant*.

- He dated his "sporadic pain left side and back" to the time

160

that he was serving at Neponset, MA, during the conversion of the USS *YP-422*.

- His duodenal ulcer appears to have started while serving on the USS *PC-815*. A report from April 1945 records that Hubbard stated "his symptoms first began in April 1943".[55]
- The onset of his hip and shoulder arthritis corresponds with the time of his course at Princeton, of which he said that the "slush and icy cold' had caused "rheumatic chills."[56]

Hubbard made no mention of any combat injuries in his disability claim.

Through the course of Hubbard's medical examinations from March 1942 onwards, he made consistent complaints of eye problems, pains in his body – which he attributed variously to accidental injury or arthritis – and stomach problems, caused by his ulcer. A medical report from November 1945, just before the end of his active service, raised the possibility that he was suffering from what was then called Reiter's Syndrome and is now known as reactive arthritis.[57]

Conjunctivitis is a classic symptom of the syndrome. It presents early in the course of reactive arthritis and can recur periodically. The onset of reactive arthritis can be caused by an infection, most commonly the sexually transmitted disease chlamydia, but also from stomach infections and food poisoning.[58] It is possible that Hubbard may have acquired an infection in Brisbane that manifested itself around the time of his return to the continental US. Clearly, though, nothing that Hubbard suffered from can be described as a combat injury and the man himself does not appear to have to have ever claimed to his doctors that he was wounded in battle.

One curious final footnote to his war service was provided by Hubbard himself in a letter that he sent in 1965 to the Board of Inquiry into Scientology, an official inquiry into the Church of Scientology conducted for the State of Victoria, Australia. He stated that he had been "once trained as the Provost Marshal of Korea", a claim that made its way into a 1969 Scientology publication as *serving* as the Provost Marshal of Korea.[59] The latter claim was unequivocally false – as his record shows clearly, he was never assigned to Korea. He is not known to have visited the country at any point in his life.

However, it is possible that he might have been slated for an eventual assignment in Korea following his course in military government at Princeton University. After completing the course, he was assigned to the Civil Affairs Staging Area in Monterey, California in preparation for duty with a civil affairs team outside the continental limits of the United States. Although no such overseas assignment is recorded in his record, a post in the Office of the Provost Marshal – the head of the military police – might have been a possibility for an officer trained in military administration. But as Hubbard would have known perfectly well, he never served in that capacity.

CHAPTER 13

Mustering Out

Hubbard never again performed active duty for the US Navy, but he still remained a commissioned officer until October 30, 1950. The intervening period was colorful, to say the least: he befriended the brilliant JPL scientist and black magician Jack Parsons, participated in sex magic, married Parsons' girlfriend bigamously, returned to writing pulp fiction stories, earned a conviction for petty theft and invented a mental therapy which he declared to be "a milestone for Man comparable to his discovery of fire and superior to his inventions of the wheel and the arch."

Some aspects of Hubbard's new life are documented in the remainder of his naval records. On April 1, 1946, Hubbard wrote to request permission to visit South and Central America for the purposes of "collecting writing material auspices Allied Enterprises, Pasadena, Calif." commencing April 10, 1946. The address given, 1003 South Orange Grove Avenue, Pasadena, CA., was Jack Parsons' house, at which Hubbard was a lodger.

Allied Enterprises was a business partnership between Hubbard, Parsons and Parsons' girlfriend (soon to be Hubbard's girlfriend and eventual second wife) Sara Northrup. Their original idea was to buy yachts on the East Coast and sail them to California to sell at a profit. Parsons appears to have been unaware of Hubbard's alternative plans to sail away to South America. In the event, Hubbard never did go to South and Central America and instead deprived Parsons of his girlfriend and $10,000 in cash. Parsons' occult "master" Aleister Crowley concluded: "Suspect Ron playing confidence trick. Jack evidently weak fool. Obvious victim [of] prowling swindlers."

After his liaison with Parsons was exposed in the London *Sunday Times* in 1969, Hubbard drafted a statement of rebuttal which the newspaper printed in a later issue. Writing in the third person, he claimed that his involvement with Parsons was part of a covert operation for the US Navy:

> *Hubbard broke up black magic in America: Dr. Jack Parsons of Pasadena, California, was America's Number One solid fuel rocket expert. ... Parsons was head of the American branch [of the Ordo Templi Orientis] located ... [in] a huge old house which had paying guests who were the U.S.A. nuclear physicists working at Cal. Tech. Certain agencies objected to nuclear physicists being housed under the same roof.*
>
> *L. Ron Hubbard was still an officer of the U.S. Navy because [sic] he was well known as a writer and a philosopher and had friends amongst the physicists, he was sent in to handle the situation. He went to live at the house and investigated the black magic rites and the general situation and found them very bad. ...*
>
> *Hubbard's mission was successful far beyond anyone's expectations. The house was torn down. Hubbard rescued a girl they were using. The black magic group was dispersed and destroyed and has never recovered. The physicists included many of the sixty-four top U.S. scientists who were later declared insecure and dismissed from government service with so much publicity.*

As Hugh B. Urban has noted, however, "neither the Church of Scientology nor any independent researcher has ever produced any evidence for this claim."[1]

In June 1947, Hubbard was sent a notification that he had been promoted to Lieutenant Commander. He had actually been appointed to that rank with effect from October 3, 1945 but the appointment had not been delivered and accepted while he was still on active service. The slow-moving wheels of naval bureaucracy did not get around to confirming his promotion until June 25, 1947.[2]

Strangely, though, his promotion seems to have been forgotten about by the Navy. No further correspondence in his file refers to him in that rank. Hubbard himself continued to use his old title of Lieutenant and there is no sign that he was ever aware that he had been promoted. It is not mentioned in any Scientology biographies. He may not have received the letter of appointment, as it was sent to Jack Parsons' residence. By the time it arrived, Hubbard had moved to a rented trailer in North Hollywood where he lived with Sara Northrup. One can only speculate what happened to the letter – perhaps the embittered Parsons tore it up when it arrived at his house. It is unclear why the Navy forgot about the promotion, but it is possible that it may have resulted from the letter of appointment being misfiled and thus escaping the notice of those subsequently administering Hubbard's affairs.

The Cold War was in full swing by this time. War had already broken out in Vietnam between the French colonial authorities and Ho Chi Minh's Moscow-supported communist guerrillas. Germany's postwar division was hardening into a military confrontation between Allied and Soviet forces, while at home Senator Joe McCarthy and Vice-President Richard Nixon were whipping up an anti-communist frenzy. War with Russia or its proxies seemed highly likely. World War II ships which had been slated for decommissioning, such as Hubbard's old vessel the USS *Algol*, were brought back into full service. It seemed more than likely that the US Naval Reserve would sooner or later be reactivated. Against this background, in November 1947, Hubbard submitted his resignation from the United States Naval Reserve.

Hubbard later claimed that his resignation was prompted by an attempt by the US Navy to seize control of Dianetics "to make people more suggestible".[3] This, he said, "immediately predated, by one week, the opening of the Hubbard Dianetic Research Foundation of Elizabeth, New Jersey" – in other words, late May or early June 1950.[4] He gave a number of versions of this story in lectures delivered in the 1950s.

> *They said, "You know you're still in the reserves and we can call you back to active duty on research in the field of the mind."*
>
> *"You're still in the service," this admiral said. "Ha-ha. You change your mind any time, you know, about coming in. You can volunteer. Of course, I can put you back on active duty at any time, so you'd better volunteer." ...*
>
> *And I said, "Well," I said, "if you put it that way," I said, "I'm overwhelmed." I said, "There's nothing much I can do." ...*
>
> *Of course, it was impossible at that time to resign from the service. A reserve officer had to continue as a reserve officer from there on out. But I was down to the Potomac River Naval Command, and I was through Bureau of Naval Personnel. It was Monday when he came to see me, and he was going to come back and see me Thursday. And when he came back and saw me Thursday he said, "Well," he said, "you've decided to come into the service as a civilian?"*
>
> *And I said, "No, I haven't. I decided not to."*
>
> *And he said, "Well," he said, "I'll have to call you back to active duty."*
>
> *And I says, "Try and do it," and handed him my resignation, accepted. He was crushed.[5]*

He provided another version of the same story a few months later, claiming that the officer who tried to recruit him had not realized Hubbard's papers were held by the Washington Navy Yard rather than in New York. This, Hubbard said, enabled him to resign quickly before the New York-based officer could do anything about it.[6] The Church of Scientology claims that as a result of refusing the Navy's advances, the US government "never forgave him for this and soon began vicious, covert international attacks upon his work, all of which were proven false and baseless."[7]

But his correspondence with the Navy suggests a very different scenario. On November 14, 1947 – two and a half years before he later claimed to have resigned, and a year before he had even written his book on Dianetics – he wrote to the Secretary of the Navy with his first letter of resignation:

1. I herewith tender my resignation from the United States Naval Reserve.

2. As an officer on inactive duty, I have no further reason to be connected with the Navy.

3. In view of my bad health for which I was separated from the Navy and the improbability of the Navy's needing my services, in my condition, in the future, I urge the acceptance of this resignation.[8]

The Office of the Chief of Naval Personnel wrote back to Hubbard with a letter regretting his decision and enclosing a pamphlet, "Your Place in the Postwar Naval Reserve". Hubbard responded positively, requesting on February 19, 1948 that his letter of resignation be disregarded in the light of the reply.

Hubbard changed his mind two years later and again tendered his resignation, only a month before the outbreak of the Korean War. On May 27, 1950, three weeks after the publication of Dianetics – he wrote to the Secretary of the Navy outlining his reasons:

1. I desire to resign my commission as lieutenant senior grade in the United States Naval Reserve as of this date.

2. Since the latter part of my active service in the war was served in a hospital, under treatment for nine months and since I have been before survey boards and the retiring board, I do not believe I could further serve in event of further emergency. Retirement was not granted but I am still considered to be 50% disabled by the Veteran's Administration.

3. As a writer, I sometimes must write on technical subjects and while these have no bearing on naval matters or government security of any kind I would feel much freer were I not a commissioned officer in the naval reserve.

4. In 1948 [sic, actually 1947] I tendered a resignation which was answered with a request from the secretary that I consider the matter again. I have duly considered this action and discover that I still find it expedient to resign.

5. As I would not be of use in the event of war, as I have taken no part in post war naval activities, it is certain that my continued commissioned status is of no benefit to the navy. It is therefore respectfully requested and urged that this resignation be accepted.[9]

The date of his letter is consistent with his claim to have resigned shortly before the establishment of the first Dianetic Foundation in New Jersey. There is no evidence from his file to support his contention that he was ever approached regarding Dianetics, and he made no reference to it in his letter of resignation.

This time the request was granted. On October 30, 1950, Hubbard received an honorable discharge from the United States Naval Reserve, which he acknowledged under the letterhead of the Dianetic Foundation on December 5, 1950. (In contradiction to Hubbard's claim of submitting a resignation on a Monday and having it accepted four days later, there was a five-month wait and a lengthy exchange of internal correspondence within the Navy bureaucracy to effect it.) His service with the US military was finally over.

CHAPTER 14

Ron the Veteran

The story of L. Ron Hubbard's naval career would not be complete without describing his protracted dealings with the Veterans Administration. One day after being mustered out of the US Naval Reserve, on December 6, 1945, Hubbard submitted a claim for a pension and disability benefits, claiming that he was earning up to $650 a month before the war but now had a monthly income of $0.00. He claimed in a later lecture that when he was released from active service in February 1946, the US Government

> *suddenly gave me an enormous amount of compensation pay. I was badly disabled, they said, and they gave me all of my back compensation pay all in one lump sum. And it was enough money to set up an office in Hollywood and which, by pushing a typewriter and keeping the office running on office expenses with fiction stories, I could keep running very handsomely.*[1]

The reality was very different. The VA rated Hubbard as only 10% disabled and awarded him a monthly pension of just $11.50, commencing February 17, 1947. Not surprisingly, he lodged an appeal. He explained that his need to obtain milk and a special diet for his ulcer "results in me having to abandon my old profession as ship master and explorer". (In fact, prior to the war, Hubbard made his living through writing pulp fiction; his supposed career as a "ship master and explorer" likely refers to his 1940 sailing holiday to Alaska.)

He also referred to his eye problems, attributing them to a far less dramatic cause than the latter claims of "muzzle flash" injuries:

I cannot now read for more than three to four minutes without suffering from headache [sic]. I have attempted to have glasses fitted by such an eminent opthamologist [sic] as the head of the Mt. Sinnai [sic] Eye Clinic without any relief ... My eyesight when I entered the service was very good. It began to fail after prolonged exposure to tropical sunlight in the Pacific in the spring of 1942. The diagnosis was "conjunctivitis actinic" and I was hospitalized for it at the Brooklyn Naval Hospital until I returned to duty on my own request. My eyesight failed until I found it very difficult to read.[2]

He also referred to his limb problems. Rather than attributing them to machine-gun fire or shrapnel fragments, he offered a much more prosaic explanation of how they were sustained:

A chronic infection in my right hip has lamed me ... This infection was contracted at Princeton University in 1945, January, according to record. Sudden transition from the tropics to the slush and icy cold of Princeton caused rheumatic chills which seem to have settled in the right hip. Warm weather slightly mitigates but does not banish this injury. I cannot walk on pavement [sic] without suffering severely ... This also prevents me from working at sea where one must stand much of the time.[3]

Robert Heinlein later recalled Hubbard's difficulty in walking, adding that Hubbard had said that both his feet had been broken when his last ship was bombed. When Heinlein introduced him to Jack Parsons, Hubbard claimed to have been "the captain of a ship that had been downed in the Pacific and he was weeks on a raft and had been blinded by the sun and his back had been broken", according to his later wife Sara.[4]

Despite claiming to be unable to "work at sea", Hubbard was at the time buying yachts in Florida on behalf of Parsons with the intention of sailing them to California via the Panama Canal and reselling them there for a profit.[5]

At the end of the appeal, Hubbard reiterated his present financial situation, incidentally inflating his claimed pre-war salary by a third to "one thousand dollars a month". To support his case, he got his new girlfriend Sara to write to the VA posing as an old friend who wished to provide independent corroboration of his rapidly deteriorating health. She put her parents' address in Pasadena on the top of the letter.

I have known Lafayette Ronald Hubbard for many years [in reality they first met in August 1945] and wish to testify as to the condition of his health as I have observed it since his separation from the Navy.

Before the war, he was an extremely energetic person in excellent health and spirits... Since his return in December last year he is entirely changed. He cannot read because of his eyes, which give him much pain. He is rather lame and cannot take his accustomed hikes ... He has tried to work at three different jobs and each he has had to leave because of an increase in his stomach condition. He seems to need an enormous amount of rest ...

I do not know what he is going to do for income when his own meagre savings are exhausted, because I see no chance of his condition improving to a point where he can regain his old standards. He is becoming steadily worse, his health impaired again by economic worries.[6]

Hubbard's efforts earned him a fresh medical examination on July 20, 1946. The doctor who examined him (and, unaccountably, described him as a captain) accepted most of his claims. The VA was informed that "it does not seem to us that a disability of 10% adequately expresses the amount of infirmity present and we feel that his rating should be markedly increased." The VA sought con firmation and summoned Hubbard to a further examination on September 19 at its medical center in Los Angeles. The subsequent report quotes the litany of problems claimed by Hubbard at the session:

Eyes are sensitive to bright sunlight and I can't read very much and I have severe headaches which radiate backwards. This handicaps me in my research work when I'm working on my writings. My stomach trouble keeps me on a very rigid diet – can only eat milk, eggs, ground meat and strained vegetable [sic]. Can't tolerate anything fried. This stomach trouble restricts my activities considerably in that I have to eat at home where these foods are not available – such as restaurants, etc. I tire quickly and become nauseated when I work hard. My left shoulder, hip – in fact the entire left side is bothered with arthritic pains – can't sit any length of time (at typewriter or desk) and restricts me to warm climates.[7]

However, the doctors were unable to find anything more serious than that Hubbard had "signs of sub deltoid bursitis", walked with "a hobble-like gait" and had only a "minimal duodenal deformity". The report noted specifically that there were no "residuals of gunshot wounds or other [combat] injuries".

Hubbard's so-called "Affirmations", entered into evidence in the 1984 Armstrong case, shed a fascinating light on his state of mind. They comprise a set of statements in which Hubbard affirms various positive physical and mental states, apparently in an attempt to boost himself through positive thinking:

- *Your ulcers are all well and never bother you. You can eat anything.*
- *You have a sound hip. It never hurts.*
- *Your shoulder never hurts.*
- *Your sinus trouble is nothing.*
- *The [foot] injury is no longer needed. It is well. You have perfect and lovely feet.*
- *When you tell people you are ill, it has no effect upon your health. And in Veterans Administration examinations you'll tell them how sick you are; you'll look sick when you take it; you'll return to health one hour after the examination and laugh at them.*
- *No matter what lies you may tell others, they have no physical effect on you of any kind. You never injured your health by saying it is bad. You cannot lie to yourself.*[8]

The "Affirmations" indicate that Hubbard likely genuinely regarded himself as suffering from a number of ailments, though they were all apparently fairly minor complaints. They also suggest that Hubbard purposefully played up his ailments in order to convince the VA that he was sicker than he really was. The science fiction writer L. Spague De Camp wrote to his fellow author Isaac Asimov around this time warning that Hubbard, who he knew well, was intent on preying on people's sympathies with a "poor-wounded-veteran racket":

He will probably soon thereafter arrive in these parts [Los Angeles] with Betty-Sarah [Northrup], broke, working the poor-wounded-veteran racket for all its worth, and looking

for another easy mark. Don't say you haven't been warned.
Bob [Robert Heinlein] thinks Ron went to pieces morally as
a result of the war. I think that's fertilizer, that he always
was that way, but when he wanted to conciliate or get
something from somebody he could put on a good charm
act. What the war did was to wear him down to where he
no longer bothers with the act.[9]

Hubbard's pre-war friend Robert MacDonald Ford saw him after the war while he was undergoing treatment, meeting up in Los Angeles over the course of several days. Ford later commented that Hubbard "was never wounded. He might have had some complaints. He was trying to tie down a pension."[10]

John W. Campbell, however, was much more taken by Hubbard's apparent fragility. When the two met on November 25, 1946, Campbell was dismayed at his friend's appearance: "He was a quivering psychoneurotic wreck, practically ready to break down completely. When he got out of service, he had the quivers – literally. He also had several bad wounds, and was in bad physical shape. His conversation was somewhat schizoid at points, wandering in not-always lucid organization."[11] He wrote later that Hubbard "had the shakes, a limp, and was a distorted imitation of the fellow I knew in 1941."[12]

Robert A. Heinlein and his wife Ginny were also firm believers in Hubbard's wartime heroics, despite having rocky relations with him. During a period in 1946 when Hubbard was in what he called "the Heinlein doghouse", after the two had fallen out for a while, Heinlein wrote, "I no longer trust you. I think a lot of those ribbons on your chest … You're an authentic hero, even though a phony gentleman. I'll give you money to get you out of a jam but I don't want you in my house."[13] Heinlein was as good as his word. When Hubbard wrote to him in February 1949 requesting a $50 loan, Heinlein promptly sent him the money. He wrote to Hubbard:

"[Ginny] won't turn down a shipmate. As for me, it's partly because I remember you floating around out there in that salt water with your ribs caved in."[14]

Despite his supposedly parlous financial state, Hubbard repeatedly failed to show up at further VA examinations. He wrote on December 8, 1946 from the Hotel Belvedere in New York to acknowledge receiving orders to report for another examination and explaining his change of address by saying that a friend had financed his trip back East in return for his advice on an expedition then being planned. It was never quite clear who this friend was or where the expedition was supposed to go. (It never happened.) In the meantime, despite the eye problems, rheumatism and other ailments suffered by Hubbard, he nonetheless managed to sell a number of short stories.

By this time the Veterans Administration was subsidizing ex-servicemen's educational activities. In October 1947, Hubbard signed up to a course at the Geller Theater Workshop in Los Angeles and thereby obtained an extra $90 a month subsistence. There is no record of whether he actually went to the course in question.

Only two weeks later he wrote a dramatic appeal for help:

Gentlemen;
   This is a request for treatment...
   After trying and failing for two years to regain my equilibrium in civil life, I am utterly unable to approach anything like my own competence. My last physician informed me that it might be very helpful if I were to be examined and perhaps treated psychiatrically or even by a psychoanalyst. Toward the end of my service I avoided out of pride any mental examinations, hoping that time would balance a mind which I had every reason to suppose was seriously affected. I cannot account for nor rise above long periods of moroseness and suicidal inclinations, and have

newly come to realize that I must first triumph above this
before I can hope to rehabilitate myself at all.

   I cannot leave school or what little work I am doing for
hospitalization due to many obligations, but I feel I might
be treated outside, possibly with success. I cannot, myself,
afford such treatment.

   Would you please help me?
   Sincerely, L. Ron Hubbard

This may have been an entirely justified claim – many of those close to Hubbard in the following decades described him as mentally unstable, with a psychology-trained girlfriend characterizing him as manic depressive in 1950.[15] However, there is no evidence that Hubbard ever did receive psychiatric treatment. The VA instead invited him to yet another medical examination at its Birmingham hospital in Van Nuys, California.

Hubbard's lengthy medical history was again reviewed but his examiner, Roy H. Nyquist, noted a previously undocumented injury which Hubbard claimed to have sustained: "Fell down a ladder on SS *Pennent* [sic] in 1942 injuring his back, r[igh]t hip, left knee and right heel."[15] The doctors found no sign of the injuries claimed by Hubbard, or even of his old duodenal ulcer, but instead diagnosed him with arthritis and myositis, an inflammation of the muscle tissue.

In the meantime, Hubbard had received a demand from the VA for $51 which he had been overpaid in subsistence. He had dropped out of college on 14 November, claiming he was too ill to continue studying, but had nonetheless collected subsistence until the end of the month. (Today it is claimed by Scientology that he spent this period conducting research on the human mind using funds earned through writing.) He promptly sent another pleading letter to the VA:

I cannot imagine how to repay this $51 as I am nearly penniless and have but $28.50 to last me for nearly a month to come. Since leaving school in mid-November I have made $115 from various sources – about $40 from the sale of two bits to magazines in late November and the repayment of a bad debt for $75. These comprise my income to date except for the sale of a typewriter tonight for the above $28.50. My expenditures consist of $27 a month trailer rent and $80 a month loud for my wife and self, which includes gas, cigarettes and all incidentals. I am very much in debt and have not been able to get a job but am trying to resume my pre-war profession of professional writing. My health has been bad and I feel that if I could just get caught up financially I could write a novel which has been requested of me and so remedy my finances. It would take me three months and even then I would not be able to guarantee solvency. Is there any provision in the Veteran's Administration for grants or loans or financing so that I could get back on my feet?[17]

Hubbard's pleas evidently met with sympathy. Despite the fact that his list of verified complaints had shrunk in the most recent medical examination, his pension was actually increased to $55.20 a month and his disability rating was re-assessed as 40%. He was not satisfied, however, and wrote back in March 1948 with another pleading letter in which he drew attention to what he called his "useless condition", well after he is supposed in Scientology accounts to have recovered fully:

I was rendered physically incapable by service with the navy. I was separated from the service as being of no further use to it regardless of the wordings of the orders I received. No proper diagnosis of illness or physical condition was ever made by the Navy beyond a duodenal ulcer despite my complete inability to perform any part of my naval duties. ... I spent the ensuing year in civilian hospitals at my own expenses. I am without income or means of support and have been rendered an invalid by my naval service. All my disabilities are service connected. I could perform no part of my duty as a naval officer. I cannot follow my profession or earn my living as a civilian. I owe my present useless condition to my service as a naval officer, and I look to the United States Navy to make proper and adequate recompense in accordance with the laws of Congress, customs and regulations of service and the honor of government.[18]

Much of this was, of course, untrue. He had said in October 1945 before being discharged from the Navy that his only complaint was a "duodenal ulcer, not acute" and that he was fit enough to request sea duty.[19] Instead of spending a year in civilian hospitals at his own expense, he spent it practising ritual sex magic in Pasadena.[20]

It was true that Hubbard was "following his profession" – writing – once again, but the real problem was that he was not earning enough money to support himself or his dependents. He complained to Robert Heinlein that "I never was so many places in print with less to show for it. I couldn't buy a stage costume for Gypsy Rose Lee." He appealed for an increased pension from the VA, though apparently without success.[21]

A few months before Hubbard resigned from the Naval Reserve in October 1950, he at last managed made a name for himself. His new mental therapy, Dianetics, briefly became a nationwide craze and made him rich. His Dianetics Foundations earned a reported $1m in their first year (equivalent to over $10m today). Hubbard claimed that Dianetics would cure many conditions, amongst them arthritis, bursitis, poor eyesight, ulcers, and even the common cold.

He presented himself as an example of what Dianetics could do for an individual, though his "war wounds" were not mentioned.

In *Look* magazine's December 5, 1950 issue, he said that had suffered from "ulcers, conjunctivitis, deteriorating eyesight, bursitis and something wrong with my feet," which matches well with his Naval medical record.[22] Similarly, in a 1952 lecture, he said that his disability was "arthritis and ulcers and a couple of other minor things", which he claimed Dianetics had "knocked out" and had resulted in the loss of his "naval retirement".[23]

Yet despite having supposedly been cured of all these afflictions, and even though he was now earning thousands of dollars a month, Hubbard still continued to claim a disability pension. On August 1, 1951, he was re-examined and claimed that his ulcer had flared up again. The examining physician noted:

> *He states that he spent approximately thirteen months in hospitals during his navy service, and that a duodenal ulcer was demonstrated by x-ray on several occasions .... He says that he has been forced to follow a modified ulcer diet continuously since his initial gastrointestinal disturbance in 1943. The spring and the fall of the year are the most troublesome times for him, and he states that he has exacerbations lasting usually about a week with rather severe distress during these months .... The patient states that he invariably has trouble with his stomach when he is working long hours and under nervous stress. He is a poor sleeper, and states that he has been unable to take the usual soporifics because they seem to upset his stomach. He smokes very little, and then only intermittently. He believes that smoking definitely aggravates his epigastric distress.*

Under the heading "Impression," the doctor wrote: "duodenal ulcer, chronic." Under the heading "Diagnosis," he wrote: "Duodenal ulcer, not found on this examination."

A second specialist examination was carried out on the same day by an orthopedist who noted:

> He also gives a history of injuring his right shoulder, just how is not clear, and of developing numerous other things including duodenal ulcer, actinic conjunctivitis, and a highly nervous state. He has applied for retirement from the navy [more specifically, from the Reserve list] which was eventually turned down .... He is a writer by profession and states he has some income from previous writing that helps take care of him .... This is a well nourished and muscled white adult who does not appear chronically ill ... .
>
> He has a history of some injury to the right shoulder and will not elevate the arm above the shoulder level. However, on persuasion, it was determined at this time that the shoulder is freely movable and unrestricted. It is noted that he has had a previous diagnosis of BURSITIS WITH CAL-CIFICATION. X-rays will be repeated. It is not believed that this is of significant incapacity .... Records show a diagnosis of MULTIPLE ARTHRITIS. However, no clinical evidence of arthritis is found at this time.

Between 1975 and 1980, Kima Douglas – a Scientologist who had been trained as a nurse – served as Hubbard's "Medical Officer". She later testified in court that she had observed him suffering from arthritis, bursitis and coronary trouble – all conditions that Dianetics and Scientology were supposed to alleviate.

Photographs of Hubbard from his war years show him wearing glasses. In July 1951, his doctors reported: "eyes tire easily has worn all types of glasses but claims he sees just as well as without as with glasses." After creating Dianetics in 1950 – which he promoted as able to cure eye problems – he only wore them in private.

He continued sending letters to the VA at least as late as 1958. During the 1984 Armstrong case, a letter from Hubbard to the Veterans Administration, dated April 2, 1958, was produced. Gerry Armstrong had this to say of it:

> *In my mind there was a conflict between the fact that here he is asking to have his V.A. [Veterans Administration] checks sent to a particular address in 1958, and in all the publications about Mr. Hubbard he had claimed that he had been given a perfect score, perfect mental and physical score by 1950, and by 1947 had completely cured himself, and here he is still drawing a V.A. check for this disability. … It seems like there is at least a contradiction and possibly an unethical practice on his part.*[24]

Hubbard's medical file certainly demonstrates that he claimed to have various physical ailments well after he told his followers that his mental techniques had cured him. It is unclear, however, why he felt the need to continue pursuing the VA for a few tens of dollars a month when he was earning thousands a month. It may simply have been that he felt that Uncle Sam owed him a debt that he was due.

CHAPTER 15

Ron's Medals

One of the most glaring anomalies in the Hubbard/Scientology account of his war years is the question of what medals L. Ron Hubbard was awarded. The Church of Scientology has distributed a document which purports to be Hubbard's official notice of separation (the form completed on leaving active duty). This document, US Navy form DD214, lists 21 awards, broken down as follows:

Purple Heart with palm	2
Victory Medal	1
Letter Commendation	1
Dist. Marksman	1
Unit Citation	1
Rifle, Pistol Exp.	2 (1 each)
European Theater (1 star)	2
American Theater (2 stars)	2
Marine Medal	1
American Defense, British & Dutch Vict Medals	3 (1 each)
Asiatic-Pac. Theater (3 stars)	4
TOTAL	21

The Church of Scientology has also circulated a photograph showing a variety of medals and ribbons, which are claimed to be those awarded to Hubbard for his war service. Curiously, Scientology has never detailed exactly for what the decorations were purportedly awarded.

Another oddity is that the number and type of medals claimed has varied over the years. Scientology has claimed that Hubbard received 29 awards[1] or alternatively 21[2]. Hubbard himself claimed 27 medals. In 1974 he ordered his staff to write to the Navy to request the medals that he had claimed but had apparently not received. His claims were detailed in an internal Scientology memorandum[3] (the list is considerably different to that circulated by Scientology today).

- Navy Commendation Medal with 1 Bronze Star.
- Purple Heart.
- Naval Reserve Medal.
- Organized Marine Corps Reserve Medal.
- (British) The 1939-45 War Medal.
- (French) Medaille Commemorative Française 1939-45.
- (Netherlands) Bronzen Kruis.
- Philippine Defence with 3 Silver Stars.
- American Defence Service Medal with 1 Bronze Star.
- American Campaign Medal with 2 Bronze Stars.
- Asiatic-Pacific Campaign Medal with 2 Bronze Stars.
- European African Middle Eastern Campaign Medal (ETO Medal) with 1 Bronze Star.
- WWII Victory Medal.
- National Defence Medal.
- Armed Forces Reserve Medal.
- Navy Expert Rifleman.
- Navy Expert Pistol Shot.

In reply, the Navy observed that Hubbard's service record showed that he had only been awarded four decorations – the American Defense Service Medal, American Campaign Medal, Asiatic-Pacific Campaign Medal and World War II Victory Medal – and sent only those four medals back to the Church of Scientology.

The purported notice of separation distributed by Scientology does not appear in Hubbard's naval service record, which is today held by the US National Archives and Record Administration. Instead, a quite different version of the same document is present. The only known source for the first document is the Church of Scientology. Regardless of the document's or the Church's merits, this in itself is enough to cast suspicion on its authenticity. The National Archives version of Hubbard's notice of separation at least has an auditable trail – we know where it has been (in the possession of the US Navy and the US National Archives), we know who produced it (the Bureau of Naval Personnel) and we know how and when it was obtained (on various occasions through the Freedom of Information Act). The origins of the Scientology notice of separation are wholly unclear, as the Church has not said where it got the document from.

Analysing the Scientology notice of separation reveals numerous discrepancies which cast doubt on its authenticity. The most obvious is its tally of medals awarded to Hubbard, which differs greatly from that held in Hubbard's official file. Some of the medals' names also appear to be abbreviated or incorrect, and in two cases the medals listed do not exist. Some other medals could not possibly have been awarded to Hubbard as he would not have qualified for them.

Only five of the medals listed correspond with those in his naval record. Notably, he was neither awarded nor claimed a Navy Good Conduct Medal. This was given to personnel who had served at least three years and had not been disciplined and had recorded above average scores in various aspects of military fitness. It is likely that Hubbard's disciplinary hearing following the Coronados affair disqualified him from this award.

The medals listed on Scientology's version of the notice of separation are as follows:

American Defense Medal

The full title of this medal, which is also represented by a ribbon, is the American Defense Service Medal. It was awarded to all who served during the pre-war Limited National Emergency (September 8, 1939 – May 26, 1941) or the Unlimited National Emergency, which ran from the onset of the Battle of the Atlantic to Pearl Harbor (May 27, 1941 – December 7, 1941). As Hubbard had been commissioned on July 19, 1941 during the Unlimited National Emergency, he qualified for and received this medal. This is confirmed in the records in his file and is listed in the National Archives version of the notice of separation.

American Theater (2 stars)

This probably refers to the American Campaign Medal. It was instituted on November 6, 1942 for service between December 7, 1941 and March 2, 1946, on land or aboard certain ships within the American Theater of Operations (ATO), for an aggregate period of one year within the continental United States, or for thirty consecutive or sixty non-consecutive days outside the continental limits but within the ATO. A star was awarded for certain specified operations such as escort duty or anti-submarine actions.

Hubbard served in the continental US for all but a few months of his four years of active service. As such, he qualified for and was awarded this ribbon, which is reflected in the National Archives version of the notice of separation. He was not deemed to have qualified for any stars and they do not appear in his Navy record. However, contradictory evidence exists on this point. Hubbard's second-in-command aboard the USS *PC-815*, Thomas Moulton, testified in 1984:

> *We were allowed, so I was advised, to wear two battle stars on our American Theater ribbon which I wore as long as I was in the service. I was told that they had been allowed by Washington.*[4]

185

It is not known who told Moulton this. It is quite possible that Hubbard himself was the source of this information, as he also claimed (but was not awarded) two battle stars. Moulton's testimony suggests that the two stars were supposed to be credit for the two Japanese submarines that Hubbard claimed to have sunk in May 1943.

Armed Forces Reserve Medal

Although the list of medals circulated by Hubbard in 1974 included the Armed Forces Reserve Medal, he could not have been awarded this decoration as he did not qualify for it. The medal was only in-augurated in September 1950, a month before he resigned from the Naval Reserve. It is awarded to reserve personnel who have completed ten years' honorable and satisfactory service. Hubbard served nine years, three months and 12 days, and so fell about eight and a half months short of qualifying for it.

Asiatic-Pacific Theater (3 stars)

The Asiatic-Pacific Campaign Medal was awarded to all officers and enlisted men of the US Armed Forces who, between December 7, 1941 and March 2, 1946, served in active duty in the prescribed area or upon certain ships. Hubbard qualified for and received this ribbon, as the National Archives version of the notice of separation confirms, but not the accompanying stars that he also claimed.

One of Hubbard's ships, the USS *Algol*, won two stars in the APAC theatre for April 1–10, 1945 and July 10 – August 3, 1945. Only one star was awarded for each engagement; Hubbard would have had to have been in both battles to have been awarded both stars. However, Hubbard had left the ship on September 28, 1944 and was ineligible for the stars. The US Navy and Marine Corps Awards Manual and the relevant Ship's Movement Card shows that his other Pacific vessel, the USS *PC-815*, took part in no engage-ments and was awarded no battle stars.

British Victory Medal

This medal simply does not exist. No mention of it appears on Hubbard's official record. Furthermore, the British Ministry of Defence has no record of Hubbard ever having been awarded a British decoration, and Hubbard's naval service record has no indication that he ever served with or alongside British forces. The only known time that he possibly had contact with the British was in 1943 when he may have been instructed by a British sonar officer, if his own account is to be believed.[5]

Dist. Marksman

This is presumably the Distinguished Marksman and Pistol Shot Ribbon. There is no record of Hubbard having been awarded this decoration, although it is clearly visible in the Church of Scientology's photograph of the decorations that he supposedly received.

Dutch Victory Medal

Like its supposed British counterpart, this medal simply does not exist. It does not appear on Hubbard's official record and there is no indication that he ever served with or alongside Dutch forces. Had he done so, it would most likely have been in the then Dutch East Indies, but his naval record shows that he got no closer to that region than Brisbane in Australia.

A Scientology spokesperson has said that the medal is actually the Dutch Cross of Merit (*Kruis van Verdienste*), awarded to "those working in the interest of the Netherlands while faced with enemy actions and distinguishing oneself through valor and resolute behavior". According to the Chancellor of Dutch Orders, which manages the Netherlands' various orders of merit, Hubbard's name does not appear among the 2,083 recipients of the Cross of Merit, nor of other Dutch medals of World War II.[6]

European Theater (later)

This probably refers to the European-Africa-Middle Eastern Campaign Medal, as a photograph published by the Church of Scientology shows Hubbard wearing this medal. However, he did not qualify for it. He might have qualified if he genuinely had participated in the Battle of the Atlantic, but not if he had stayed on the USS *YP-422*. The decoration was awarded for service east of a line drawn down the middle of the North Atlantic, which neither Hubbard nor *YP-422* ever crossed during the war.

Letter of Commendation, Unit Citation

It is unclear what these two items may refer to. "Letter of Commendation" may refer to the Navy Unit Commendation, established by the Secretary of the Navy in December 1944 and awarded to any ship, aircraft, detachment, or other unit of the US Navy or Marine Corps which, subsequent to December 6, 1941, distinguished itself by outstanding heroism in action against the enemy. Even more outstanding heroism was recognized by the Presidential Unit Citation, established in February 1942 and awarded for extraordinary heroism in the face of the enemy. This may be the "Unit Citation" listed on the document.

No record exists of these having been awarded to any unit to which Hubbard was attached. There are no mentions of any such awards, nor of any action which might have merited them, on Hubbard's own conduct reports. Neither Scientology nor Hubbard have detailed to which unit and for what action the award was supposedly bestowed.

Marine Medal

There are several possibilities for this, but the most likely is that it represents the Navy and Marine Corps Medal (also represented as a ribbon). This was instituted on August 7, 1942 for personnel of the US Navy and Marine Corps who, since December 6, 1941, had distinguished themselves by heroism not involving actual combat with the enemy. There is no record of Hubbard having been awarded this medal nor of having done anything to earn it.

Purple Heart (with palm)

The modern Purple Heart is of surprisingly recent origins, considering its revered status. Originally a short-lived Revolutionary War decoration, it was revived in 1932 for the US Army. It was not until December 3, 1942 that it was extended to the Navy and Marine Corps by an Executive Order issued by Present Roosevelt.[7] Its eligibility was also changed, so that now it was (and still is) awarded exclusively to those killed or wounded as a result of enemy action, rather than also for meritorious service.

There is no indication from Hubbard's medical record that any of his complaints were the result of enemy action. The only recorded incident in which he was involved in anything that might have been considered an action was his "battle" against two supposed Japanese submarines off Oregon in 1943. However, as no enemy vessels were involved, this did not count as combat and neither he nor his crew sustained any injuries meriting a Purple Heart. Even if serious injuries had been sustained, as it was not a combat engagement, they would not have qualified for a Purple Heart in any case.

Furthermore, the Navy does not award Purple Hearts "with palms". According to the Military Order of the Purple Heart, if someone is wounded in action more than once they are recognized with gold and silver stars, rather than palms.

Rifle, Pistol Exp.

This presumably refers to the Navy Expert Pistol Shot and Navy Expert Rifleman medals. Both are awarded on attainment of rigidly prescribed marksmanship standards established in the Navy Landing Party Manual. The National Archives version of the notice of separation indicates that Hubbard was awarded these medals. Curiously, though, the Navy's official summary of his war record omits them.

Victory Medal

The World War II Victory Medal was awarded to all members of the US Armed Forces who served on active duty at any time between December 7, 1941 to December 31, 1946. It was also awarded to members of the Philippine Armed Forces. Hubbard clearly qualified for, and was duly awarded, this medal, as confirmed by the National Archives version of his notice of separation.

The Scientology version also shows a number of other strange anomalies:

Section 6 – Character of Separation

Both versions of the document list Hubbard's character of separation as "Honorable", but only the US Navy version shows that he was released to inactive duty, rather than being discharged completely.

Section 16 – Means of Entry

This section lists how and when Hubbard joined the US Navy. The archived version of the notice of separation shows Hubbard as enlisting in April 1941 (when he volunteered) and receiving a permanent commission on "7/5/41". This matches the dates given elsewhere in his record. The Scientology version only checks the box for Hubbard's commissioning and does not give any dates.

The commissioning or enlistment date was one of the most important dates in the entire document. It was essential for calculating Hubbard's length of service and therefore his pay and pension rights. Its absence is startling, and it seems inconceivable that this information would have been omitted from a genuine notice of separation.

Sections 20 & 23 – Qualifications, certificates held etc. & Service Schools Completed

The Scientology version of the notice of separation lists a completely different set of information for both of these sections from that given in the National Archives version. According to the Scientology version, Hubbard qualified in "Navigator, Radar, Anti-Sub Warfare; General Intelligence; Military Govt. Officer". The archived version instead lists Hubbard's qualifications as "Intelligence Officer; Commander, Escort Vessels; Navigator". This corresponds to the training that he completed at the start of his career when inducted into the Office of Naval Intelligence and his courses at the Subchaser Training Center in Miami and the Fleet Sound School in Key West. It lists his qualifications more specifically and in the correct chronological order, unlike the Scientology version.

The Scientology version goes on to list his training establishments as the Office of Naval Intelligence in New York City, the Sub Chaser Training Center in Miami, "CIC, Treasure Is., Calif.", and "Military Govt, Princeton, N.J." Curiously, the archived version omits both the Fleet Sound School and the Princeton School of Military Government from his list of training establishments.

Section 24 – Service (vessels and stations served on) – lists "C.O. USS Howland" and "CO USS Mist".

The USS *Howland* does not appear to have ever existed – it is not recorded in the United States Naval Vessel Register. Hubbard's service record shows no mention of any vessel by that name, civilian or military.

The USS *Mist* was a motor launch converted during World War I into a guard boat. She was returned to her owner in February 1919, when Hubbard was only seven years old. She did not serve in World War II. However, Hubbard's first command, the USS *YP-422*, was a converted trawler formerly named *Mist*. She did not carry her civilian name into military service and was given only a hull number. She was never called the USS *Mist*. A fitness report from September 1942 refers to "the conversion of the Mist (USS YP422)" but correctly does not call the vessel the USS *Mist*.[8]

Section 35 – Signed by Lt Cdr Howard D. Thompson, US Naval Reserve.

No officer of this name is listed in the 1944 or 1945 Registers of Commissioned and Warrant Officers of the United States Naval Reserve. The US Navy's copy of the notice of separation is signed by J.C. Rhodes, the same officer who signed Hubbard's detachment paperwork. "Howard D. Thompson" does not appear anywhere else in Hubbard's navy records.

Section 41 – Non-Service education (years successfully completed) – claims that he spent 4 years at college.

In fact, Hubbard dropped out of George Washington University in 1932 after two years of a three-year course. The National Archives version of Hubbard's notice of separation correctly states two years of college.

Section 42 – Degrees – lists the award of C.E. (for Civil Engineer).

Hubbard never gained an academic qualification, as he dropped out of the Civil Engineering course he undertook at George Washington University in 1930-31. This was recorded in Hubbard's service record, as the Navy obtained a copy of his college grades when he enlisted and noted that he was "deficient in academic educational background." In the early days of Scientology, however, Hubbard liked to add the letters "C.E." to his name on Scientology publications, before renouncing all claims to doctorates and titles in the 1960s. The National Archives version of the notice of separation has a line struck through the box for recording his degrees, correctly indicating that Hubbard did not have one.

Section 46 – Date of Separation – stated as "6 Dec. 1945"
This differs from the US Navy's copy of Hubbard's notice of separation, which gives the date of February 16, 1946. December 6, 1945 was the date of Hubbard's detachment, when he was allowed to leave active duty. He had two months and ten days of accumulated leave which he took immediately after his detachment. His official separation took place on February 16, 1946. Hubbard would not have noticed any practical difference between the two dates and may have forgotten, or not been aware, that he did not formally separate until nine weeks after he returned to civilian life.

These inconsistencies – especially the signature of an apparently non-existent officer – make the authenticity of the document very doubtful. By contrast, the copy contained in Hubbard's official file does not include any undocumented or otherwise inexplicable entries. The archived copy is also much more obviously worn and has seen much more use than the nearly pristine document circulated by the Church of Scientology. The amount of wear and tear on the Navy's version of the document is consistent with something that has been repeatedly handled and used over the years, as might be expected of a document that would have been consulted many times by Navy administrators and archivists.

The most likely explanation for the inconsistencies is that the Scientology document is a poorly executed forgery concocted to support Hubbard's claims to have been a highly-decorated war hero. It is unclear when the document might have been forged, though it is reportedly surfaced in a court case in 1979. It could have been created after Hubbard sent his 1974 request for medals, perhaps in an attempt to rebut the US Navy's assertion that he had earned only a handful of decorations. According to Gerry Armstrong, Hubbard had in his possession a number of blank US Navy forms. If this is true then it makes it much more likely that the forgery was Hubbard's own work.

As for the 21 decorations shown in the photograph circulated by

Scientology, their provenance is a mystery. Hubbard evidently did not have them in 1974, as his request to the US Navy indicates. The US Navy only sent him four; so where did the other seventeen in Scientology's possession come from? The most probable answer is that Hubbard or his agents obtained them from others and then claimed falsely that they were his.

CHAPTER 16

Uncovering the Truth

L. Ron Hubbard's service record remained hidden in the US National Archives for many years after his departure from the Service. In the 1960s he became an increasingly controversial figure as newspapers focused on what they called his "mind-bending cult" and governments scrutinized his financial dealings. Questions about Hubbard's service career began to arrive at the Bureau of Naval Personnel.

The first recorded query was from a Miss Marjorie Holburn of Sydney, Australia in March 1964, requesting an overview of Hubbard's career. Further enquiries followed from a variety of sources, including the British *Daily Mail* newspaper, Dr. William V. Joel, "Consulting Scientologist" of New York City and Britain's Granada Television. In each case the information sought was a corroboration of Hubbard's basic claims about wounds and awards of medals. Each time, though, the reply was the same: no personal information could be released without the permission of the individual involved.

Hubbard's wall of myth was eventually breached by the US Government itself. In the course of investigating a massive clandestine espionage operation which the Church of Scientology had instigated against Federal and State agencies across the country, in August 1976 the US Department of Justice requested the Navy to provide a summary of Hubbard's service. This was very brief – only one page – but was the first officially-released statement of Hubbard's service.

It is somewhat strange that it took the Church of Scientology until

1979 to obtain Hubbard's record; there is no indication that the man himself ever attempted to do so despite the access afforded by the Freedom of Information Act, for which Scientology had vigorously campaigned. Nonetheless, officials of Scientology's "Ministry of Legal Affairs" were granted powers of attorney to obtain the records on Hubbard's behalf, as part of the Church's drive to obtain every record on Scientology or Hubbard held by the US Government.

The records were finally released to the public in 1986 following Hubbard's death on January 24 that year. Privacy concerns were now no longer an issue and enquiries were not long in coming. The first media organization to obtain a full copy of the records was the *Los Angeles Times*, which submitted a request on September 9, 1986. The Navy also received requests from the British writers Russell Miller (author of *Bare-Faced Messiah*) and Jon Atack (*A Piece of Blue Sky*), as well as from many other people subsequently.

In June 1988, Scientology made a move of long-term significance. The Church attempted to block publication of Russell Miller's book *Bare-Faced Messiah* in Britain, Canada and the United States. It issued a subpoena against the US Navy for any correspondence with Miller and demanded a copy of what the Navy had sent to Miller concerning Hubbard's war record. The Navy was under a strict legal obligation to provide Scientology with true and accurate copies of all the documents requested. It did so, and no complaints from Scientology about the outcome are recorded. Despite the Church's later claims that Hubbard's records have been falsified by the US government, it does not appear to have ever attempted to dispute them through official channels.

The first version of this book, published online in 1999, identified for the first time the likely falsification of Hubbard's notice of separation. This has been highlighted by subsequent commentators, notably in 2011, when the author and Pulitzer Prize-winning journalist Laurence Wright wrote an article on Scientology for *The New*

Yorker. Wright discussed Hubbard's war record with Tommy Davis, at that time the chief spokesman for the Church of Scientology, who insisted that "[t]he fact of the matter is that Mr. Hubbard was a war hero." Archivists at the National Archives in St. Louis assisted Wright in reviewing the documentation that Davis provided and identified multiple discrepancies.[1]

Since then, and despite all of the challenges to Hubbard's war record, the Church of Scientology has continued to make provably false claims about Hubbard's military career. Its advertisements and websites still state that Hubbard "commanded corvettes during World War II", that he was "multiply decorated for service under fire" and that he ended his war "in military hospital for wounds sustained in combat". Although the truth about Hubbard's career may have been established by others, there is evidently a long way to go before the Church accepts it in full.

CHAPTER 17

Ron the Secret Agent?

Hubbard's time with the US Navy was, as he recognized himself, "not too glorious".[1] But what if the inglorious account documented in his service record was just a cover for working as a daring secret agent behind enemy lines on Japanese-occupied Java?

Perhaps the most curious thing about his supposed mission to Java is that it appears nowhere in Hubbard's published lectures and written work. He gave many anecdotes about his time in the region but does not seem to have made any claim to have been engaged in secret missions or to have served anywhere in the region other than Australia. The claim comes instead from Thomas S. Moulton, who testified in a California court in 1984 that Hubbard said he was

> in Surabaya [in Java] at the time the Japanese came in or in the area of Surabaya and that he spent some time in the hills in back of Surabaya after the Japanese had occupied it ... He had been landed, so he told me, in Java from a destroyer named the Edsall and had made his way across the land to Surabaya, and that is when the place was occupied. When the Japanese came in, he took off into the hills and lived up in the jungle for sometime until he made an escape from there ...
>
> He had been landed by the Edsall and she was sunk shortly after that. He was, as far as I know, the only person that ever got off the Edsall because he wasn't aboard when it happened. She was sunk within a few days after that.[2]

Hubbard told Moulton that he had been injured by fire from a Japanes machine gun, which damaged his urinary system, "some time during his chasing up and around through the jungle before he made his escape". The escape was effected when "he and another chap sailed a life raft, I believe, to near Australia where they were picked up by a British or Australian destroyer ... 75 miles off Australia."[3]

This account was unknown before Moulton's testimony but it has enthusiastically been accepted as canonical by the Church of Scientology. One Scientology account says that Hubbard "saw action on the island of Java, and only eluded capture through a daring escape on a raft."[4] In March 1997, a worldwide audience of Scientologists heard about Hubbard's time on Java "in search of stockpiled weapons and fast, shallow-draft vessels". According to Dan Sherman, his official biographer, Hubbard said he "met some people who were not on my side" – the Imperial Japanese Army – so "we had to leave the battle". Hubbard was said to have missed the last Allied plane out of Java "and was only able to escape the island after scrambling into a rubber raft and paddling out to meet an Australian destroyer."[5]

The vagueness of this account is striking, not least in the fact that Moulton and Sherman disagree about when was it was supposed to have actually happened. Moulton said that Hubbard told him he was in Surabaya when the Japanese bombed Pearl Harbor. This was, as Moulton noted, "on the 8th of December [1941] which corresponded to December 7th, the other side of the dateline." In his account, Sherman arbitrarily moved the date to some unspecified time "in the closing days of February 1942" and stated that Hubbard missed the last Allied plane out of Java on March 6 – therefore his escape happened at some unspecified point afterwards.

Neither Moulton's nor Sherman's timeframes are realistic. Both are contradicted by other evidence about what Hubbard and the

Japanese were doing at the time. Moulton's placement of the episode at the time of Pearl Harbor is contradicted by Hubbard's own account that he heard about the attack while he was in New York City.[6] This presumably is why Sherman moved the episode to late February, shortly after the *Don Isidro* affair. At that time, Hubbard appears to have been in a temporary post in the Office of the Naval Observer in Brisbane. There is no documentary evidence that Hubbard went anywhere other than Brisbane or Melbourne during his time in Australia.

Three events mentioned in Moulton and Sherman's testimony allow the range of possible dates to be narrowed down. The USS *Edsall* was sunk on March 1, 1942 around 250 miles (400 km) south of Christmas Island and the Japanese landed on the same date 100 miles (160 km) west of Surabaya.[7] The last Allied aircraft left on March 6, according to Sherman, and the city fell on March 7, 1942.[8] Hubbard's supposed drop-off near Surabaya therefore had to have happened some time before March 1 and his escape had to have happened after March 6 in order for Hubbard to have missed the last plane out.

Sherman's account falls apart, however, when the movements of *Edsall* are considered. During January 1942, when we know from Hubbard's report of February 5 that he was in Brisbane routing ships, *Edsall* was in northern Australian waters. She travelled on February 3 to Cilacap (then known as Tjilatjap) on the south central coast of Java, on the same date that Hubbard was returning to Brisbane from his disciplinary interview in Melbourne. She had been damaged by a premature depth charge explosion the month before, causing a persistent leak in the stern that limited her ability to carry out anti-submarine escort duties, and remained in Cilacap throughout February.

On February 26-27, *Edsall* and her sister destroyer USS *Whipple* left to escort the aircraft carrier USS *Langley to* Cilacap but came under attack from Japanese aircraft. The two destroyers rendezvoused the next day with a fuel ship off Christmas Island, several hundred miles to the south, but were forced into the open ocean by more Japanese attacks. On 1 March *Edsall* turned back alone to return to Java. She was caught and sunk by a Japanese task force about 250 miles south-southwest of Christmas Island. Although a few of her crew were rescued by the Japanese, they were later executed and none of those aboard the vessel survived the war.[9]

As this account demonstrates, *Edsall* never went near Surabaya, which is on the north-east coast of Java hundreds of miles away from Cilacap. Her continuous presence in Cilacap is attested by naval orders and the logs of other warships that were in the port at the time. So Hubbard could not have been dropped off by *Edsall*. He clearly could not have served as her Gunnery Officer, as his name does not appear in her muster roll and he had no training in naval gunnery. Nor could he have had any contact with *Edsall* after 26 February, as she was at sea in the open ocean from then until her sinking four days later. During that four-day period *Edsall* was constantly engaged in escort operations in conjunction with *Whipple*, so there was no point at which she could have made a round trip of at least 400 miles to drop Hubbard off near Surabaya.

Sherman's claimed timeframe for Hubbard's return is also impossible. He claimed that Hubbard encountered Japanese forces, and Moulton said that Hubbard had been injured by enemy machine-gun fire, but this could not have happened before the Japanese landings on March 1. With no air route to safety, the badly wounded Hubbard would have had to have crossed mountains and dense jungle to reach an unidentified point on Java's south coast, find a boat in the company of another officer whose name has never been disclosed, sail hundreds of miles across the Indian Ocean to within 75 miles of the Australian coast, be rescued by a vessel that has never been identified, transfer to an equally unidentified Australian port, recuperate and return to Brisbane. All of that had to have happened between March 1 and March 8, when his presence is recorded in the war diary of the USS *New Orleans* on the day before Hubbard departed from Australia aboard the *Pennant*. Needless to say, no records support that physically impossible scenario.

Moulton thought Hubbard's supposed voyage was a remarkable feat of navigation, which it certainly would have been. The shortest distance between the south-easternmost point of Java and Australia is about 700 miles (1,100 km) across the shark-infested waters of the eastern Indian Ocean. Had Hubbard crossed from the south coast opposite Surabaya, it would have been closer to 900 miles (1,300 km) and would have involved crossing rugged terrain on Japanese-occupied Java. As the Australian writer Steve Cannane points out, the crossing was supposedly made in the middle of the monsoon season, "the most dangerous period to attempt a sea crossing to northern Australia. Fishing boats carrying asylum seekers struggle to make it to Australia via this route, let alone men in rubber life rafts."[10]

In short, the idea that Hubbard was a secret agent on Java is completely lacking in credibility as well as any physical or documentary evidence. But for Hubbard's apologists, the claim has one great advantage. What if his inglorious service record was in fact faked to cover up the heroic work that he did in secret?

This claim seems to have originated with Moulton during his testimony in 1984. It was entirely possible, he said, that the records had been falsified to provide a cover story for Hubbard's intelligence activities:

Moulton: [This record] says January 16; however, this could be meaningless. It is not to be relied on. If something you said just now is true – said he was an intelligence officer, I believe – if that is so, this would be meaningless.
Michael Flynn, attorney: That could be false?
Moulton: Not false, but an intelligence officer, as far as I know, has all sorts of spurious letters stating where he is

sent to, when he got there. I did not know he was an intel-
ligence officer. But if he was, this would be meaningless.[11]

Hubbard's naval record again came under scrutiny in a 1985 trial involving a former Scentologist, Julie Christofferson Titchbourne of Portland, Oregon. The church's lawyers turned to ex-US Air Force Colonel L. Fletcher Prouty, who had written articles for the Church's magazine *Freedom*. Prouty argued that the records were purposefully incomplete and had been "sheep-dipped" to cover up Hubbard's wartime activities.

More recently, an "independent Scientologist" (i.e. someone who still believes and practices Scientology outside of the confines of the Church of Scientology) called Margaret Lake has published an online analysis of Hubbard's war record. She argues that he could in fact have participated in secret operations on Java and he could have sustained injuries in combat there.[12]

So how plausible are these claims? Moulton and Prouty both based their claims on the belief that the records of someone working for US Naval Intelligence would be falsified to conceal what they were really doing. Moulton's brief testimony was clearly drawn only from personal belief – "as far as I know". The judge hearing the case pointed out: "The witness isn't competent to testify about the way in which Naval intelligence records were kept."[13]

Prouty, who died in 2001, put forward a more comprehensive theory. He produced an affidavit for the Church of Scientology "to provide proof of the fact that the records, data and related materials ... of Mr. L. Ronald Hubbard, formerly Lt. Commander, U.S. Navy Reserve, are incomplete ... [and] to attest to the fact that those materials and records provided give ample evidence that proves the existence of other records that have been concealed, withheld and overlooked."[14] He also wrote to the producers of the CBS *60 Minutes* program in 1985 and to the publishers of *Bare-Faced Messiah* in 1987. His claims were amplified by the Church in a 1985 television interview, in which its attorney Earle Cooley claimed "that there are more than one set of military records on Mr. Hubbard" and that "his military records have been doctored ... by God knows whom".[15]

Prouty cited his experience as a former US Army and Air Force officer in support of his claims. He served in both services from 1941 through 1964, when he served as a pilot and a Pentagon desk officer in a variety of operational, administrative and intelligence posts. After retiring from the service he worked in banking and public relations, writing on intelligence matters and focusing in particular on the 1963 assassination of President Kennedy.[16]

He became known for his conspiracy theorizing, claiming among other things that President Franklin D. Roosevelt was assassinated, that the 1978 Jonestown mass suicide was perpetrated by the CIA with the knowledge of the Joint Chiefs of Staff, that the CIA assassinated Princess Diana and that oil is not a fossil fuel but is in fact a plentiful resource covertly monopolized by the oil companies, with the aid of the Israelis. He was perhaps best known for his claims about the Kennedy assassination and was the prototype for the "Mr. X" character in Oliver Stone's film *JFK*.

By the 1970s and 1980s he relied on fringe outlets such as the far-right Liberty Lobby and the Church of Scientology's *Freedom* magazine to publicize his work. He served on the advisory board of the Liberty Lobby's Populist Action Committee, alongside various white nationalists, Christian supremacists and Holocaust deniers. He was also associated with the Institute for Historical Review, a notorious Holocaust denial group, and spoke at their conferences.

Prouty claimed to have personally carried out the type of "sheep-dipping" that he said was visible in Hubbard's service rcord. He claimed in a 1973 book that sheep-dipping is

an intricate Army-devised process by which a man who is in the service as a full career soldier or officer agrees to go

*through all the legal and official motions of resigning from
the service. Then, rather than actually being released, his
records are pulled from the Army personnel files and transferred to a special Army intelligence file. Substitute but
nonetheless real appearing records are then processed, and
the man 'leaves' the service.*[17]

Prouty's claims in his letters and affidavits are, however, notably
short of evidence. He never served with the Navy and provided no
evidence that the Navy had ever engaged in "sheep-dipping". It is
not even clear that the practice existed as long ago as the 1940s.
According to the Canadian-American journalist Elie Abey, writing
in 1966, sheep-dipping was used by the CIA to conceal the identities
of the pilots of U-2 aircraft conducting reconnaissance flights over
Cuba in the early 1960s. Abey wrote: "The U-2 planes were being
flown by Air Force officers who had been transferred to the CIA
payroll, ostensibly as civilians, after a process of quasi-separation
known in the trade as 'sheep-dipping'."[18] Prouty claimed that the
practice was subsequently used in the secret US air campaigns in
Laos and Cambodia later in the decade and in the early 1970s.
However, he provided no evidence that it was used thirty years
earlier in World War II. Abey's 1966 description of 'sheep-dipping"
appears to have been the first time the term was used in print,
according to a Google Books search.

As his main piece of evidence, Prouty claimed that a particular
designation in Hubbard's records indicated that he was on intelligence duties throughout the war, not just in the first six months of
his career when he was a member of the Office of Naval
Intelligence:

*In the upper left hand corner there is a correspondence code
"NAV-1651-EZ". You should know that all "16—" series correspondence pertains to intelligence matters. Of course, it*

is sometimes omitted to protect security interests, and when
it is used it means "Intelligence". Your sources say nothing
about that although this same, official "16—" designator
appears on countless LRH documents through the years of
his military service.[19]

This claim was investigated by Jon Atack, the author of *A Piece of Blue Sky*, a history of Hubbard and Scientology. He wrote:

The most significant error in Prouty's work was his
assertion that the code '16' on Hubbard's orders signified
that he was a member of US Navy Intelligence. In fact, the
files themselves show that the code number indicates simply
'Naval Reserve', and of course Hubbard was commissioned
as a member of the Naval Reserve. Prouty offers no source
for his drastic presumption.

This conclusion was confirmed by Atack and a retired US naval officer who had served at the same time and in similar circumstances in Hubbard. As Atack puts it, "The retired naval officer who helped me to check the records showed me his own records. His orders also carried the number "16," yet he had never served in Intelligence and he was – yes, you guessed it – a naval reserve officer."[20] Atack points out another obvious problem: if the US Navy really wanted to falsify Hubbard's records, why did it not portray Hubbard's career as uneventful, rather than depicting an officer who repeatedly had issues with poor conduct and judgment?

Prouty's credibility was not helped by the major factual errors that he made in discussing Hubbard's service record. He wrote that "L. Ron Hubbard ran corvettes in Australia"[21] (in fact, Hubbard did not serve on corvettes anywhere, let alone Australia, where the US Navy did not deploy any corvettes). He also made a series of claims about Hubbard's war medals, apparently based on Scientology's version of Hubbard's notice of separation. Prouty highlighted some of the medals listed:

> *The official U.S. Navy record establishes that Hubbard had sustained wounds in action [and was awarded a Purple Heart with Palm] before Dec 1945.*
>
> *Something most important that Miller chose to overlook was the fact that Hubbard has been awarded (see document cited above) a "Unit Citation". This award is most important and special. Unit Citations are made only by the President of the United States …*
>
> *From that same Section 34, see above, there is the citation "Br. & Dtch. Vict. Medals." This citation is found on very few U.S. military records and signifies notable service with the British and the Dutch during WW II. From what we know of Hubbard's Naval Intelligence Service in the Pacific it is beyond question that these awards were earned in and around Indonesia (Dutch at the time) and in Australia and the seas around it (British Zone).*
>
> *It is important to note that Hubbard had been awarded the "Marine Medal". This medal is awarded rarely to Navy line officers, least of all to those serving with Intelligence. To back up this unusual award you will note that this Naval Intelligence officer also held "Rifle, Pistol Expert" marksmanship ratings. Both of these awards signify ground action that is not typical of the sea duty expected of Navy officers.[22]*

Prouty failed to spot that the record on which he based his claims was almost certainly forged. In particular, he cited a number of decorations – the Purple Heart "with Palm" and the British and Dutch "Victory Medals" – as evidence of Hubbard's "unique service record" without realising that those decorations did not exist. This could readily have been checked with any reference guide to World War II military medals. His inability to detect such a basic error suggests that he did little or any research to back up his claims, and relied instead on his own, very faulty, personal knowledge and belief.

Prouty also made other demonstrably false claims about Hubbard's career. He claimed that Hubbard's "special training at Princeton for select Navy Intelligence personnel was to groom them for unique duties in the Far East. The course at Monterey was the higher grade training." In fact, as the official record of the United States Naval Administration in World War II reveals, the School of Military Government which Hubbard joined in September 1944 was not for "select Navy Intelligence personnel" but for officers from throughout the US armed forces. Hubbard's application was in reply to a general Navy request for applicants "for intensive training with eventual assignment to foreign duty as civil affairs officers in occupied areas." Nor, as Prouty should have spotted, was Hubbard a member of Naval Intelligence at the time; he had left the Office of Naval Intelligence nearly three years earlier in May 1942.

Perhaps the most fundamental problem with Prouty's claims, though, is that they are utterly inconsistent with the nature of Hubbard's record. Prouty himself claimed that "sheep-dipping" was used to hide the records of military officers being loaned to the CIA for intelligence duties. The officers secretly remained members of the armed forces but went through what Abey called "quasi-separation" to make it appear that they had left.

This was a completely different scenario to that shown in Hubbard's service record. At all times between enlisting in 1941 and separating in 1946, he was overtly under military command (even in the Office of Censorship, where his section was staffed and run by US Navy Reserve officers). He was openly enrolled as a member of the Office of Naval Intelligence and his departure from the ONI was simply the result, as a record at the time stated, of the fact that the ONI's censorship responsibilities had been transferred to the

Office of Censorship and were no longer considered to be intelligence duties.

Despite Prouty's lack of credibility, the Church of Scientology still promotes his claims about Hubbard's war record. In September 2010, Lawrence Wright and a team of fact-checkers from *The New Yorker* sat down with the Church of Scientology's then chief spokesman, Tommy Davis, to discuss a range of issues including Hubbard's war record. Wright says that Davis "totally stood up for Fletcher Prouty and the whole intelligence gambit."[23] Davis told the *New Yorker* team, "We finally got so frustrated with this point of conflicting medical records that we took all of Mr. Hubbard's records to Fletcher Prouty. He actually solved the conundrum for us" with his theory of "sheep-dipping".[24] Prouty's claims thus seem to serve a prophylactic function for the church, providing it with a way of reconciling the contradictions between records and claims.

Despite the Church's claims that Hubbard's records were falsified, it has so far not publicly indicated *which* records it considers suspicious. In fact, the Church's most recent accounts of Hubbard's naval career are fairly close to the Navy's records. It accepts, for instance, that Hubbard served on the USS *YP-422*, *PC-815* and *Algol*, though it systematically fails to acknowledge anything which sheds a less-than-positive light on Hubbard's service.

Margaret Lake takes a different approach to Prouty's argument that Hubbard's war records were falsified, which she calls "weak". She points out that while Prouty claimed the existence of a "second record" of Hubbard's supposed true war service, it has never turned up in the National Archives. She argues instead that Hubbard's intelligence activities are hidden by the gaps in his record, of which the biggest relates to his months in Australia. She paints a picture of Hubbard's war service that is built on improbable assumptions and leaps of faith that are unsupported by hard evidence.

Like Sherman, Lake is constrained by the timeframe around the

Japanese invasion of Java and Hubbard's departure from Australia. She similarly locates the period of Hubbard's supposed secret operations on Java as being in late February-early March 1942. To make that case, she argues:

> *Based on what is known about Hubbard's timeline while in Australia and the known timeline of the EDSALL, however, Hubbard would likely have been first flown to Darwin in mid-February, and then flown (or took passage on a ship) to western Timor. From there, he could have picked up the EDSALL (or possibly another ship or destroyer, such as the USS ALDEN or the USS PAUL JONES) for transport to Java, which were known to be providing escort service and making deliveries between Timor and Java in mid-February 1942.*

The sole basis for that argument is the existence of the letter from Colonel Johnson to the commander of US Army Base Section One in Darwin on February 13, 1942 in which he recommended Hubbard's personal qualities and asked for an unspecified request to be granted. Lake argues that the letter and request "may have been in relation to providing Hubbard transport to Timor and/or Java. And these may have all been in relation to Hubbard carrying out senior Navy orders to go to Java, for an as-yet undetermined reason."

There is no documentary evidence of any kind to support this supposition. Nothing in Hubbard's record and no known records from any source indicate that he ever went near Java, Timor or any ships in the area. Lake also cites as "circumstantial evidence" Hubbard being issued a Thompson sub-machine gun in Brisbane and claiming "recent experience with … .30 and .50 machineguns, also Thompsons and Vickers" while in the South Pacific, and even

Hubbard ordering a new or repaired uniform (that he did not pay for despite the tailor's complaints). She argues that Hubbard's need for a new uniform may indicate that he had "damaged his existing one somehow during a mission to Java, as described in Moulton's testimony". The gun was not even US property in the first place – it was borrowed from the Australians – and Hubbard's claimed experience with machine guns was far more likely to have been gained in gunnery practice sessions conducted in Brisbane.

One of the biggest unanswered questions for Hubbard's apologists is: *why would Hubbard be chosen for a secret mission to Java?* He had never been to Java before; he did not speak Javanese, or claim any familiarity with the country; he had no obvious qualifications for a secret mission. Just days before the time of the supposed mission, he had been disciplined by two of the most senior Army and Navy officers in Australia, described as unfit for independent duty and ordered back to the United States. The likelihood that he would have *then* been entrusted with a secret mission in Java seems remote at best.

There is also no clarity from any of Hubbard's apologists about what he was supposedly doing on Java in the first place. Moulton said nothing about the goals of the supposed secret mission. Sherman referred to Hubbard going "in search of stockpiled weapons and fast, shallow-draft vessels", though it is not clear whether that was meant to be Hubbard's mission – in which case what was the point of it? – or his response to supposedly being cut off by the Japanese and seeking a means of escape. Lake for once does not speculate and says only that Hubbard's purpose on Java was "as yet undetermined".

Hubbard himself did not claim in his published lectures or written works to have gone to Java or performed any secret missions there. He described himself as a "mail officer"[25] and described his work as involving administrative tasks for the US Army, including ship-routing. This matches his records. Prior to coming to Australia, his only recorded work for the Navy was writing articles for its Public Relations office and cataloging photographs for the Hydrographer's Office. Nothing in his background would suggest he had any qualifications of any sort that would have been of use in a covert mission.

So why did Hubbard make that claim to Moulton in the first place? The context is essential to understanding his reasons for doing so. Moulton said in his testimony that Hubbard made the claim "in Miami which would have been in the fall of '42". The injuries Hubbard claimed to have sustained from Japanese machine-gun fire supposedly damaged his urinary system, which Moulton testified caused him "a great bit of difficulty in urinating".[26] The timing of this claim closely matches Hubbard's admission in his later "Affirmations" that he had caught gonorrhea from a girl while at the Sub Chaser Training Center in Miami.[27] One of the disease's most typical symptoms is pain while urinating. The likelihood is that Hubbard invented the story to explain away one of the more embarrassing consequences of catching a sexually transmitted disease.

Hubbard was known for telling tall stories about his experiences to impress his friends, several of whom later wrote about this aspect of his personality. In the mid-1930s he would spin tales of his adventures to his writer friends in New York City. As Russell Miller writes, one of them, Frank Gruber, eventually grew tired of hearing about Hubbard's escapades:

> One evening Gruber sat through a long account of Ron's experiences in the Marine Corps, his exploration of the upper Amazon and his years as a white hunter in Africa. At the end of it he asked with obvious sarcasm: 'Ron, you're eighty-four years old aren't you?'
> 'What the hell are you talking about?' Ron snapped.
> Gruber waved a notebook in which he had been jotting

figures 'Well,' he said, 'you were in the Marines seven years, you were a civil engineer for six years, you spent four years in Brazil, three in Africa, you barnstormed with your own flying circus for six years... I've just added up all the years you did this and that and it comes to eighty-four.'

Ron was furious that his escapades should be openly doubted. 'He blew his tack,' said Gruber.[28]

Hubbard was doing the same thing a decade later. The science fiction writer Jack Williamson recalled that in Philadelphia in 1944, Hubbard regaled his friends and colleagues with the claim that he had recently seen action aboard a Navy destroyer in the Aleutians.[29] Hubbard's supporters do not seem to mention this particular claim, perhaps because it is so clearly disprovable (he was on the USS *Algol* at the time). Nelson Himmel, with whom Hubbard shared a room around August 1945, described Hubbard as

very sharp and quick, a fascinating story-teller, and he could charm the shit out of anybody. He talked inter-minably about his war experiences and seemed to have been everywhere. Once he said he was on Admiral Halsey's staff. I called a friend who worked with Halsey and my friend said "Shit, I've never heard of him."

... Another time he said he was in the Aleutians in command of a destroyer and a polar bear jumped from an ice floe onto his ship and chased everyone around. I recognized it as an old, old folklore story that goes way back.[30]

At some point, Hubbard also told A. E. van Vogt that he "had been in command of a gunboat in the Pacific. Once he sailed right into the harbour of a Japanese occupied island in the Dutch East Indies. His attitude was that if you took your flag down the Japanese would not know one boat from another, so he tied up at the dock, went ashore and wandered around by himself for three days. Everyone else was scared except Hubbard."[31] Three decades later, Hubbard was in hiding in New York City with a pair of Scientologist aides. One of them, Jim Dincalci, recalled that at some point in 1973 during his nine-month stay there, Hubbard told them about his wartime experiences:

> *He said that when Pearl Harbor was bombed he was on some island in the Pacific and he was the senior person in charge because everyone else had been killed. He was con-trolling all the traffic through the island until a bomb exploded right by him at the airport and he was sent home, the first US casualty of World War Two. He had a big fatty tumour, a lymphoma, on the top of his head which he said had slivers of shrapnel in it. We had it X-rayed once and had the film enlarged fifty times to find the shrapnel, but there was nothing there.*[32]

Both of these reported claims by Hubbard – which are contradicted by his own words elsewhere, as well as his service record – have conveniently been forgotten about by his supporters. Hubbard himself appears to have been aware of his tendency to tell tall stories about his naval career. In his 1946 "Affirmations", he wrote:

> *You have no urge to talk about your navy life. You do not like to talk of it. You never illustrate your point with bogus stories. It is not necessary for you to lie to be amusing and witty.*[33]

The final strand of evidence cited by Lake is Hubbard's supposed injuries, in particular the actinic conjunctivitis with which he was diagnosed and the injury to his ankle and/or foot that he reported in his May 11, 1942 medical examination at the US Naval Hospital in Brooklyn. These, she claims, indicate that Hubbard could have suffered combat injuries. She cites Hubbard's claim to Moulton that he was injured by the flash of a gun on the USS *Edsall* while serving as her Gunnery Officer and also proposes as an alternative that he might have been injured in Darwin during Japanese air raid.

However, Lake unaccountably ignores Hubbard's own statements about his ailments. In his request for a pension in December 1945, Hubbard said that the onset of his actinic conjunctivitis dated to March 1942[34] – that is, *after* the sinking of the *Edsall* and the bombing of Darwin – and he told his doctor that it was the result of exposure to "strong sunlight".[35] Five years later, he told his followers that he had been "struggling to get my eyes up from a bomb blast that knocked them flat in early 1942".[36] His service record shows that he made no mention at any time of gun flash or bomb blast injuries, nor does it suggest that he was in any locations where he might have been at risk of either.

Ultimately, Prouty, Sherman and Lake's accounts all suffer from the same flaw. Rather than following the evidence, they were written principally to prove Hubbard's claims. As a result, all three have found themselves making arguments that lack evidence to support them, relying on assumptions and ignoring contradictory evidence including Hubbard's own statements. Rather than proving that Hubbard was a war hero, all three have shown all the more vividly that his claims cannot be reconciled with reality.

CHAPTER 18

Ron's War

Once the layers of exaggeration and obfuscation are stripped away from the story of L. Ron Hubbard's war service, the account that emerges is far from heroic. It reveals, instead of a war hero, a man who repeatedly tripped himself up through his poor decision-making. He had barely advanced in his career by the end of his service; in important respects, such as the loss of his commands, he had gone backwards. His physical ailments, while inconvenient, were a far cry from the war wounds he later claimed. The man who wrote before the war that he had "high hopes of smashing my name into history so violently that it will take a legendary form even if all books are destroyed"[1] found at the end of the war that he had achieved little in nearly five years of military service.

The story of Ron's war revealed by his service records can be told fairly simply and briefly. After receiving his commission he spent a few months doing low-level and fairly unimportant administrative work. When war broke out, he was sent abroad but was unable to reach his designated post. He was given temporary assignments by the Army but took on duties for which he was unqualified and made poor decisions. His failures and personal conduct resulted in him being disciplined and sent home.

While this might have ended his career in peacetime, the Navy's desperate shortage of personnel led to him being given command of a small patrol vessel on the East Coast. However, his poor decision-making and personal conduct again led him to be removed from his post within a short time. After a period of training, he was given command of a small warship on the West Coast. Yet again, though, his poor decision-making led to him being removed from his post within only a few months. His repeated failures led to the Navy's senior leadership finally recognizing and responding to his deficiencies. As a result, he did not get another command.

The last two years of his naval career were devoid of any significant achievements. His service aboard a naval cargo ship ended at his volition before it left American waters. He spent the next year and a half in training for a future post that he never took up and receiving treatment in hospital for his ulcers.

His repeated failures caused him much stress and depression and were the likely cause of his ulcers. He worried a good deal about his health, especially after contracting gonorrhea, which may have worsened some of his other health problems. His various ailments resulted in him undergoing repeated stays in hospitals. He was not, however, above playing up the seriousness of his ailments, presumably to avoid returning to tedious duties.

What kind of officer was Hubbard? His fitness reports over the course of the five and a half years of his service provide a unique insight into his character and personal qualities. The war represented the only time in his adult life that he worked for someone else and was under close and regular observation. A handful of his colleagues and subordinates, tracked down in later years by the Church of Scientology, gave very positive views of him. This is perhaps not a surprise, though, given that their views have publicized by the Scientologists precisely because they were so positive. His commanding officers were also mostly positive about his performance, though with occasional reservations.

Hubbard did not receive a full evaluation for all of his assignments as they did not all offer an opportunity to judge him against the Navy's criteria. The ten fitness reports that did provide full evaluations him illustrate what the Navy thought of him. Five of his reports rated him to be above average, four more rated him average and one below average. One reporting officer said they would like to have him serve under them, four more reports stated that they would be pleased to have him serve, another four said they would be satisfied and one said they did not want to have him serve with them. Considered against a performance range of 0 to 4 points, Hubbard's average was a respectable 3.4. In all but one report, he received satisfactory grades for each of the 13 categories of conduct assessed by the Navy, from personal intelligence to "military bearing and neatness of person and dress".

The exception, predictably, was Rear Admiral Braisted's scathing report following the Coronados incident in 1943. Perhaps surprisingly, given its otherwise critical tone, the report was quite favorable towards Hubbard in terms of grading. Braisted gave him grades of 3.5 for his administrative ability and ship handling, but rated him lower for his ability to command. Hubbard received exceptional or above average grades for most of the criteria and Braisted gave him only one failing grade, assessing Hubbard's ability to make judgments as being that he "[f]requently draws wrong conclusions." Hubbard was given a below-average score overall, in the context of a comparison "with other officers of his rank and approximate length of service".

This was the only below-average report that Hubbard received during his career. Although it was very much justified by the incompetence that Hubbard had displayed at the Coronados, he would undoubtedly have felt hard done-by after the favorable reports he had received from previous commanding officers. However, the other two major failures he experienced during his career – his removal from Australia and from his command of YP-422 – are not reflected in his fitness reports. Had they been properly recorded, which seems not to have happened due to glitches in the naval bureaucracy in the first months of the war, he would likely have had a significantly lower average.

The picture that emerges from the reports is that Hubbard was possibly a better officer than he has sometimes been portrayed. He seems to have served competently for most of his duties, successfully oversaw the commissioning of two vessels and contributed to the commissioning of a third. He was generally rated as being of average to above average ability. His failures generally had more to do with flaws in his personality than lack of ability.

The criticisms of his commanding officers highlighted consistent and recurrent problems, in each case focusing on his temperament rather than his technical ability: "He is garrulous and tries to give impressions of his importance. He also seems to think that he has unusual ability in most lines."[2] "He is not temperamentally fitted for independent command",[3] ... "lacking in the essential qualities of judgement, leadership and cooperation. He acts without forethought as to probable results",[4] ... "very temperamental and often has his feelings hurt."[5]

In other words, Hubbard suffered from an unfortunate combination of a thin skin, an unduly large ego and a lack of good judgment. These traits were all very much visible in his post-war years and nearly led to disaster for him and his organizations on several occasions. The Navy needed Hubbard to subordinate himself to people who had more experience and knowledge than he had – not a situation with which he was familiar or comfortable. While he would probably still not have become the war hero of his imagination, if he had been able to exercise more self-control and possessed more awareness of his own limitations it is likely that he would have been able to enjoy a much more successful career.

There is no doubt that Hubbard lied a great deal about his wartime service. He did not save Australia. He did not serve on corvettes. He did not sink any submarines. He never went to Java or the Aleutians on secret missions. He did not suffer any war wounds. He was not crippled and blinded. He was not awarded most of the medals that he claimed.

Yet truths can be detected beneath the layers of exaggeration, like grains of sand at the heart of rotting pearls. As this book has shown, many of the anecdotes told by Hubbard in his books and lectures can be linked to specific events recorded in his service history and other related documents. Hubbard was a serial exaggerator who took the fairly humdrum reality of his war and presented it as something exceptional.

By the end of the war, Hubbard had come back to more or less the same point at which he had been at its beginning. He had little to tell for his years of service other than a collection of physical maladies, a handful of commonplace medals, a lingering resentment of his superiors and a palpable sense of failure. He wrote in his *Affirmations* in 1946: "You did a fine job in the Navy. No one there is now "out to get you." You are through with its [sic] Navy and will utterly forget any derogatory instances."[6]

Only a few years later, he was to make his fortune with the creation of Scientology. His naval experience came to define many aspects of his new movement: from the complex bureaucracy through which he managed it to the creation of his own pseudo-navy, the Sea Org, which imitated many aspects of the US Navy including military-style uniforms and ranks. The legacy of Hubbard's time in the Navy can still be seen today on the streets of Scientology's "Mecca", the Florida town of Clearwater, where Scientologists in quasi-naval uniforms re-enact Hubbard's military career on a daily basis.

Bibliography
Scientology Sources

Hubbard, L. Ron

- *A History of Man* (1968 ed.) Copenhagen : American Saint Hill Organization.
- *Mission into Time* (1973). Copenhagen : American Saint Hill Organization. ISBN 978-87-87347-56-3
- *All About Radiation* (1979 ed.). Los Angeles : Bridge Publications. ISBN 978-0-88404-446-8
- *Research & Discovery Series,* vol. 1. (1980). Copenhagen : Scientology Publications. ISBN 978-0-88404-931-9
- "Affirmations" (or "Admissions"). Undated, circa 1946.
- http://scientology-research.org/the-admissions-of-l-ron-hubbard/
- "Autobiographical notes for Peter Tompkins", June 6, 1972. Unpublished work.
- "Agreements and Postulates of the Eight Dynamics", lecture of January 8, 1957
- "Auditing Techniques: Games Conditions", lecture of February 1, 1957
- "Civil Defense", lecture of June 27, 1951
- "Definition of Organization, Part I", lecture of November 8, 1956
- "E-Meter Talk and Demo", lecture of May 7, 1961
- "Flows: Characteristics of", lecture of December 9, 1952
- "The Game of Life (Exteriorization and Havingness)", lecture of February 7, 1956
- "Group Dianetics", lecture of November 9, 1950
- "Introduction to 9th ACC: Havingness", lecture of December 6, 1954
- "The Key Words (Buttons) of Scientology Clearing – Question and Answer Period", lecture of July 21, 1958

- "Miracles in Dianetics", lecture of December 27, 1951
- "Motion and Emotion", lecture of August 16, 1951
- "Obnosis", lecture of January 9, 1957
- "Political Dianetics", lecture of September 5, 1940
- "Routine IA-Problems", lecture of July 3, 1961
- "Safeguarding Dianetics", lecture of June 28, 1951
- "Self-Determined Effort Processing", lecture of October 1, 1951
- "Space", lecture of April 29, 1954
- "The Story of Dianetics & Scientology", lecture of October 18, 1958
- "Study: Evaluation of Information", lecture of August 11, 1964
- "Welcome Address", lecture of November 7, 1959
- "Withholds and In-session-ness", lecture of January 24, 1961

Other Scientology works

- "Facts About L. Ron Hubbard – Things You Should Know", Flag Divisional Directive 69RA of 8 March 1974, revised 7 April 1974
- "A Short Biography of L. Ron Hubbard", *The Auditor* magazine, issue 63. East Grinstead : Church of Scientology, Saint Hill Foundation.
- "A Brief Biography of L. Ron Hubbard." *Ability* magazine, issue 111, January 1959. Washington, D.C : Church of Scientology.
- "An interview granted to the Australian Press on January 10th 1963 at Saint Hill Manor... by L. Ron Hubbard." Washington, D.C. : Founding Church of Scientology press release, November 30, 1963.
- "LRH Conference with the Investigators" (August 17, 1966)
- *What Is Scientology?* (1992 ed.) Los Angeles : Bridge Publications. ISBN 978-0-88404-633-2
- *L. Ron Hubbard – Images of a Lifetime: A Photographic Biography* (1996). Los Angeles : Bridge Publications. ISBN 978-1-57318-028-3
- "Merchants of Sensationalism: The *Boston Herald* Exposed" (1997). Los Angeles : Church of Scientology International
- *What Is Scientology?* (1978 ed.) Los Angeles : Church of Scientology of California. ISBN 0-88404-061-5

- *A Report to Members of Parliament on Scientology* (1969). East Grinstead : Church of Scientology World-Wide Public Relations Bureau.
- *L. Ron Hubbard – A Chronicle* (1990). L. Ron Hubbard Library. Los Angeles : Bridge Publications.
- *L. Ron Hubbard: A Profile* (1995). "The Friends of Ron". Los Angeles : Bridge Publications. ISBN 978-08-840-4995-1
- *L. Ron Hubbard: Master Mariner/Yachtsman* (1996). L. Ron Hubbard Library. Los Angeles : Bridge Publications.
- *Ron: Master Mariner – At The Helm Across Seven Seas* (2012). L. Ron Hubbard Library. Copenhagen : New Era Publications. ISBN 978-87-649-3479-3
- *Ron: Freedom Fighter – Articles and Essays* (2012). L. Ron Hubbard Library. Copenhagen : New Era Publications. ISBN 978-87-649-3475-5
- *Ron: Poet/Lyricist – The Aesthetics of Verse* (2012). L. Ron Hubbard Library. Copenhagen : New Era Publications. ISBN 978-87-649-3482-3
- L. Ron Hubbard Library (2012). *Ron: Adventurer/Explorer – Daring Deeds & Unknown Realms*. Copenhagen : New Era Publications. ISBN 978-87-649-3474-8
- L. Ron Hubbard Library (2012). *Ron: Humanitarian – Restoring Honor and Self-Respect*. Copenhagen : New Era Publications. ISBN 978-87-649-3484-7
- L. Ron Hubbard Library (2012). *Ron: Humanitarian – Education, Literacy & Civilization*. Copenhagen : New Era Publications. ISBN 978-87-649-3485-4

Other Books and Articles

- **Abel, Elia** (1969). *The Missiles of October: The Story of the Cuban Missile Crisis, 1962.* London : MacGibbon & Kee. ISBN 978-0-261-63162-5
- **Atack, Jon** (1990). *A Piece of Blue Sky: Scientology, Dianetics, and L. Ron Hubbard exposed.* New York : Carol Publishing Group. ISBN 0-8184-0499-X
- **Banyai, Richard** (1974). *Money and Banking in China and Southeast Asia During the Japanese Military Occupation 1937–1945.* Taipei : Tai Wan Enterprises Co.
- **Brown, Louis** (1999). *A Radar History of World War 2: Technical and Military Imperatives.* Bristol : Institute of Physics Publishing. ISBN 978-0-7503-0659-1
- **Bruce, Anthony** (2014). *Encyclopaedia of Naval History.* Hoboken : Taylor and Francis. ISBN 978-1-135-93534-4
- **Bruning, John R.** (2013). *Battle for the North Atlantic: The Strategic Naval Campaign that Won World War II in Europe.* Minneapolis : Zenith Press. ISBN 978-0-7603-3991-6
- **Cannane, Steve** (2016). *Fair Game: The Incredible Untold Story of Scientology in Australia.* Sydney : Harper Collins. ISBN 978-1-74309-675-8
- **Cowart, Virginia E.** (2006). *Gas Masks & Palm Trees: My Wartime Hawaii.* Victoria, British Columbia : Trafford Publishing. ISBN 978-1-4251-9589-2
- **Cutler, Thomas** (2015). *The U.S. Navy Reserve.* Annapolis, MD : Naval Institute Press. ISBN 978-1-61251-991-3
- **De Camp, L. Sprague** (1976) "El-Ron and the City of Brass", in *Literary Swordsmen and Sorcerers: The Makers of Heroic Fantasy.* Sauk City, WI : Arkham House Publishers. ISBN 0-87054-076-9
- **Dod, Karl C.** (1966) *The Corps of Engineers: The War Against Japan.* Government Printing Office, Washington, D.C. ISBN 978-0160018794

- **Douglass, Darren & Stacey** (1992). *Diving Offshore California.* New York : Aqua Quest Publications. ISBN 978-0-9623389-5-3
- **Dunn, Peter (2006).** Australia at War – Headquarters, U.S. Army Base Section No. 3 – Brisbane Somerville House, APO 923. https://www.ozatwar.com/ozatwar/basesection3.htm
- **Edmonds, Walter D.** (1951). *They Fought With What They Had: The Story of the Army Air Forces in the Southwest Pacific, 1941-1942.* Boston : Little, Brown.
- **Ellsberg, Helen** (1970). *Los Coronados Islands.* Glendale, CA : La Siesta Press.
- **Erickson, Hal** (2012). *Military Comedy Films: A Critical Survey and Filmography of Hollywood Releases Since 1918.* Jefferson, NC : McFarland & Company. ISBN 978-0-7864-6290-2
- **Forty, George** (2006). *US Marine Corps Handbook 1941-1945.* Stroud : Sutton. ISBN 978-0-7509-4196-9
- **Friedman, Norman** (2006). *British Destroyers & Frigates: The Second World War and After.* London : Chatham. ISBN 978-18-617-6137-8
- **Gkotzardis, Evi** (2006). *Trials of Irish History: Genesis and Evolution of a Reappraisal.* London : Routledge. ISBN 978-1-86176-137-8
- **Haines, Gerald K & Langbart, David A.** (1993). *Unlocking the Files of the FBI: A Guide to its Records and Classification System.* Wilmington, DE : Rowman & Littlefield. ISBN 978-0-8420-2338-2
- **Heden, Karl** (2006). *Sunken Ships World War II: US Naval Chronology, Including Submarine Losses of the United States, England, Germany, Japan, Italy*, p. 67. Boston, MA : Branden Books. ISBN 0-8283-2118-3
- **Kehn, Donald M.** (2008). *A Blue Sea of Blood: Deciphering the Mysterious Fate of the USS Edsall.* Minneapolis : MBI Publishing Company. ISBN 978-0-7603-3353-2
- **Lake, Margaret** (2013). "L. Ron Hubbard, the Navy and World War II: Revisited". http://scientologymyths.com/hubbardww2.htm
- **La Du, Robert** (2017). *Her Finest Hour: Shipbuilding in the*

Portland Area during World War II. Page Publishing, Inc. ISBN 978-1-68348-801-9

- **Leighton, Richard M. & Coakley, Robert W.** (1955). *The War Department – Global Logistics And Strategy 1940–1943*. Washington, D.C. : Center of Military History, U.S. Army. ISBN 978-0-16-001901-2
- **Malia, Joseph**. 'Scientology Unmasked'. *Boston Herald*, March 1, 1998
- **Mayo, Lida** (1968). *The Ordnance Department, On Beachhead and Battlefront*. Washington, D.C. : Center of Military History, U.S. Army.
- **Miller, Russell** (1987). *Bare-Faced Messiah*. New York : London : Michael Joseph. ISBN 978-0-7181-2764-0
- **Monsarrat, Nicholas** (1943). HM Corvette. London : Cassell.
- **Nienhuys, Jan Willem** (2003). "Hubbards heldendom". *Skepsis* 16.1. https://skepsis.nl/hubbard
- **Packard, Wyman H. (1996)** A *Century of U.S. Naval Intelligence*. Naval Historical Center, Washington D.C. ISBN 978-0945274254
- **Parascandola, John** (2008). *Sex, Sin, and Science: A History of Syphilis in America*. Westport, CT : Praeger. ISBN 978-0-275-99430-3
- **Patterson Jr., William H.** (2011). *Robert A. Heinlein: In Dialogue with His Century: Volume 1: Learning Curve 1907-1948*. New York : Tom Doherty Associates. ISBN 978-0-7653-1962-3
- **Pendle, George** (2006). *Strange Angel: The Otherworldly Life of Rocket Scientist John Whiteside Parsons*. London : Phoenix. ISBN 978-0-7538-2065-0
- **Price, Bryan** (November 1945). *A Report on the Office of Censorship*. Washington, D.C. : US Government Printing Office.
- **Prouty, Leroy Fletcher** (1973). *The Secret Team: The CIA and Its Allies in Control of the United States and the World*.
- **Reitman, Janet** (2011). *Inside Scientology: The Story of America's Most Secretive Religion*. Boston : Houghton Mifflin Harcourt. ISBN 978-0-547-54923-1

- **Scheina, Robert L.** (1982). *U.S. Coast Guard Cutters & Craft of World War II*. Annapolis : Naval Institute Press. ISBN 0-87021-717-8
- **Segen, J.C.** (2012). *The Dictionary of Modern Medicine*.
- **Sturgeon, Theodore** (1986). *Godbody*. New York : Fine. ISBN 978-0-917657-61-0
- **Takemae Eiji** (2003). *The Allied Occupation of Japan*. New York : London : Continuum. ISBN 978-0-8264-1521-9
- **Underbrink, Robert L.** (1971) *Destination Corregidor*. Annapolis; United States Naval Institute. ISBN 0-87021-142-0
- **Wallace, Schuyler C.** "The Naval School of Military Government and Administration". *The Annals of the American Academy of Political and Social Science*, Vol. 231, Higher Education and the War (Jan., 1944), pp. 29-33
- **Williamson, Jack** (1984). *Wonder's Child: My Life in Science Fiction*. New York : Bluejay Books. ISBN 978-0-312-94454-4
- **Williford, Glen** (2013). *Racing the Sunrise: The Reinforcement of America's Pacific Outposts*, 1941—1942. Annapolis : Naval Institute Press. ISBN 978-1-61251-256-3
- **Womack, Tom** (2015). The Allied Defense of the Malay Barrier, 1941–1942. Jefferson, NC : McFarland & Company. ISBN 978-1-4766-2267-5
- **Wright, Lawrence** (February 14 & 21, 2011). "The Apostate". *The New Yorker*. http://www.newyorker.com/magazine/2011/02/14/the-apostate-lawrence-wright
- **Wright, Lawrence** (2013). *Going Clear: Scientology, Hollywood and the Prison of Belief*. New York : Alfred A. Knopf. ISBN 978-03-077-0066-7
- *Annual Report of the Surgeon General, U.S. Navy* (1942). Washington, D.C. : U.S. Government Printing Office
- *German, Italian and Japanese U-Boat Casualties during the War: Particulars of Destruction*. Command Paper 6843. HM Admiralty. (London, June 1946). London: His Majesty's Stationary Office
- *Glossary of U.S. Naval Abbreviations* (OPNAV 29 P1000). Fifth Edition (revised April 1949). Washington, D.C. : Office of Naval

Records and History, Office of the Chief of Naval Operations, Navy Department

- *Japanese Naval and Merchant Shipping Losses during World War II by All Causes* (February 1947). United States Joint Army-Navy Assessment Committee. Washington, D.C. : U.S. Government Printing Office
- "Ex-Portlander Hunts U-Boats – Guides New 'Hell Howler'". *Oregon Journal*, April 22, 1943
- CBS News (December 22, 1985). *60 Minutes* – "Scientology".

Index

233

235

Notes

Introduction

1   Janet Reitman (2011). *Inside Scientology: The Story of America's Most Secretive Religion*, p. 9

2   Lawrence Wright (2013). *Going Clear: Scientology, Hollywood and the Prison of Belief*, p. 350

3   Evi Gkotzardis (2006). *Trials of Irish History: Genesis and Evolution of a Reappraisal*, p. 207

Chapter 1: Scientology's account

1   Quoted in L. Ron Hubbard Library (2012), *Ron: Master Mariner – At The Helm Across Seven Seas*, p. 83

2   L. Ron Hubbard Library (1997). *Ron – Letters and Journals..* http://legacyimgs.lronhubbard.org/eng/journal/page38.htm

3   Hubbard, "Search for Research" (undated, 1930s) – http://writer.lronhubbard.org/page51.htm

4   *A Brief Biography of L. Ron Hubbard. Ability* magazine, Church of Scientology Washington, D.C. Issue 111, January 1959.

5   Bridge Publications (1992). *What Is Scientology?*, p. 119

6   Hubbard, "Political Dianetics", lecture of September 5, 1940

7   L. Ron Hubbard Library (2012). *Ron: Adventurer/Explorer – Daring Deeds & Unknown Realms*, p. 100 http://adventurer.lronhubbard.org/page59.htm

8   Hubbard, "Autobiographical notes for Peter Tompkins", June 6, 1972

9   Bridge Publications (1996). *Master Mariner: At the Helm Across Seven Seas*

10 L. Ron Hubbard Library (1996). *L Ron Hubbard – Master Mariner/Yachtsman.* http://legacyimgs.lronhubbard.org/yachtsmn/voyage8.htm

11 Church of Scientology of California (1978). *What Is Scientology?*, p. 122

12 L. Ron Hubbard Library (2012). *Ron: Freedom Fighter – Articles and Essays*, p. 2

13 "Military & War". Galaxy Press.
   http://galaxypress.com/books/military-war/

14 *Church of Scientology v. Armstrong*, 21 May 1984; also Dan
   Sherman, LRH Biographer, quoted in *Freedom* magazine, Spring
   1997

15 "Insight into a Remarkable Life". *Freedom* magazine, 1996.
   http://www.freedommag.org/english/la/issue01/page18.htm

16 L. Ron Hubbard Library (1990). *L. Ron Hubbard – A Chronicle*

17 L. Ron Hubbard Library (1995). *L. Ron Hubbard: A Profile*, p. 106

18 L. Ron Hubbard Library (1996). *L. Ron Hubbard: The Poet/Lyricist*.

19 Thomas Moulton testimony, Church of Scientology v. Armstrong,
   May 31, 1984.
   http://www.gerryarmstrong.org/50k/legal/a1/5131.php

20 *L. Ron Hubbard: The Poet/Lyricist*, op. cit.

21 John W. Campbell, letter to Robert Heinlein (May 13, 1942)

22 Hubbard, "The Story of Dianetics & Scientology", taped lecture of
   October 18, 1958

23 L. Ron Hubbard Library (2012). *Ron: Humanitarian – Restoring
   Honor and Self-Respect*, p. 10.
   http://legacyimgs.lronhubbard.org/human/respect3.htm

24 *An interview granted to the Australian Press on January 10th
   1963 at Saint Hill Manor... by L. Ron Hubbard.* Founding Church
   of Scientology press release, November 30, 1963.

25 Hubbard (1973). *Mission into Time,* p. 10

26 A.E. van Vogt, interview with Russell Miller, July 22, 1986.

27 *L. Ron Hubbard: The Poet/Lyricist*, op. cit.

28 Hubbard (1958), "The Story of Dianetics & Scientology"

29 *A Brief Biography of L. Ron Hubbard*, op. cit

30 "A Short Biography of L. Ron Hubbard", *The Auditor* magazine,
   issue 63

31 "L. Ron Hubbard: Educator – An Introduction". Applied
   Scholastics. http://www.appliedscholastics.org/l-ron-
   hubbard.html

32 "Who Was L. Ron Hubbard?" Church of Scientology
   International. http://www.scientology.org.uk/faq/scientology-
   founder/who-was-lronhubbard.html

33 *L. Ron Hubbard: The Humanitarian,* op. cit.

34 *Ron The Poet/Lyricist,* op. cit.

35 "Facts About L. Ron Hubbard – Things You Should Know", Flag Divisional Directive 69RA of 8 March 1974, revised 7 April 1974

36 *Ron The Poet/Lyricist,* op. cit.

37 *L. Ron Hubbard – A Chronicle,* 1990; *Ron The Poet/Lyricist,* 1996; "L. Ron Hubbard as a Naval Officer", factsheet circulated by Church of Scientology in the 1990s

38 *L. Ron Hubbard – A Chronicle,* op. cit.

39 L. Ron Hubbard Library (2012). *L. Ron Hubbard – Humanitarian : Education, Literacy & Civilization.* http://education.lronhubbard.org/page14.htm

40 Church of Scientology World-Wide Public Relations Bureau (1969). *A Report to Members of Parliament on Scientology*

41 *L. Ron Hubbard – A Chronicle,* op. cit.

42 Hubbard (October 18, 1958). "The Story of Dianetics & Scientology"

43 *L. Ron Hubbard: Master Mariner/Yachtsman,* 1996

44 Bridge Publications (1996). *L. Ron Hubbard – Images of a Lifetime,* p. 103

45 *A Brief Biography of L. Ron Hubbard,* 1960; also Hubbard, "Autobiographical notes for Peter Tompkins", 6 June 1972

46 *A Report to Members of Parliament on Scientology,* op. cit.

47 *Who's Who in the South and Southwest,* ca. 1963 – entry on Hubbard; also *L. Ron Hubbard – A Chronicle,* 1990

48 *Ron The Humanitarian,* 1996

49 Jack Williamson (1984). *Wonder's Child: My Life in Science Fiction,* p. 185

50 *A Report to Members of Parliament on Scientology,* 1968

51 L. Ron Hubbard Library (2012). *Ron: Freedom Fighter – Articles and Essays,* p. 2

52 Letter to Hubbard family, quoted by L. Ron Hubbard Jr. in letter of 26 January 1973

53 Church of Scientology v. Armstrong, 21 May 1984; also *Ron – Letters and Journals,* 1997

54 L. Ron Hubbard Library (1997). *Ron – Letters and Journals*

55 "A Glimpse into the Life of L. Ron Hubbard". *Freedom* magazine (1997). http://www.freedom.org.uk/mag/issuea01/page04c.htm

56 Hubbard (1968 ed.) *A History of Man*

57 Hubbard (1965) *"My Philosophy"*

58 Hubbard (1973). *Mission into Time*, p. 11

59 Hubbard (1980), *Research & Discovery Series* vol. 1, pp. 695-6

60 Hubbard (1979 ed.) *All About Radiation*

61 Church of Scientology of California (1978). *What Is Scientology?*, p. 324

62 Hubbard (1968 ed.) *A History of Man*

63 Hubbard, *"My Philosophy"*, 1965

64 Bridge Publications (1996). *L. Ron Hubbard – Images of a Lifetime*, p. 104

65 *Facts About L. Ron Hubbard – Things You Should Know*, 1974

66 Flag Operations Liaison Memo of May 28, 1974

67 Church of Scientology International (1994). *The Church of Scientology: 40th Anniversary*

68 "Who Was L. Ron Hubbard?" Church of Scientology International. http://www.scientology.org.uk/faq/scientology-founder/who-was-lronhubbard.html

69 Bridge Publications (1992). *What Is Scientology?*

70 *FSM* magazine, vol. 1 no. 1, 1968.

71 Cooper, quoted in Atack (1990), *A Piece of Blue Sky*, pp. 45-6

72 Shannon, quoted in Atack, p. 46

73 Note to Mr. Showalter, May 5, 1980

74 Russell Miller (1987). *Bare-Faced Messiah*, p. 5

75 *Ibid.* pp. 370–371

Chapter 3: Ron the Warrior

1 US Navy, summary service record of Harry Ross Hubbard (September 6, 1979)

2 *Ibid.*, p. 42

3 Miller (1987). *Bare-Faced Messiah*, p. 33

4 "Statement of Prior Service", 9 October 1943. US Navy.

5 Hubbard, "Statement concerning age error on both Mont. N.G. and FMCR enlistment papers". Notarized declaration of April 26, 1941.

6   DIS-16 work sheet. US Navy, 16 December 1949.

7   L. Ron Hubbard Library (1997). *Ron – Letters and Journals.*. http://legacyimgs.lronhubbard.org/eng/journal/page38.htm

8   George Forty (2006). *US Marine Corps Handbook 1941-1945*

9   "RE: HUBBARD, Ronald". Memorandum of April 22, 1941.

10 Hubbard, "Statement concerning age error on both Mont. N.G. and FMCR enlistment papers". Notarized declaration of April 26, 1941.

11 US Marine Corps Reserve, Service Record of Lafayette Ronald Hubbard.

12 Hubbard, "Statement concerning age error on both Mont. N.G. and FMCR enlistment papers". Notarized declaration of April 26, 1941.

13 Atack (1990). *A Piece of Blue Sky*, p. 57

14 Lawrence Wright (2013). *Going Clear*, p. 34.

15 Hubbard, "Motion and Emotion", lecture of August 16, 1951

16 L. Ron Hubbard Library (1997). *Ron: Letters and Journals*, http://legacyimgs.lronhubbard.org/eng/journal/page56.htm

17 Hubbard, letter to US Marine Corps, July 18, 1931

18 L. Cronmiller Jr. "To Whom It May Concern". Letter of 23 October 1941.

19 DIS-16 work sheet. US Navy, 16 December 1949.

20 Hubbard, letter to the Army Air Corps, September 1, 1939. The officer he mentioned may have been James F. Moriarity, who had been awarded two Silver Stars during World War I and went on to serve with distinction in World War II.

21 Hubbard, "Search for Research" (undated, 1930s) – http://writer.lronhubbard.org/page51.htm

22 Hubbard, "He Walked To War". *Adventure*, October 1, 1935

23 "Military & War". Galaxy Press. http://galaxypress.com/books/military-war/

24 Hubbard, *Adventure*, April 1936

25 Miller (1987). *Bare-Faced Messiah*, p. 84

26 He did eventually become a member of the Explorers' Club, but only in February 1940.

27 Hubbard, letter to the Secretary of the War Department, September 1, 1939

28 Miller (1987). *Bare-Faced Messiah*, p. 88

29 L. Ron Hubbard Library (2012). *Ron: Poet/Lyricist – The Aesthetics of Verse*, p. 95

30 L. Ron Hubbard Library (2012). *Ron: Adventurer/Explorer – Daring Deeds & Unknown Realms*, p. 100
http://adventurer.lronhubbard.org/page59.htm

31 Miller (1987). *Bare-Faced Messiah*, pp. 89-91

32 *Ibid*. pp. 90, 93

33 L. Ron Hubbard Library (1996). *L Ron Hubbard – Master Mariner/Yachtsman.*
http://legacyimgs.lronhubbard.org/yachtsmn/voyage8.htm

34 Louis Brown (1999). *Technical and Military Imperatives: A Radar History of World War 2*, p. 430

35 Hubbard, "Introduction to 9th ACC: Havingness", lecture of December 6, 1954

36 U.S. Government Printing Office (1939). *The Code of Federal Regulations of the United States of America*, p. 1743

37 Miller (1987). *Bare-Faced Messiah,* pp. 90–91

38 Letter from Jimmy Britton, KGBU Radio, March 15, 1941

39 Letter from Cdr W.E. McCain, March 25, 1941

40 Russell Miller interview with Robert MacDonald Ford, Olympia, Washington, September 1, 1986

41 Letter from Rep. Robert M. Ford (written by L. Ron Hubbard), May 1, 1941

42 Miller (1987). *Bare-Faced Messiah*, p. 92

43 Letter from Sen. Warren G. Magnuson, April 8, 1941

44 Letter from Prof. Arthur F. Johnson and records of interviews with Prof. Johnson and Prof. Douglas Bement

45 Quoted in Atack (1990), *A Piece of Blue Sky*, p. 69

46 Memo from Cdr Lucius C. Dunn, June 4, 1941

47 Hubbard, "Political Dianetics", lecture of September 5, 1940

48 Letter from Senator Pat McCarran to L. Ron Hubbard, June 30, 1941

49 L. Ron Hubbard Library (1996). *L. Ron Hubbard: Adventurer*.
http://adventurer.lronhubbard.org/page59.htm

50 Endorsement by Geo. Pettengill, June 10, 1941

51 Articles of Commission for Lt. (jg) L. Ron Hubbard, July 2, 1941

Chapter 4: Ron the Intelligence Officer

1   L. Ron Hubbard Library (1996). *Ron The Poet/Lyricist*
2   Memorandum for Reserve Section, Office of Naval Intelligence, Navy Department. April 21, 1941.
3   *Glossary of U.S. Naval Abbreviations, OPNAV 29 P1000.* Fifth Edition (revised April 1949). Office of Naval Records and History, Office of the Chief of Naval Operations, Navy Department, Washington, DC
4   Memo from Cdr. Lucius C. Dunn, June 4, 1941
5   Wright (2013). *Going Clear*, p. 26
6   Miller (1987). *Bare-Faced Messiah*, p. 74
7   *United States Naval Institute Proceedings*, Volume 65 (1939), p. 471
8   *Ibid.*, p. 96
9   *Ibid.*
10 Memorandum for the Assistant Hydrographer, October 22, 1941
11 Hubbard, "Autobiographical notes for Peter Tompkins", June 6, 1972
12 Name and Subject Index to the General Correspondence to the Secretary of the Navy, 1930-1942 (also includes Office of Chief of Naval Operations, Microfilm Publication M1067, United States National Archives
13 Patterson Jr., William H. (2011). *Robert A. Heinlein: In Dialogue with His Century: Volume 1: Learning Curve 1907-1948*, p. 409
14 Wyman H. Packard (1996), *A Century of U.S. Naval Intelligence*, p. 302.
15 "Active duty with full pay and allowances". Memo of November 19, 1941.
16 "L. Ron Hubbard Discusses The Development of His Philosophy". Interview with Dr. Stillson Judah, November 1958. http://www.ronthephilosopher.org/phlspher/page40.htm
17 Hubbard, "Miracles in Dianetics", lecture of December 27, 1951.

Chapter 5: Ron the Saviour of Australia

1   Hubbard, "The Melbourne Enquiry into Scientology", Executive Letter of 6 October 1965
2   Hubbard, "Ron's Journal 1968 Australian – Anzo Supplement for issue at tape play BP", Information Letter of 17 February 1969

3   Richard M. Leighton & Robert W. Coakley (1995). *The War Department – Global Logistics And Strategy 1940–1943. United States Army in World War II*, p. 150; Glen Williford (2010). *Racing the Sunrise — Reinforcing America's Pacific Outposts 1941—1942*, p. 257

4   *An interview granted to the Australian Press on January 10th 1963 at Saint Hill Manor... by L. Ron Hubbard.* Founding Church of Scientology press release, November 30, 1963.

5   Hubbard, "Welcome Address", lecture of November 7, 1959

6   Karl C. Dod (1966), *The Corps of Engineers: The War Against Japan*, p. 112

7   Underbrook, pp. 32-33

8   *Ibid.*

9   *Ibid.*

10 Hubbard, "Welcome Address"

11 Hubbard, "The Key Words (Buttons) of Scientology Clearing – Question and Answer Period", lecture of July 21, 1958

12 Memorandum of June 28, 1943

13 Hubbard, "Definition of Organization, Part I", lecture of November 8, 1956

14 Robert L. Scheina (1982). *U.S. Coast Guard Cutters & Craft of World War II*, p. 44.

15 "USS Chicago (CA-29)". *Dictionary of American Naval Fighting Ships*. Office of Naval Records and History, Office of the Chief of Naval Operations, Navy Department, Washington, DC

16 Peter Dunn, Australia at War – Headquarters, U.S. Army Base Section No. 3 – Brisbane Somerville House, APO 923. https://www.ozatwar.com/ozatwar/basesection3.htm

17 L. Ron Hubbard Library (1996) *L. Ron Hubbard: The Poet/Lyricist.* http://www.ronthepoet.org/poet/thewar1.htm

18 Robert L. Underbrook (1971). *Destination Corregidor*, p. 22

19 Underbrook, pp. 32-33

20 L. Ron Hubbard, "Subject: Intelligence report". February 5, 1942

21 Lida Mayo (1968). *United States Army in World War 2, The Technical Services. The Ordnance Department, On Beachhead and Battlefront*, p. 37.

22 Glen M. Williford (2013). *Racing the Sunrise: The Reinforcement of America's Pacific Outposts, 1941-1942.*

23 L. Ron Hubbard, "Subject: Intelligence report". February 5, 1942

24 "View Shipwreck – Don Isidro USAT" . Australian National Shipwreck Database. http://archive.is/20130630205048/https://apps5a.ris.environm ent.gov.au/shipwreck/public/wreck/wreck.do;jsessionid=374975 75AB67A73C9AD1EB2CF67BE955?key=3424&action=expandAll

25 L. Ron Hubbard, "Subject: Intelligence report". February 5, 1942

26 Underbrook, p. 67

27 *Ibid.*

28 *Ibid.*

29 Memo from US Naval Attaché Australia to Commandant 12th Naval District, February 14, 1942

30 Atack (1990). *A Piece of Blue Sky*, p. 72

31 Telegram from US Naval Attaché Australia, February 17, 1942

32 Lawrence Wright (2013). *Going Clear*, p. 35.

33 Jon Atack (1990). *A Piece of Blue Sky*, p. 73.

34 Russell Miller (1987). *Bare-Faced Messiah*, p. 98.

35 Walter D. Edmonds (1951). *They Fought With What They Had: The Story of the Army Air Forces in the Southwest Pacific, 1941-1942*, p. 377.

36 Underbrook, pp. 32-33

37 Lida Mayo (1968). *United States Army in World War 2, The Technical Services. The Ordnance Department, On Beachhead and Battlefront*, p. 37.

38 Government of the Northern Territory (2016) "Territory Remembers – USAT *Don Isidro*". http://www.territoryremembers.nt.gov.au/history/don-isidro

39 Glen Williford (2010). *Racing the Sunrise—Reinforcing America's Pacific Outposts 1941—1942*, p. 257

40 *Ibid.*

41 Underbrook, p. 122

42 *Ibid.*, p. 123

43 Hubbard, "The Key Words (Buttons) of Scientology Clearing – Question and Answer Period", lecture of July 21, 1958

44 *Ibid.*

45 War Diary – USS *New Orleans*, March 1943

46 "Lieutenant L.R. Hubbard, USN, non-payment of bills." Office of United States Naval Observer, Brisbane to Bureau of Navigation, Washington. April 9, 1942

47 Paul S. Slawson Navy service records, National Personnel Records Center (NPRC), St. Louis, MO.

48 Tom Womack (2015). *The Allied Defense of the Malay Barrier, 1941–1942*, p. 28.

49 Hubbard, "The Key Words (Buttons) of Scientology Clearing – Question and Answer Period", lecture of July 21, 1958

50 *An interview granted to the Australian Press on January 10th 1963 at Saint Hill Manor... by L. Ron Hubbard.* Founding Church of Scientology press release, November 30, 1963.

51 Hubbard (1973). *Mission into Time*, p. 10

52 Hubbard, "The Key Words (Buttons) of Scientology Clearing – Question and Answer Period", lecture of July 21, 1958

53 Scientology.org, "Melbourne Congress". https://www.scientology.org/store/item/melbourne-congress-lectures.html

54 "Lieutenant L.R. Hubbard, USN, non-payment of bills." Office of United States Naval Observer, Brisbane to Bureau of Navigation, Washington. April 9, 1942

55 *Ibid.*

56 "Soldiers in Bunks on Army Transport, S.S. Pennant". The World War II Multimedia Database. http://worldwar2database.com/gallery/wwii1035

57 L. Ron Hubbard medical assessment report, December 11, 1947

58 War Diary – USS *New Orleans*, March 1943

59 Miller (1987). *Bare-Faced Messiah*, p. 87

60 *Ibid*, p. 180

61 *Ibid*, p. 221

62 War Diary – USS *New Orleans*, March 1943

63 Hubbard, "The Story of Dianetics and Scientology"

64 Hubbard, "The Game of Life (Exteriorization and Havingness)", lecture of February 7, 1956

65 Hubbard, "Definition of Organization, Part I", lecture of November 8, 1956

66 "Form H-8 Medical History – Hubbard Lafayette R." Lt Cdr L.K. Gay, March 23, 1942.

67 "Index to Vessels Arriving in San Francisco, 1882-1957", Microfilm Publication no. M1437, Record Group 85. United States National Archives.

68 "Form H-8 Medical History – Hubbard Lafayette R." Lt Cdr L.K. Gay, March 23, 1942.

69 *Segen's Medical Dictionary* (2012)

70 "Accurate Diagnosis of Influenza and Acute Catarrhal Fever", Krueger A.P. et al. *U.S. Naval Medical Bulletin*, Vol. 42 (1944).

71 *Annual Report of the Surgeon General, U.S. Navy*, p. 111 (1942)

72 Atack (1990). *A Piece of Blue Sky*, p. 73

73 *Ibid.*

74 Hubbard, "The Key Words (Buttons) of Scientology Clearing – Question and Answer Period", lecture of July 21, 1958

75 Hubbard, "Safeguarding Dianetics", lecture of June 28, 1951

76 Hubbard, "Cause and Effect: Full Responsibility", lecture of December 3, 1951

77 *Ibid.*

78 "L. Ron Hubbard Discusses The Development of His Philosophy". Interview with Dr. Stillson Judah, November 1958. http://www.ronthephilosopher.org/phlspher/page40.htm

79 Hubbard, "The Game of Life (Exteriorization and Havingness)", lecture of February 7, 1956

80 John W. Campbell, letter to Robert Heinlein (May 13, 1942)

81 Report on the Fitness of Officers, L. Ron Hubbard #113392, May 11 1942 – June 24 1942. Dated June 29, 1942.

82 "[D]eck officers, commissioned and warrant, including boatswains and ship's clerks, qualified for specialist duties."– *Glossary of U.S. Naval Abbreviations, OPNAV 29 P1000* (April 1949)

83 Hubbard (February 17, 1966). "LRH Conference with the Investigators".

84 Gerald K. Haines, David A. Langbart. (1993). *Unlocking the Files*

of the FBI: A Guide to its Records and Classification System, p. 18.

85 Hubbard, "Withholds and In-session-ness", lecture of January 24, 1961

86 Hubbard (February 17, 1966). "LRH Conference with the Investigators"

87 Bryan Price (November 1945). *A Report on the Office of Censorship,* p. 11.

88 *Ibid.*, p. 45

89 Report on the Fitness of Officers, L. Ron Hubbard #113392, May 11 1942 – June 24 1942. Dated June 29, 1942.

90 Hubbard, "Sea duty, request for". Memo to Chief Censor, June 10, 1942

91 Bryan Price, *A Report on the Office of Censorship*. November 1945.

92 Fenn, H.K. "Lieut. (jg) LaFayette Ronald Hubbard, D-V(S), USNR – Sea duty training request for". Memo of June 20, 1942

93 Letter from First National Bank of Ketchikan to US Navy, August 20, 1942

94 Letter from Hubbard to First National Bank of Ketchikan, October 28, 1942

95 Naval Message PERS-33-RAY 49009, June 22 1942

Chapter 6: Ron in the Atlantic

1 Thomas Cutler (2015). *The U.S. Navy Reserve*, p. 79

2 John R. Bruning (2013). *Battle for the North Atlantic: The Strategic Naval Campaign that Won World War II in Europe*, p. 186

3 Cutler (2015), *ibid.*

4 Anthony Bruce (2014). "Corvette." *Encyclopedia of Naval History*, p. 90

5 NavSource Online – USS *YP-422*. http://www.navsource.org/archives/14/31422.htm

6 L. Ron Hubbard Library (1996). *L. Ron Hubbard: The Humanitarian*

7 *L. Ron Hub*bard Library (1996). *Ron The Poet/Lyricist*

8 Mailgram from Comdt 1st Navdist, July 29, 1942

9   Joseph Malia (March 1, 1998). 'Scientology Unmasked'. *Boston Herald*

10 "Correction of False Reports in 'Scientology Unmasked', *Boston Sunday Herald* March 1, 1998" – statement by Church of Scientology, March 1998

11 Report on the Fitness of Officers, L. Ron Hubbard #113392, June 25 1942 – July 28 1942. Dated September 5, 1942.

12 Hubbard, "Affirmations". Undated, circa 1946. http://scientology-research.org/the-admissions-of-l-ron-hubbard/

13 Miller (1987). *Bare-Faced Messiah*, p. 99

14 *Ibid.*

15 *Ibid.*

16 Cable from Commandant Boston Yard, September 25, 1942

17 Telegram from Hubbard, September 25, 1942

18 Memorandum of October 1, 1942

19 L. Ron Hubbard Library (2012). *Ron: Humanitarian – Restoring Honor and Self-Respect*, p. 10

20 Hubbard, "Withholds and In-session-ness", lecture of January 24, 1961

21 USS *YP-422* Muster Rolls, September 30, 1942

22 L. Ron Hubbard Library (2012). *Ron: Humanitarian – Restoring Honor and Self-Respect*, p. 10.
    http://legacyimgs.lronhubbard.org/human/respect3.htm

23 Hubbard, "Space", lecture of April 29, 1954

24 War Diary of Commander Destroyer Squadron Five, entries for April 24 & 25, 1943

25 CINCPAC war diary, Operations – Daily Summary, June 13, 1944

26 Memorandum of October 8, 1942

27 Memorandum of October 9, 1942

28 Hubbard, "Agreements and Postulates of the Eight Dynamics", lecture of January 8, 1957

29 Hubbard, "Study: Evaluation of Information", lecture of August 11, 1964

30 Thomas Moulton testimony, Church of Scientology v. Armstrong, May 31, 1984.
    http://www.gerryarmstrong.org/50k/legal/a1/5131.php

31 Cutler (2015), pp. 76-8

32 Report on the Fitness of Officers – Hubbard, LaFayette Ronald. Nov 9, 1942 to Jan 1, 1943. Dated January 25, 1943

33 Hubbard, "Affirmations". Undated, circa 1946. http://scientology-research.org/the-admissions-of-l-ron-hubbard/

34 John Parascandola (2008). *Sex, Sin, and Science: A History of Syphilis in America*, p. 107

35 Hubbard, "Routine 1A-Problems", lecture of July 3, 1961

Chapter 7: Ron the Sub Hunter

1 Order from Chief of Naval Personnel assigning Hubbard to duty aboard *USS PC-815*, January 19, 1943

2 Robert La Du (2017). *Her Finest Hour: Shipbuilding in the Portland Area during World War II*. Page Publishing, Inc.

3 *The Log*, Vol. 38, 1943, p. 105

4 Ship Building History – Albina Engine & Machine Works, Portland OR. http://shipbuildinghistory.com/shipyards/large/albina.htm

5 Thomas Moulton testimony, Church of Scientology v. Armstrong, May 31, 1984. http://www.gerryarmstrong.org/50k/legal/a1/5131.php

6 Report on the Fitness of Officers – Lafayette Ronald Hubbard 113392. May 29, 1943 – July 7, 1943

7 Hubbard, "E-Meter Talk and Demo", lecture of May 7, 1961

8 Ship Building History – Albina Engine & Machine Works, Portland OR. http://shipbuildinghistory.com/shipyards/large/albina.htm

9 Nicholas Monsarrat (1943). *HM Corvette*, p. 16

10 Memo from Chief of Naval Personnel concerning Hubbard's indebtedness, February 5, 1943

11 Thomas Moulton testimony, Church of Scientology v. Armstrong, May 31, 1984. http://www.gerryarmstrong.org/50k/legal/a1/5131.php

12 Report on the Fitness of Officers, L. Ron Hubbard #113392, January 15, 1943 – April 20, 1943

13 *Oregon Journal*, April 22, 1943

14 "A Short Biography of L. Ron Hubbard", *The Auditor* magazine, issue 63

15 "Scientology Founder L. Ron Hubbard", Church of Scientology video published on July 19, 2011

16 L. Ron Hubbard Library (1997). *Ron The Poet/Lyricist*; original claim made in Hubbard lecture of 1958, "The Story of Dianetics and Scientology"

17 Hubbard, "Welcome Address"

18 Hubbard, "Space", lecture of April 29, 1954

19 Hubbard, "Orders – request for". Memorandum of October 19, 1943

20 Hubbard, "Auditing Techniques: Games Conditions", lecture of February 1, 1957

21 Norman Friedman (2006). *British Destroyers & Frigates: The Second World War and After*, p. 132

22 Quoted in Clay Blair (2010). *Hitler's U-Boat War: The Hunters 1939-1942.*

23 Lance E. Davis, Stanley L. Engerman (2006). *Naval Blockades in Peace and War: An Economic History since 1750.*

24 The three submarines sunk by US Navy PC-class subchasers were: *U-521* (German) by USS *PC-565*, off the US Atlantic coast, 2 June 1943; *I.9* (Japanese) by USS *PC-487*, off the Aleutian Islands, Pacific Ocean, 10 June 1943; *U-375* (German) by USS *PC-624*, in the Mediterranean, off Tunisia, 30 July 1943. Source: Command Paper 6843 (June 1946). *German, Italian and Japanese U-Boat Casualties during the War.*

Chapter 8: Ron's Battle

1   War Diary, Fleet Airship Wing 31. Entry for May 19, 1943.

2   *Ibid.*

3   *Ibid.*

4   Hubbard, "Auditing Techniques: Games Conditions", lecture of February 1, 1957

5   War Diary, Fleet Airship Wing 31. Entry for May 19, 1943.

6   *Ibid.*

7   *Ibid.*

8   *Ibid.*

9   *Ibid.*

10   Hubbard, "Auditing Techniques: Games Conditions", lecture of February 1, 1957

11   Thomas Moulton testimony, Church of Scientology v. Armstrong, May 31, 1984.
     http://www.gerryarmstrong.org/50k/legal/a1/5131.php

12   *Ibid.*

13   *Ibid.*

14   Memorandum from Commander North-West Sea Frontier to CINCPAC, June 8, 1943

15   Hubbard, of unknown date; quoted in *Ron The Poet/Lyricist* (1996)

Chapter 9: The Mystery of the Missing Submarines

1   Nicholas Monsarrat (1943), *HM Corvette*, p. 80

2   *Ibid.*, p. 153

3   Thomas Moulton testimony, Church of Scientology v. Armstrong, May 31, 1984.
     http://www.gerryarmstrong.org/50k/legal/a1/5131.php

4   *German, Italian and Japanese U-Boat Casualties during the War: Particulars of Destruction*, Command Paper 6843 (London, June 1946*); Japanese Naval and Merchant Shipping Losses during World War II by All Causes* (Washington, DC, February 1947)

5   This was the *RO.35*, lost sometime during June 1942. Its cause of sinking was described as an "operational accident" but where and when this happened was not determined by the Allies in their contemporary reports. According to Lt. Cdr. Shizuo Fukui of the Imperial Japanese Navy, the *RO.35* was sunk in October 1943 in the Solomon Islands.

6   Karl Heden (2006). *Sunken Ships World War II: US Naval Chronology, Including Submarine Losses of the United States, England, Germany, Japan, Italy*, p. 67

7   A group called the Oregon Coast Project (not associated with the Scientologists, but motivated by a former crewman on the USS

SC-536) has been trying since 2007 to prove the existence of the supposed submarines. Despite carrying out sonar surveys and dives it has yet to find anything.
https://www.facebook.com/Oregon-Coast-Project-258560794346933/ .

8   Thomas Moulton testimony, Church of Scientology v. Armstrong, May 31, 1984,
http://www.gerryarmstrong.org/50k/legal/a1/5131.php

9   "Correction of False Reports in 'Scientology Unmasked', *Boston Sunday Herald* March 1, 1998" – statement by Church of Scientology, March 1998

Chapter 10: The Coronados Affair

1   Darren & Stacey Douglass (1992), *Diving Offshore California*, p. 26; Helen Ellsberg (1970), *Los Coronados Islands*, p. 11

2   Transcript of Board of Investigation on the circumstances attending the firing of 3 shots from the USS *PC-815*, 30 June-3 July 1943

3   *Ibid.*

4   *Ibid.*

5   *Ibid.*

6   Letter of admonition to Lt L. Ron Hubbard, Rear Adm F.A. Braisted, July 15, 1943

7   USS *Laffey* (DD724), War Diary for September 1945 (October 24, 1945)

8   COMNOWESTSEAFRON War Diary, entry for September 11, 1945

9   Virginia E. Cowart (2006). *Gas Masks & Palm Trees: My Wartime Hawaii.*

10 Report on the Fitness of Officers – Lafayette Ronald Hubbard 113392. 29 May 1943-7 July 1943

11 Hubbard, "Affirmations". Undated, circa 1946.
http://scientology-research.org/the-admissions-of-l-ron-hubbard/

Chapter 11: "Mister Roberts" and the USS *Algol*

1   Notification of Hubbard's hospitalization with "diagnosis 371" (duodenal ulcer), 24 July 1943

2   Hubbard, "Affirmations". Undated, circa 1946. http://scientology-research.org/the-admissions-of-l-ron-hubbard/

3   *Ibid.*

4   *Ibid.*

5   Autobiographical notes for Peter Tompkins, 6 June 1972

6   Letter from L. Ron Hubbard Jr., 26 January 1973

7   Hubbard, "Flows: Characteristics of", lecture of December 9, 1952

8   *Ibid.*

9   L. Ron Hubbard Library (2012). *Ron: Humanitarian – Education, Literacy & Civilization*, p. 16. http://education.lronhubbard.org/page14.htm

10 Report on the Fitness of Officers – Lafayette Ronald Hubbard 113392. 29 May 1943-7 July 1943

11 Letter from Hubbard to Chief of Naval Personnel, October 19, 1943

12 Hubbard request for sea duty, 19 October 1943

13 Report on the Fitness of Officers – Lafayette Ronald Hubbard 113392. 29 May 1943-7 July 1943

14 Response from Rear Admiral Braisted, 10 November 1943

15 L. Ron Hubbard notice of posting to USS *Algol*, 25 November 1943

16 Hubbard, of unknown date – see *Ron the Writer* (1989)

17 L. Ron Hubbard Library (1996). *L. Ron Hubbard: Master Mariner/Yachtsman.*

18 Hubbard, "Obnosis", lecture of January 9, 1957

19 L. Ron Hubbard Fitness Report, 21 July 1944 – 28 September 1944

20 Deck Log, USS *Algol*, September 27, 1944

21 L. Ron Hubbard Library (2012). *Ron: Freedom Fighter – Articles and Essays, p. 76.* http://freedom.lronhubbard.org/page041.htm

22 Church of Scientology (1997). "Merchants of Sensationalism: The *Boston Herald* Exposed".

23 Hubbard, "The Game of Life (Exteriorization and Havingness)", lecture of February 7, 1956

24 Hubbard, "Autobiographical notes for Peter Tompkins", 6 June 1972

25 Church of Scientology Washington, D.C. (January 1959). "A Brief Biography of L. Ron Hubbard". *Ability* magazine, Issue 111.

26 Robert Macdonald Ford interview with Russell Miller, September 1, 1986

27 Hal Erickson (2012), *Military Comedy Films: A Critical Survey and Filmography of Hollywood Releases Since 1918*, pp. 160–1

Chapter 12: "Crippled and Blinded"

1   "A Report to Members of Parliament on Scientology", Church of Scientology, 1968

2   Takemae, Eiji (2003). *The Allied Occupation of Japan*, p. 206

3   *Ibid.*

4   Schuyler C. Wallace. "The Naval School of Military Government and Administration". The Annals of the American Academy of Political and Social Science, Vol. 231, Higher Education and the War (Jan., 1944), pp. 29-33

5   L. Ron Hubbard Library (1996). *Ron The Humanitarian*

6   Campbell, letter to Robert Swisher, November 30, 1944

7   Takamae, *ibid.*

8   Hubbard, "Group Dianetics", lecture of November 9, 1950

9   Hubbard, "Civil Defense", lecture of June 27, 1951

10 Robert A. Heinlein, foreword to *Godbody* by Theodore Sturgeon (1986)

11 *Ibid.*

12 L. Sprague de Camp (1976) "El-Ron and the City of Brass", in *Literary Swordsmen and Sorcerers: The Makers of Heroic Fantasy.*

13 Jack Williamson (1984). *Wonder's Child: My Life in Science Fiction*, p. 185

14 Campbell, letter to Robert Swisher, November 30, 1944

15 Hubbard, "Affirmations". Undated, circa 1946

16 Hubbard, "A First Word on Adventure", circa 1945. http://legacyimgs.lronhubbard.org/eng/journal/page10.htm

17 Hubbard, "Communication and Is-ness". Professional Auditor's Bulletin of November 15, 1957

18 "Report on the Fitness of Officers", 28 Sept 1944 – Jan 27 1945

19 Oak Knoll Coalition – Timeline.
http://www.oakknollcoalition.org/timeline/

20 California State Military Museums – Naval Regional Medical Center, Oakland.
http://www.militarymuseum.org/NavHospOakland.html

21 L. Ron Hubbard Library (2012). *Ron: Humanitarian – Restoring Honor and Self-Respect*, p. 29.
http://legacyimgs.lronhubbard.org/human/ethics1.htm

22 Hubbard, "My Philosophy", 1965

23 *L. Ron Hubbard: The Philosopher* (1996),
http://www.ronthephilosopher.org/page82.htm

24 Hubbard, "Special Effect Cases, Anatomy – Q&A Period", lecture of July 23, 1958

25 L. Ron Hubbard Library (1996) *L. Ron Hubbard: The Philosopher*, http://www.ronthephilosopher.org/page40.htm

26 L. Ron Hubbard Library (1997). *Ron – Letters and Journals*

27 *Freedom* magazine (1997). "A Glimpse into the Life of L. Ron Hubbard".
http://www.freedom.org.uk/mag/issuea01/page04c.htm

28 Hubbard, "Affirmations". Undated, circa 1946

29 Hubbard (1958). "The Story of Dianetics and Scientology"

30 Thomas Moulton testimony, Church of Scientology v. Armstrong, May 31, 1984.
http://www.gerryarmstrong.org/50k/legal/a1/5131.php

31 *Ibid.*

32 Report of Medical Survey, 10 September 1945

33 Hubbard (1973). *Mission into Time*, p. 11

34 Church of Scientology (1998). "The People Behind 'Secret Lives'"

35 Hubbard letter of appeal, July 4, 1946

36 *Ibid.*

37 Hubbard, "The Game of Life (Exteriorization and Havingness)", lecture of February 7, 1956

38 *What is Scientology?* 1992 edition – see
http://www.scientology.org/wis/wiseng/wis1-3/wis3_1t.htm

39 Tape-recorded lecture of July 23, 1951, transcribed in Research &

Discovery Series, vol. 6, p.409; HCO Bulletin of November 15, 1957, in *Technical Bulletins of Dianetics & Scientology*, vol. 3, p.146

40 Hubbard, "Basic Programming", lecture of July 23, 1951

41 Notice of Temporary Additional Duty for Lt Lafayette R. HUBBARD, October 6, 1945

42 Medical History – HUBBARD, Lafayette Ronald 113392. Entry for 11-28-45

43 Hubbard, "Introduction to 9th ACC: Havingness", lecture of December 6, 1944.

44 Hubbard, "Affirmations". Undated, circa 1946. http://scientology-research.org/the-admissions-of-l-ron-hubbard/

45 Hubbard, "Autobiographical notes for Peter Tompkins", June 6, 1972

46 Hubbard, "Special Effect Cases, Anatomy – Q&A Period", lecture of July 23, 1958

47 Telegram from L. Ron Hubbard to Chief of Naval Personnel, October 12, 1945

48 Telegram from L. Ron Hubbard to Chief of Naval Personnel, October 13, 1945

49 Air mail letter to Hubbard from BuNavPers, October 19, 1945

50 Hubbard claim for pension, December 6, 1945

51 "Form H-8 Medical History – Hubbard Lafayette R." Lt Cdr L.K. Gay, March 23, 1942.

52 Hubbard medical history, entry for July 15, 1943

53 *Ibid.*

54 *Ibid.*

55 Report of Medical Survey, April 11, 1945

56 *Ibid.*

57 Hubbard medical history, entry for November 28, 1945

58 Hill Gaston JS, Lillicrap MS (2003). "Arthritis associated with enteric infection". *Clinical Rheumatology*. 17 (2): 219–239.

59 Church of Scientology World-Wide Public Relations Bureau (1969). *A Report to Members of Parliament on Scientology*

Chapter 13: Mustering Out

1 Hugh B. Urban, (2014). "The Secrets of Scientology: Concealment, Information Control and Esoteric Knowledge in the World's Most Controversial New Religion", in *Contemporary Esotericism*, p. 186. Eds. Egil Asprem, Kennet Granholm

2 "Promotion Status", letter from Bureau of Navy Personnel, June 25, 1947

3 Hubbard, "The National Academy of American Psychology", lecture of December 31, 1957

4 The Foundation was established June 7, 1950, according to the chronology in James Lewis's *Handbook of Scientology* (2017)

5 Hubbard, "A Postulate out of a Golden Age", lecture of December 6, 1956

6 Hubbard, "How We Have Addressed the Problem of the Mind", lecture of July 4, 1957

7 Church of Scientology of California (1978). *What is Scientology?*

8 Hubbard, letter of November 14, 1947

9 Hubbard, letter of May 27, 1950

Chapter 14: Ron the Veteran

1 Hubbard, "Additional Remarks: Energy Problems", lecture of December 15, 1953

2 Hubbard, letter of appeal, July 4, 1946

3 *Ibid.*

4 Wright (2013). *Going Clear*, p. 43

5 Miller (1987), *Bare-Faced Messiah*, p. 120

6 Letter from Sara Northrup to Veterans Administration, July 4, 1946

7 VA report of physical examination, September 19, 1946

8 Hubbard, "Affirmations". Undated, circa 1946. http://scientology-research.org/the-admissions-of-l-ron-hubbard/

9 Letter from L. Sprague De Camp to Isaac Asimov, August 27, 1946. Quoted in George Pendle (2006). *Strange Angel*, p. 271

10 Robert MacDonald Ford, interview with Channel 4 *Secret Lives*, 1997. https://www.youtube.com/watch?v=xbYCihzzTOU

11 Campbell, letter to Robert Heinlein, March 24, 1953
12 Campbell, letter to Don Purcell, May 18, 1953
13 Heinlein, letter to Hubbard, February 19, 1949
14 Miller (1987). *Bare-Faced Messiah*, p. 175
15 L. Ron Hubbard medical assessment report, December 11, 1947
16 Hubbard, letter of January 27, 1948
17 Hubbard letter to Chief of Naval Personnel, March 28, 1948
18 Telegram from L. Ron Hubbard to Chief of Naval Personnel, October 12, 1945
19 Wright (2013). *Going Clear*, p. 45
20 Wright (2013). *Going Clear*, p. 57; Miller (1987). *Bare-Faced Messiah*, p. 142
21 "Dianetics: Science or Hoax?", *Look* magazine (December 5, 1950)
22 Hubbard, "Running the service facsimile chain", lecture of January 16, 1952
23 Quoted in Atack (1990). *A Piece of Blue Sky*, p. 87

Chapter 15: Ron's Medals
1 "The Church of Scientology: 40th Anniversary". Church of Scientology International (1994)
2 L. Ron Hubbard Notice of Separation, Scientology version
3 Flag Operations Liaison Memo of May 28, 1974
4 Thomas Moulton testimony, Church of Scientology v. Armstrong, May 31, 1984.
   http://www.gerryarmstrong.org/50k/legal/a1/5131.php
5 Hubbard, "E-Meter Talk and Demo", lecture of May 7, 1961
6 Jan Willem Nienhuys, "Hubbards heldendom". *Skepsis* 16.1 (2003). https://skepsis.nl/hubbard
7 Executive Order 9277, *Award of the Purple Heart to Persons Serving with the Navy, Marine Corps or Coast Guard of the United States* (December 3, 1942).
   http://www.presidency.ucsb.edu/ws/?pid=60972
8 Report on the Fitness of Officers, L. Ron Hubbard #113392, June 25 1942 – July 28 1942. Dated September 5, 1942.

Chapter 16: Uncovering the Truth

1   Lawrence Wright, "The Apostate". *The New Yorker*, February 14 & 21, 2011.
    http://www.newyorker.com/magazine/2011/02/14/the-apostate-lawrence-wright

Chapter 17: Ron the Secret Agent?

1   Hubbard, "Affirmations". Undated, circa 1946.
    http://scientology-research.org/the-admissions-of-l-ron-hubbard/
2   Thomas Moulton testimony, Church of Scientology v. Armstrong, May 31, 1984.
    http://www.gerryarmstrong.org/50k/legal/a1/5131.php
3   Thomas Moulton testimony, Church of Scientology v. Armstrong, May 31, 1984.
    http://www.gerryarmstrong.org/50k/legal/a1/5131.php
4   L. Ron Hubbard Library (2012). *Ron: Poet/Lyricist – The Aesthetics of Verse*
    http://www.ronthepoet.org/poet/thewar1.htm
5   *Freedom* magazine (1997). "A Glimpse into the Life of L. Ron Hubbard".
    http://www.freedom.org.uk/mag/issuea01/page04c.htm
6   Hubbard, "Miracles in Dianetics", lecture of December 27, 1951
7   Richard Banyai (1974). *Money and Banking in China and Southeast Asia During the Japanese Military Occupation 1937–1945*, p. 87.
8   Royal Institute of International Affairs (1947) *Chronology and Index of the Second World War*, 1938-1945, p. 112.
9   Donald M. Kehn (2009). *A Blue Sea of Blood: Deciphering the Mysterious Fate of the USS Edsall*
10 Steve Cannane (2016). *Fair Game: The Incredible Untold Story of Scientology in Australia.*
11 Thomas Moulton testimony, Church of Scientology v. Armstrong, May 31, 1984.
    http://www.gerryarmstrong.org/50k/legal/a1/5131.php

12 Margaret Lake (2013). "L. Ron Hubbard, the Navy and World War II: Revisited".
http://scientologymyths.com/hubbardww2.htm

13 Church of Scientology v. Armstrong, May 31, 1984.
http://www.gerryarmstrong.org/50k/legal/a1/5131.php

14   Prouty affidavit (February 1, 1985)

15 CBS News (December 22, 1985). *60 Minutes* – "Scientology".

16 Michael Carson (June 22, 2001). "L. Fletcher Prouty – Obituary", *The Guardian*.
https://www.theguardian.com/news/2001/jun/22/guardianobituaries

17 Leroy Fletcher Prouty (1973). *The Secret Team: The CIA and Its Allies in Control of the United States and the World*, p. 172

18 Elia Abel (1966). *The Missiles of October: The Story of the Cuban Missile Crisis, 1962*, p. 27

19 L. Fletcher Prouty (November 21, 1985). 2nd letter to CBS *60 Minutes*

20 Jon Atack (September 10, 2016). "Laying to rest the obfuscations of L. Fletcher Prouty, Scientology's conspiracist-for-hire". *The Underground Bunker*. http://tonyortega.org/2016/09/10/laying-to-rest-the-obfuscations-of-l-fletcher-prouty-scientologys-conspiracist-for-hire/

21 L. Fletcher Prouty (November 21, 1985). 2nd letter to CBS *60 Minutes*

22 L. Fletcher Prouty (October 4, 1987). Letter to Michael Joseph Ltd

23 Lawrence Wright (June 30, 2017). Personal communication to the author.

24 Lawrence Wright (February 14 & 21, 2011). "The Apostate". *The New Yorker*.
http://www.newyorker.com/magazine/2011/02/14/the-apostate-lawrence-wright

25 *An interview granted to the Australian Press on January 10th 1963 at Saint Hill Manor... by L. Ron Hubbard.* Founding Church of Scientology press release, November 30, 1963.

26 Thomas Moulton testimony, Church of Scientology v. Armstrong, May 31, 1984.
http://www.gerryarmstrong.org/50k/legal/a1/5131.php

27 Hubbard, "Affirmations". Undated, circa 1946.
    http://scientology-research.org/the-admissions-of-l-ron-
    hubbard/
28 Miller (1987). *Bare-Faced Messiah*, p. 67
29 Jack Williamson (1984). *Wonder's Child: My Life in Science
    Fiction*, p. 185
30 Miller (1987). *Bare-Faced Messiah*, p. 117
31 A.E. van Vogt, interview with Russell Miller, July 22, 1986.
32 Miller (1987). *Bare-Faced Messiah*, p. 316
33 Hubbard, "Affirmations". Undated, circa 1946.
    http://scientology-research.org/the-admissions-of-l-ron-
    hubbard/
34 Hubbard claim for pension, December 6, 1945
35 "Form H-8 Medical History – Hubbard Lafayette R." Lt Cdr L.K.
    Gay, March 23, 1942.
36 Hubbard, "Self-Determined Effort Processing", lecture of October
    1, 1951

Chapter 18: Ron's War

1 L. Ron Hubbard, letter of October 1938, quoted in Miller, p. 81
2 Memo from US Naval Attaché Australia to Commandant 12th
   Naval District, February 14, 1942
3 Cable from Commandant Boston Yard, September 25, 1942
4 Report on the Fitness of Officers – Lafayette Ronald Hubbard
   113392. 29 May 1943-7 July 1943
5 L. Ron Hubbard Fitness Report, 21 July 1944 – 28 September
   1944
6 Hubbard, "Affirmations". Undated, circa 1946.
   http://scientology-research.org/the-admissions-of-l-ron-
   hubbard/

Lightning Source UK Ltd.
Milton Keynes UK
UKHW040624290123
416064UK00016B/265